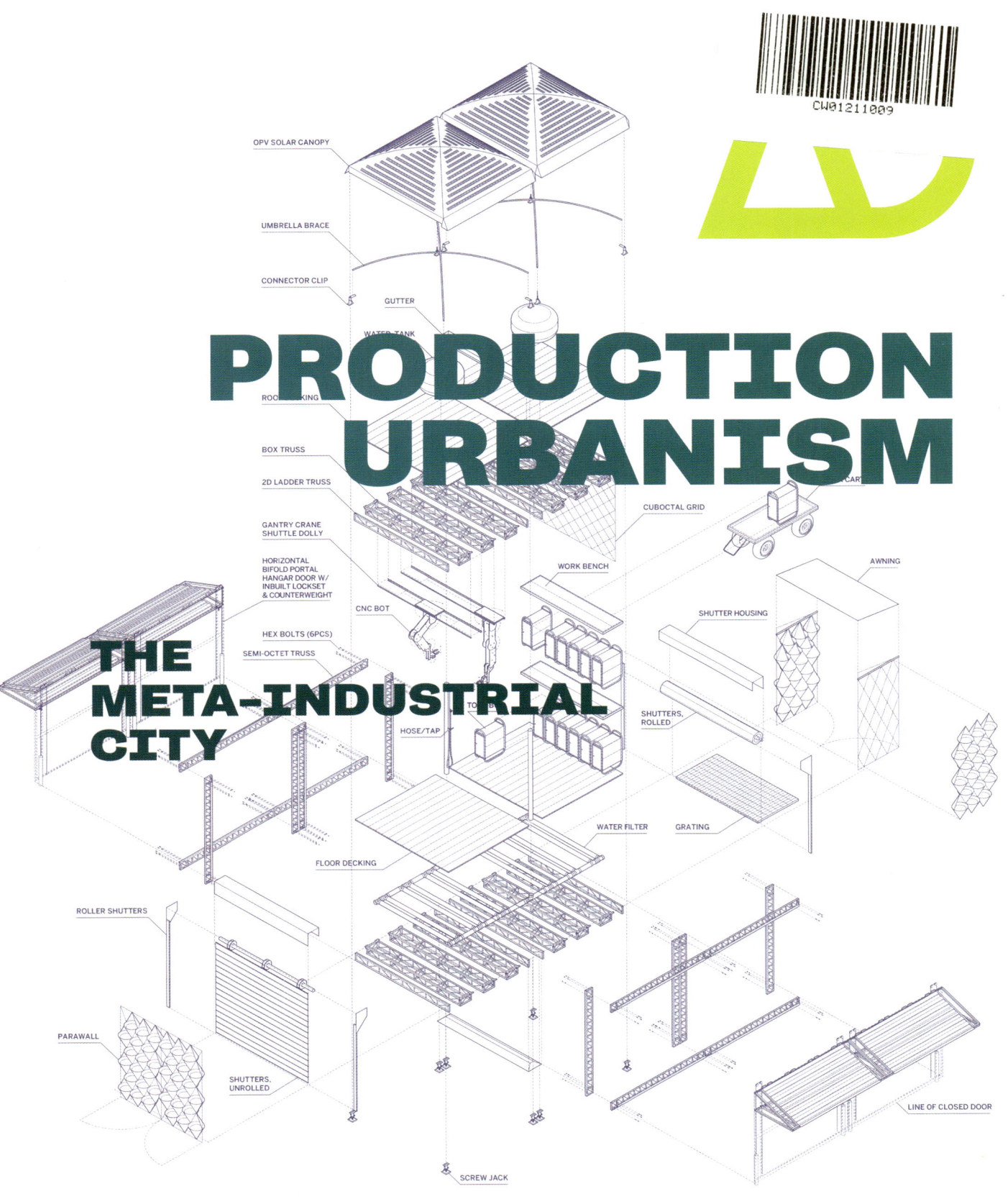

PRODUCTION URBANISM

THE META-INDUSTRIAL CITY

Guest-edited by
DONGWOO YIM AND
RAFAEL LUNA

05 | Vol 91 | 2021

PRODUCTION URBANISM:
THE META-INDUSTRIAL CITY

05/2021

About the Guest-Editors 5
Dongwoo Yim and Rafael Luna

Introduction 6
Factories for Urban Living: Retooling 21st-Century Production
Dongwoo Yim and Rafael Luna

The New Industrial Urbanism 14
Tali Hatuka

The Digital Reindustrialisation of Cities 24
Vicente Guallart

ISSN 0003-8504
ISBN 978 1119 717706

Nothing Is Automatic 32
Producing More-Than-Human Relations in the Pearl River Delta
Marina Otero Verzier

Salad Days 40
Urban Food Futures
Scott Lloyd and Alexis Kalagas

The New Industrial Commons 48
Worker-Owners and Factory Space
Nina Rappaport

From Food Hub to Food Port 56
In Conversation with OMA's Shohei Shigematsu
Rafael Luna and Dongwoo Yim

Occupying Africa 62
Prototyping a Transformal Makerspace Network
DK Osseo-Asare and Yasmine Abbas

Guest-edited by **Dongwoo Yim and Rafael Luna**

A New Paradigm for the Periphery 70

The Case Against Reuniting City and Factory

Frank Barkow

Architecture for Plateaus and Valleys 78

The Marketability of Industrial Mixing

Kengo Kuma

Urban Production in Seoul's Historic Centre 106

Choonwondang Hospital of Korean Medicine

Doojin Hwang

Seoul's Shoe Silo 114

A Vertical Smart Anchor for the Small Manufacturer

Yerin Kang and Chihoon Lee

'In an era fascinated by new technologies and hyperconnectivity, architects face the call to envision a future built environment beyond simple technocratic ideals and into complex hybrid scenarios where infrastructures of production can be repositioned as an architectural problem.'
—Dongwoo Yim and Rafael Luna

Floating Farms 84

Feeding Rotterdam from Within

Wesley Leeman

The *Danwei* System 92

Living with Production

Michele Bonino and Maria Paola Repellino

Freeland 100

How Residents Are Creating a Dutch City from Scratch

Winy Maas

Building Better Brussels 120

Production Urbanism as a Policy

Kristiaan Borret

From Another Perspective

Ottawa 2120 128

Zachary Colbert

Neil Spiller

Contributors 134

Editorial Offices
John Wiley & Sons
9600 Garsington Road
Oxford
OX4 2DQ

T +44 (0)18 6577 6868

Editor
Neil Spiller

Managing Editor
Caroline Ellerby
Caroline Ellerby Publishing

Freelance Contributing Editor
Abigail Grater

Publisher
Todd Green

Art Direction + Design
CHK Design:
Christian Küsters
Barbara Nassisi

Production Editor
Elizabeth Gongde

Prepress
Artmedia, London

Printed in the United Kingdom
by Hobbs the Printers Ltd

Front and back cover
PRAUD, Made in Seongsu, Seoul, South Korea, 2020.
© PRAUD

Inside front cover
Goldsmith.Company, Floating Farm Dairy, M4H district, Rotterdam, 2019.
© Goldsmith.Company, photo Ruben Dario Kleimeer

Page 1
Agbogbloshie Makerspace Platform, Taxonomy of the AMP spacecraft kit, 2020.
© AMP / LowDO

EDITORIAL BOARD

Denise Bratton
Paul Brislin
Mark Burry
Helen Castle
Nigel Coates
Peter Cook
Kate Goodwin
Edwin Heathcote
Brian McGrath
Jayne Merkel
Peter Murray
Mark Robbins
Deborah Saunt
Patrik Schumacher
Ken Yeang

ARCHITECTURAL DESIGN

September/October | Issue | Profile No.
2021 | 05 | 273

Disclaimer
The Publisher and Editors cannot be held responsible for errors or any consequences arising from the use of information contained in this journal; the views and opinions expressed do not necessarily reflect those of the Publisher and Editors, neither does the publication of advertisements constitute any endorsement by the Publisher and Editors of the products advertised.

Journal Customer Services
For ordering information, claims and any enquiry concerning your journal subscription please go to www.wileycustomerhelp.com/ask or contact your nearest office.

Americas
E: cs-journals@wiley.com
T: +1 877 762 2974

Europe, Middle East and Africa
E: cs-journals@wiley.com
T: +44 (0)1865 778 315

Asia Pacific
E: cs-journals@wiley.com
T: +65 6511 8000

Japan (for Japanese-speaking support)
E: cs-japan@wiley.com
T: +65 6511 8010

Visit our Online Customer Help available in 7 languages at www.wileycustomerhelp.com/ask

Print ISSN: 0003-8504
Online ISSN: 1554-2769

Prices are for six issues and include postage and handling charges. Individual-rate subscriptions must be paid by personal cheque or credit card. Individual-rate subscriptions may not be resold or used as library copies.

All prices are subject to change without notice.

Identification Statement
Periodicals Postage paid at Rahway, NJ 07065. Air freight and mailing in the USA by Mercury Media Processing, 1850 Elizabeth Avenue, Suite C, Rahway, NJ 07065, USA.

USA Postmaster
Please send address changes to *Architectural Design*, John Wiley & Sons Inc., c/o The Sheridan Press, PO Box 465, Hanover, PA 17331, USA.

Rights and Permissions
Requests to the Publisher should be addressed to:
Permissions Department
John Wiley & Sons Ltd
The Atrium
Southern Gate
Chichester
West Sussex PO19 8SQ
UK

F: +44 (0)1243 770 620
E: Permissions@wiley.com

All Rights Reserved. No part of this publication may be reproduced, stored in a retrieval system or transmitted in any form or by any means, electronic, mechanical, photocopying, recording, scanning or otherwise, except under the terms of the Copyright, Designs and Patents Act 1988 or under the terms of a licence issued by the Copyright Licensing Agency Ltd, 5th Floor, Shackleton House, Battle Bridge Lane, London SE1 2HX, without the permission in writing of the Publisher.

Subscribe to D
D is published bimonthly and is available to purchase on both a subscription basis and as individual volumes at the following prices.

Prices
Individual copies:
£29.99 / US$45.00
Individual issues on
D App for iPad:
£9.99 / US$13.99
Mailing fees for print may apply

Annual Subscription Rates
Student: £93 / US$147
print only

Personal: £146 / US$229
print and iPad access

Institutional: £346 / US$646
print or online

Institutional: £433 / US$808
combined print and online

6-issue subscription
on D App for iPad:
£44.99 / US$64.99

ABOUT THE GUEST-EDITORS

DONGWOO YIM AND RAFAEL LUNA

Dongwoo Yim and Rafael Luna are the founding partners of PRAUD, a design and research firm based in Seoul and Boston, Massachusetts. Yim graduated from Seoul National University and received his Master of Architecture in Urban Design from Harvard University, and Luna received his Master of Architecture from the Massachusetts Institute of Technology (MIT).

PRAUD researches production urbanism through an array of scales, typologies and mediums in order to investigate circular economies as catalysts of urban regeneration through hybrid architecture. Their investigations on hybrid typologies between production and housing, propelled by new manufacturing technologies, propose an alternative urban housing model for future equitable cities. Current research focuses on the Seoul megalopolitan condition, where urban manufacturing is still valid within the city, through 'makeshift' urban production typologies.

Yim and Luna's work on production urbanism extends from academia to published writings and exhibitions. Both have taught for several years at various international institutions, including the Rhode Island School of Design, Washington University in St Louis, and the Chinese Academy of Arts. Yim is currently an assistant professor at Hongik University, and Luna an assistant professor at Hanyang University, both in Seoul. Their studio topics have focused on the evolution of the socialist micro-district, which aggregates factories and dwellings in a single urban block, and adapting this model to capitalist scenarios and sites. The findings have been published in international journals, and exhibited at the Museum of Modern Art (MoMA) in New York, in the Golden Lion-winning Korean Pavilion at the 2014 Venice Architecture Biennale, and at the Seoul Biennale of Architecture and Urbanism in 2017 and 2019. PRAUD's curatorial roles have included the 'Factory for Urban Living' exhibition (Palais de Seoul, 2018) and 'Cities Exhibition' at the Seoul Biennale (2019) where they presented a collective dialogue on new industrial models. Publications include *North Korean Atlas* (Damdi, 2014), *I Want to be Metropolitan: Boston Case Study* (ORO, 2012), *City After Urbanism* (Book Journalism, 2018) and *Unprecedented Pyongyang* (Actar, 2017). They were the award-winning team of the 2013 Architectural League Prize, and the DAM Architectural Book Award in 2014. 𝔻

Text © 2021 John Wiley & Sons Ltd. Image © PRAUD

Factories for Urban Living

Retooling 21st-Century Production

INTRODUCTION

DONGWOO YIM AND RAFAEL LUNA

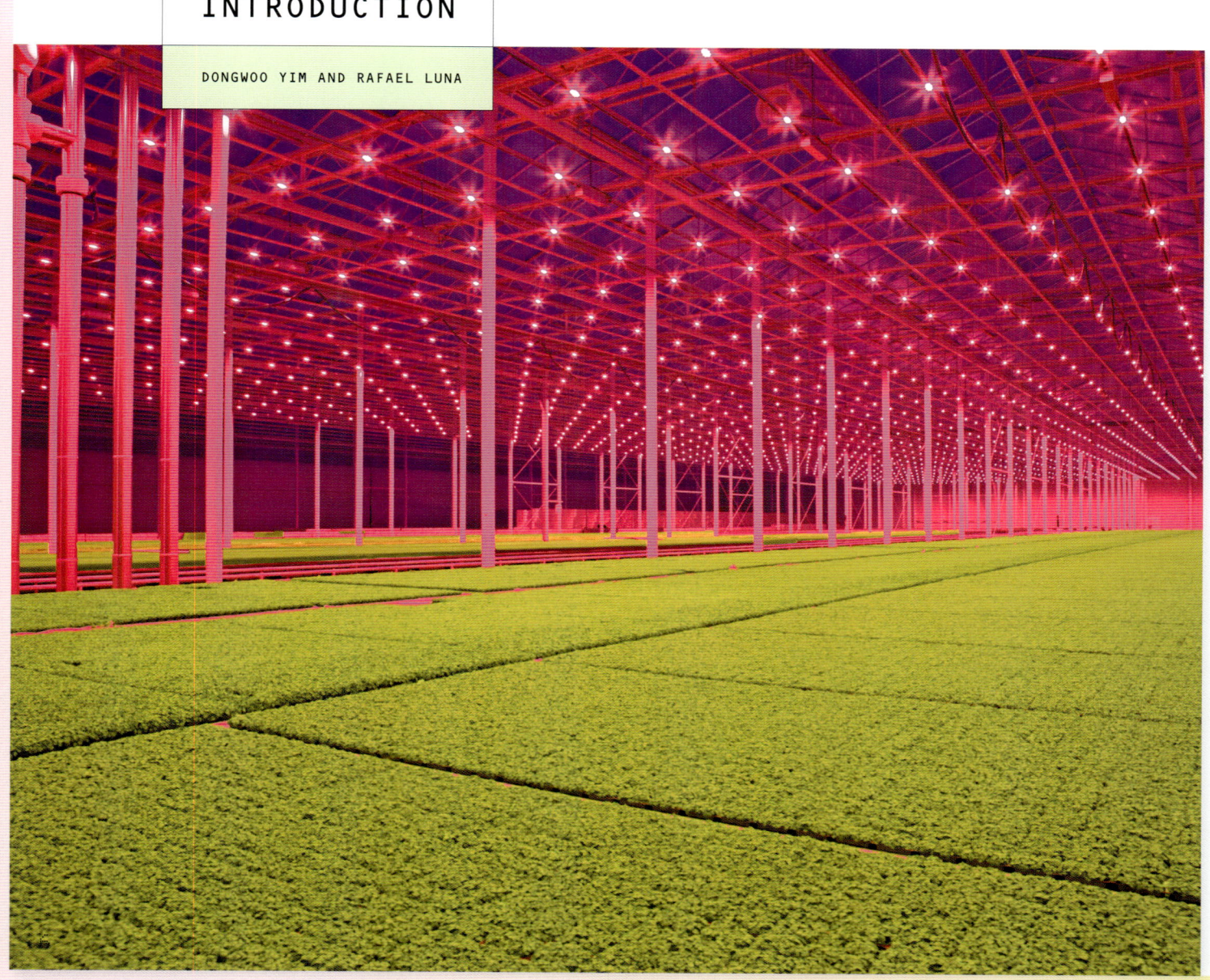

'It is a milestone clearly delimiting a past period and opening up all possible hopes ... In ten years, [your book] will be the foundation of all production and be the first rallying sign.'

— Charles-Édouard Jeanneret (Le Corbusier) in a letter to Tony Garnier on first encountering *An Industrial* City in 1919[1]

Towards the second half of the 19th century, Barcelona's Eixample district (1859) and the General Theory of Urbanisation (1867)[2] by Catalan planner Ildefons Cerdà had prompted an era of urbanisation and capitalism through the parcelisation process of the grid. New visionary counter models for city and production emerged to provide alternative equitable choices. British planner Ebenezer Howard would initiate the Garden City Movement in 1898 as a vision for a more self-sufficient city structured through an integration of industries, agriculture and cooperative landownership. French architect Tony Garnier would embrace the new technologies of the 20th century through his drawings of *An Industrial City* (1904) that would envision an integration between living and working. The factory, for Garnier, would be an indispensable typology for the formation of the city.

Just as these city models in the early 20th century would project future cities based on emerging industries, technologies and economies from an architectural perspective, our current transition into shared economies, mass customisation and algorithmic autonomous production faces the same potential for a new generation of architectural industrial solutions. This issue of △ re-evaluates the revolutionary spirit of the industrial city as a way of understanding integral values between production and living, circular economies, and the architectural response that can organise a new productive urbanity. In an era fascinated by new technologies and hyperconnectivity, architects face the call to envision a future built environment beyond simple technocratic ideals and into complex hybrid scenarios where infrastructures of production can be repositioned as an architectural problem.

Technological evolutions in energy, communication and transportation have marked transformative epochs for production in the city. These can be categorised into four industrial revolutions that have had a direct correlation between the process of production, urbanisation models and architectural typologies. The First Industrial Revolution took shape in the second half of the 18th century with the invention of the steam engine and the mechanisation of singular labour. Riverside mills would shape cities in England, as new labour would concentrate in these production typologies, causing a paradigm shift from agrarian economies to manufacturing economies and giving birth to the industrial city. The Second Industrial Revolution evolved in the second half of the 19th century with the process of electrification and mass production. The unregulated concentration of factories would corrupt the image of the city through unfiltered scenes between housing and production, eventually leading to zoning and the displacement of factories away from residential zones. The development of nuclear energy in the mid-20th century advanced the field of electronics, robotics and information technology, leading to automated production in the Third Industrial Revolution. As information technology progressed as a clean industry with innovative models of production, new factory typologies were developed that would challenge the modernist zoning. The current Fourth Industrial Revolution, spawned by the invention of the internet and the process of digitisation through the internet of things (IoT), has had an effect of decentralisation as data becomes more readily accessible. Production evolves into a 'smart' process of mass customisation, shared economies, decentralisation and prosumers, shifting back into an urban model where production can coexist with living.

The notion of the meta-industrial city reflects on how production in the 21st century is changing the way that cities are evolving from a consumption-based society, circling back to a deeper relationship between consumer and producer within the Fourth Industrial Revolution. Through architectural mutations of production a new architectural engagement can be present for a social–technocratic–economic shift that addresses a

Tony Garnier,
Blast Furnaces in an Industrial City,
1904

right: As seen in this rendering by Garnier, the industrial zone works as a city unto itself. Regardless of zoning, industry requires an intrinsic network of infrastructure that could double up to serve an urban purpose.

Koppert Cress LED Greenhouse,
Monster,
Netherlands,
2016

opposite: The digitisation process has created an industrial shift: while the number of agro-businesses are reducing, the remaining ones have expanded their footprint with the use of automation.

much-needed socially equitable urban model. This issue of △ focuses on answering the call by presenting investigations through industrial grafted typologies that are merging in dense cities, the digitisation of industries, production as a model for social equity, and questioning of modern zoning as a broken, outdated model.

Digitisation of Industry

The digitisation process of the Fourth Industrial Revolution has had the ramifications of not only producing a new virtual economy as a clean industry, but also disrupting traditional industries through new efficiencies and socio-economic agendas. 'Industry 4.0', as presented by Tali Hatuka in this issue, has generated concepts for a new 'industrial ecosystem', 'industrial urbanism' and 'industrial ecology' that reflect a new understanding of the economic and physical organisation of industry. Smart cities are moving beyond the accumulation of data for the purposes of management, to an exploration of optimisation of their infrastructure. This has allowed for underutilised areas of the city to transform into new, industrious, vibrant urban pockets through digital clean industries. Traditional industries also have been gradually changing their labour force with the aid of autonomous machines. This condition has engendered post-human architecture dominated by robotics, such as logistics and distribution centres that facilitate urban life.

Production as Equity (Cities of Inequality)

Twentieth-century Fordism propelled a new era of mass production that would sustain a new-found economy of mass consumption. Yet consumption and production represented a dichotomy for the modernist city. Production would be expelled to the fringe areas, which offered cheaper land and labour, while consumption would overwhelm urban centres. As industry moved out of the city, workers would relocate in order to live closer to the factories, disconnecting them from the growing cosmopolitan urban centres. Monoculture factory towns would develop to support labour housing outside of the city, and a disparity between consumption and production would solidify an inequity between the two in relation to culture, education and further opportunities. At the same time, these factory towns and mono-industrial cities lack the resiliency to self-sustain in the case that industry fails or factories relocate.

The hyperconnected 'smart' industry era of the 21st century has fomented the decentralisation of economies and entrepreneurial power, allowing for some of these disparities to be addressed through self-empowered innovation. Shared economies minimise initial overhead costs, allowing micro-industries to emerge in urban centres through the pixelation of industrial typologies.

Broken Zoning

In 1928, the first International Congress of Modern Architecture (CIAM) introduced the La Sarraz Declaration[3] in Switzerland as an initial manifesto for the modern city to be an economically efficient society – a

Ter Laak Orchids Greenhouse,
Wateringen,
Netherlands,
2018

Increasing land prices and labour costs have led to the optimisation of production with the aid of automation, minimising human participation in the process.

The notion of the meta-industrial city reflects on how production in the 21st century is changing the way that cities are evolving from a consumption-based society, circling back to a deeper relationship between consumer and producer within the Fourth Industrial Revolution.

General Architecture Collaborative,
ADC Workshop,
Masoro Sector,
Rulindo,
Northern District,
Republic of Rwanda,
2015

In 2014 the fashion house Kate Spade New York (KSNY) launched a social responsibility endeavour that directs profits from goods designed and crafted under their On Purpose moniker, in this Rwanda factory established by KSNY and run by local firm ADC, towards projects within the communities KSNY works with.

product of rationalisation and standardisation. Town planning had to follow an order based on the functions of dwelling, producing and relaxation. Functionalist planning would be cemented with the Charter of Athens[4] in 1933 after the fourth CIAM, themed 'Functional City', offered a solution to organise the then industrial city. This new manifesto proposed an understanding of the city as a value of four spatially separated functions: dwelling, recreation, work and transportation.

The modern model of zoning has persisted as a reference point for cities across the globe. Yet the evolution of industrial development in the 21st century disrupts this model. Denser cities where real estate is too valuable will naturally seek to redevelop industrial areas, challenging zoning codes to be transformed. When separated, distances between the different city functions have become environmental urban problems of congestion and of how to optimise use of fuel, resources and human capital. The emergence of concepts like energy microgrids, farm-to-table movement and neighbourhood fab labs are indicators of a demand for condensing mixed functions and operations within a neighbourhood unit. This calls on a re-evaluation of models like the socialist micro-district, or the Maoist *danwei* as analysed by Michele Bonino and Maria Paola Repellino in this issue.

Grafted Typologies

The need to recontextualise production as a part of an urban unit is an imminent problem as cities face supply chain challenges that will require locally produced, locally consumed goods and services. The challenge is the reintroduction of industrial architecture as part of the generic urban fabric. Just as Le Corbusier stated 'Architecture or revolution',[5] this issue calls upon architecture to reflect on mass-production and mass customisation for a mass urbanised world through the appropriation of industrial elements that can ensure the survival of the factory in the city.

The pressure for production is already evident in dense societies where the hybridisation process between production and living is organically occurring. While architecture has only just started presenting new integrated models for the 21st-century urban factory, neighbourhoods like Seongsu in Seoul have flourished through the promotion of manufacturing as something that holds cultural appeal for tourists and residents, where factories exist within a typical mixed-use urban fabric. Banal modernist buildings are grafted into factories through the assemblage of production elements à *la* Frankenstein. Vent ducts pop out of windows, commercial lifts are attached to façades, overhead doors appear on upper floors. The theoretical conception of architectural elements as once proposed by Jean-Nicolas-Louis Durand's *Précis of the Lectures on Architecture* that he gave at Paris's École Polytechnique (1805)[6] are challenged through this appropriation of 'ready-made' industrial elements that transform a modernist frame into a factory. Vent ducts, in that sense, perform the duty of being an ornamental symbol that signifies production, while at the same time are a performative element that allows for the function of a factory. In *Learning from Las Vegas* (1972), Robert Venturi, Denise Scott Brown and Steven Izenour postulated the canonic semiotic polemic between form and sign through the 'duck' and the 'decorated shed'.[7] These industrial buildings present a new taxonomy of architectural elements for the urban factory, neither 'ducks' nor 'decorated sheds', but perhaps an evolutionary blending of both.

From Post- to Meta-
The urbanisation project catapulted rapid transformations onto emerging markets around the world throughout the 20th century. The increasing speed of development paired with technological innovation in the 21st century has allowed for new urban development to leapfrog legacy industrial and infrastructural networks that were once laid out by the Modern Movement. Cities that served as testbeds for industrial revolutions are also plagued with the path dependency from initial planning experiments, having to evolve through a sequential transition from the negative connotation of an industrial city to post-industrial variations that reflect a better quality of life and seek to evoke an innovative character. Despite the post-industrial city looking to escape the negative connotation of 'industrial', industry has circled back to becoming an asset for urban innovation rather than an outcast of the city. As a self-referential process on the industrial city, this issue of ⌀ has been organised through a framework that seeks to lay down the historical background for the meta-industrial city, the role of the factory as a typology in the city, and models for production urbanism. While its contributors have been organised under this general framework, the issue seeks to ask four imminent questions.

```
Gutiérrez-delaFuente Arquitectos,
Low Line,
London, England,
2019
```

opposite: While infrastructure can be obtrusive in the urban space, this adaptive reuse project recuperates the underutilised space of the train bridge to create a productive environment.

below: The bridge is organised through the different layers of a production sequence in order to produce a circular economy within the site.

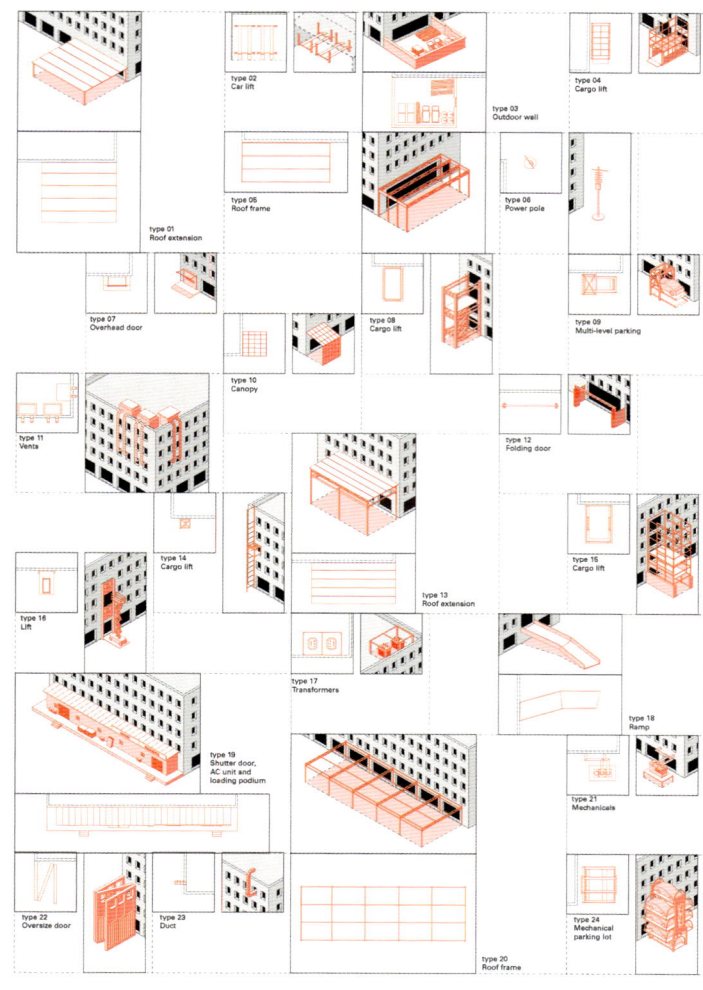

PRAUD,
Made in Seongsu,
Seoul, South Korea 2020

above: The semi-industrial area of Seongsu has been able to mix housing and industry through the use of ready-made industrial elements that attach to banal buildings.

below: The use of industrial elements as architectural components allows for the same structure to perform multiple functions, showing the capacity for a rigid structure to be flexible in its use.

First: how has the digitisation of industry in the Fourth Industrial Revolution been exercised? Professor Tali Hatuka from Tel Aviv University introduces concepts for industrial formal and economic organisation in the city. Spanish architect Vicente Guallart evaluates a new conception of smartness for a productive city. Marina Otero Verzier, Director of research at Het Nieuwe Instituut in Rotterdam, discusses how automation has formed new urban landscapes. Architect Scott Lloyd and urban strategist Alexis Kalagas reflect on the digital process of food production decentralisation.

Second: what are the potentials for a new industrial revolution to provide equitable urbanity? Architectural critic Nina Rappaport conducts a study on the cooperative factory as a transformative and socially responsible model. Shohei Shigematsu, Partner in OMA's New York office, designs a Food Hub as a hybrid between a logistics centre and a social community centre. Architect DK Osseo-Asare discusses open-source architecture that empowers an entrepreneurial spirit in Ghana's largest industrial scrapyard.

Third: is there still any value in zoning? Frank Barkow, principal at Berlin architecture firm Barkow Leibinger, frames the possibility of an industrial linear city. Kengo Kuma, founder of Kengo Kuma & Associates in Japan, reflects on the positive unintended consequences for new typologies as a result of Tokyo's zoning. Dutch Architect Wesley Leeman redefines conventional boundaries by occupying the river with a floating dairy farm. Turin Architects Michele Bonino and Maria Paola Repellino reflect on the transformations of the *danwei* system which once allowed living and working in the same unit as an urban and social model. Rotterdam-headquartered office MVRDV's principal, Winy Maas, hypothesises a free-range urbanism with no zoning, where one can build with no restrictions other than one's own funding and willing to contribute to the collective infrastructure.

Fourth and last: what are emerging industrial typologies? Korean architect Doojin Hwang reflects on the density of Seoul while showcasing the elegance of

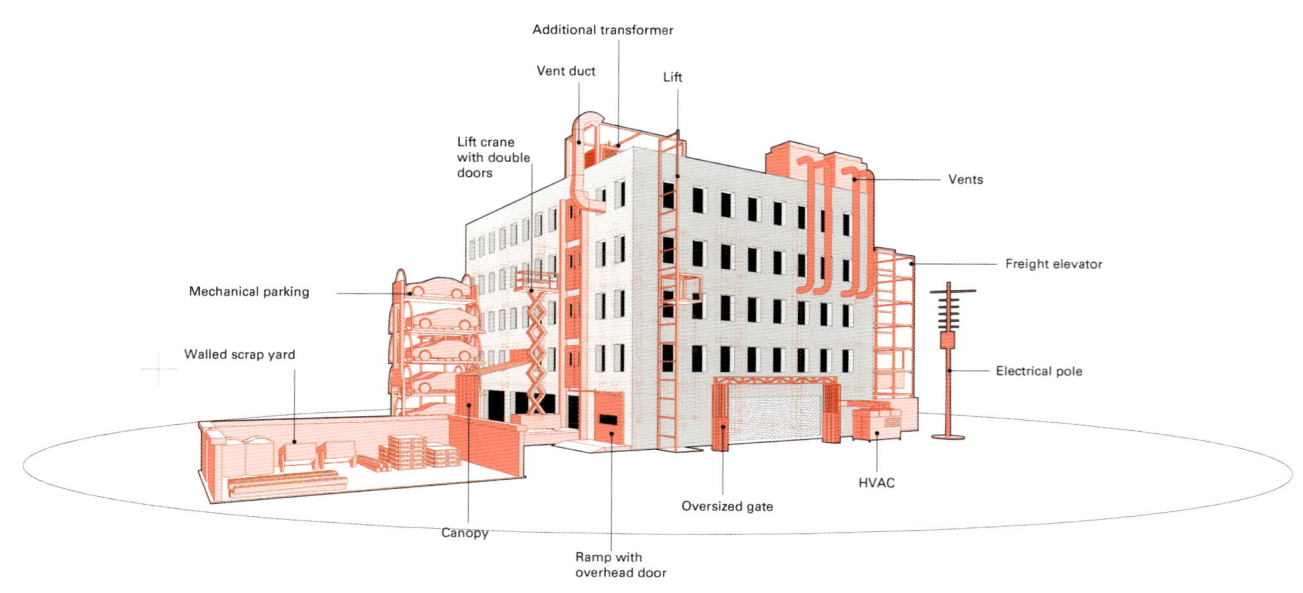

China Architecture Design Group (CADG),
Land-Based Rationalism Design & Research Centre,
Dahua Textile Mill renovation,
Xi'an, China,
2014

A bird's-eye view of the former *danwei* of the Dahua Textile Mill in Xi'an, now transformed into the new Dahua 1935 creative cluster.

industrial elements in the centre of the city. Yerin Kang and Chihoon Lee of Korean firm SoA (Society of Architecture) introduce a hybrid shoe factory in the transforming semi-industrial neighbourhood of Seongsu-dong. Kristiaan Borret, Chief Architect (Bouwmeester) of the Brussels-Capital Region, presents new typologies of factories as a strategy for redevelopment in the centre of Brussels.

The post-industrial city has focused on addressing industrial heritage, through the adaptation and reuse of industrial remnants as cultural artefacts such as the Gas Works Park in Seattle (1975) or Tate Modern (2000) in London. The aforementioned questions, instead, suggest the meta-industrial city as a 21st-century architectural and urban model that re-establishes industry as a holistic urban catalyst beyond just the economic dimension, but re-integrating industry as an intrinsic part of the built form of contemporary human settlement. ᗪ

Notes
1. Letter quoted in Sukhada Tatke, 'Reviving the Utopian Urban Dreams of Tony Garnier', Bloomberg CityLab, 11 November 2019: https://www.bloomberg.com/news/articles/2019-11-11/why-architect-tony-garnier-was-ahead-of-his-time.
2. Ildefons Cerdà, *Teoría general de la urbanización, y aplicación de sus principios y doctrinas a la reforma y ensanche de Barcelona*, Imprenta Española (Madrid), 1867.
3. Ulrich Conrads (ed), *Programs and Manifestoes on 20th Century Architecture*, MIT Press (Cambridge, MA), 1971, pp 109–14.
4. Ibid.
5. Le Corbusier, *Towards a New Architecture* [*Vers une architecture*, 1923], trans Frederick Etchells, Dover Publications (New York), 1986, p 265.
6. Jean-Nicolas-Louis Durand, *Précis of the Lectures on Architecture* [*Précis des leçons d'architecture données à l'École polytechnique*, 1805], trans David Britt, Getty Research Institute (Los Angeles, CA), 2000.
7. Robert Venturi, Denise Scott Brown and Steven Izenour, *Learning from Las Vegas*, MIT Press (Cambridge, MA), 1972, p 88.

Text © 2021 John Wiley & Sons Ltd. Images: p 6 © Jan van Berkel; pp 8–9(t) © Johannes Schwartz; pp 8–9(b) © General Architecture Collaborative; pp 10–11 © Gutiérrez de la Fuente; p 12 © PRAUD; p 13 © China Architecture Design Group (CADG) Land-based Rationalism Design & Research Center

THE NEW INDUSTRIAL URBANISM

Tali Hatuka

A hybrid, heterogeneous model of urban design, 'New Industrial Urbanism' can facilitate dynamic, innovative and vibrant sectors of the city. Architect and urban planner **Tali Hatuka**, Head of the Laboratory of Contemporary Urban Planning and Design (LCUD) at Tel Aviv University, explores its contemporary societal, economic and technological context. She describes its impact on ideas of localism, skilling up the workforce and cross-disciplinary collaboration.

Wageningen Foodvalley – campus of Wageningen University and Research, Netherlands, 2016

A rural cluster that thrives on a specialised labour force and on R&D-intensive activities.

Tali Hatuka,
Key concepts in contemporary industrial development

Forming the basis for new ideas in industrial development, these concepts are complementary, though not often perceived as linked.

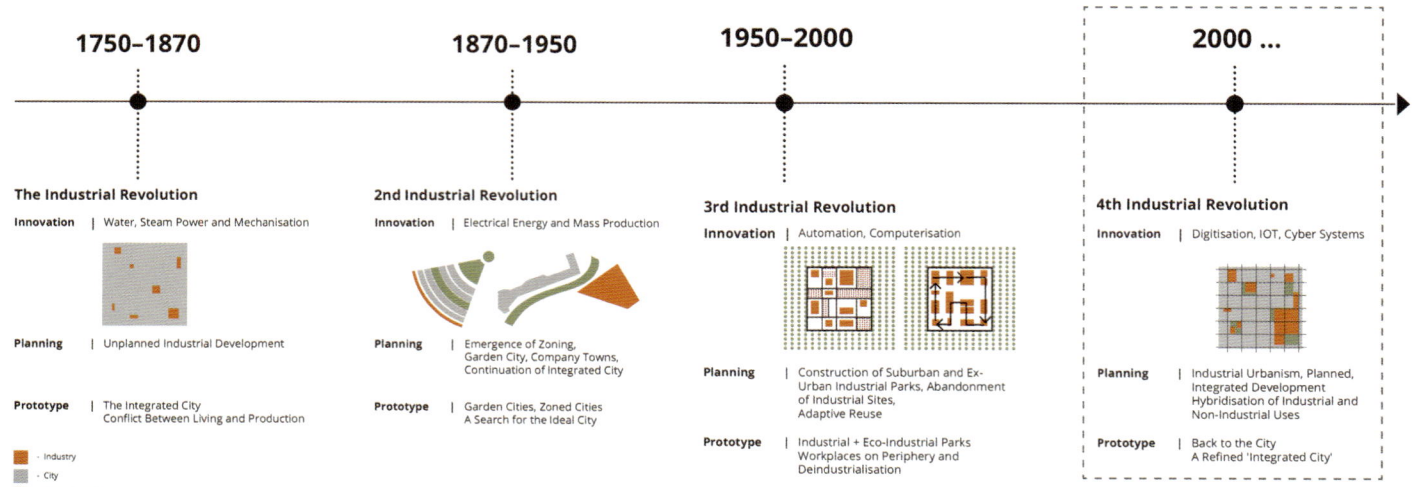

Industrialisation is present everywhere, in each product we consume and use. Yet industrial production often takes place elsewhere, distant and detached from our daily routines and living spaces. In fact, industry is something we rarely think about. This physical and perceptual distancing is connected to the way capitalism and planning have radically altered and alienated relationships between workers, products and consumers. But this process of distantiation is gradually changing with the emergence of innovative technologies that cultivate new thinking about the interface between the city and industry.

This new interface is not a radical shift but another phase in an ongoing city–industry dynamic that spans more than a century. The initial phase can be traced back to the First Industrial Revolution when water and steam were used to mechanise production. The mechanisation process changed the social and physical fabric of cities, which functioned as labour pools and logistical hubs. The period of initial industrialisation was characterised by environmental degradation and increased pollution, resulting in the desire to separate industry and manufacturing from housing – an attitude that was further enhanced during the Second Industrial Revolution, with the increased use of electric power to support mass production. Planners, architects and social reformers responded to this dynamic by putting forward propositions for a new model of an ideal industrial city. Towards the end of the 19th century, these models ranged from the design of new mill-towns to the establishment of novel sets of zoning regulations to handle factories' nuisance activities, leading to the establishment of stricter environment laws and regulations. During the mid- to late 20th century, the Third Industrial Revolution, which expanded automated production and the use of electronics and information technology, started a process of deindustrialisation especially in Europe and the US. Countries transformed their industrial activities and utilised urban planning tools to further segregate industry from other land uses. This position of disfavouring manufacturing, coupled with zoning practices that favoured residential development above all other uses (especially manufacturing), led to the development of industrial parks in rural areas and a loss of industrial land in cities.

The industrial revolutions dramatically impacted the development of cities and countryside. Each transformation left its spatial mark on the physical fabric, often without eliminating the footprints of the previous phase. This continuum resulted in three key spatial forms of industry–residential relationships: (1) integrated, in which there is a fusion or close proximity of residential and industrial uses; (2) adjacent, in which there is planned segregation between the industrial and residential areas of the city; and (3) autonomous, in which standalone industrial/business parks or large factories are isolated from any existing settlements.[1] Yet industrial changes have not stopped, but continue to have a spatial impact. The Fourth Industrial Revolution is pushing city governments, as well as planners and architects, to reconsider a more integrated city–industry dynamic in what is defined in this article as 'New Industrial Urbanism'.[2]

The Present Phase of City–Industry Dynamic
New Industrial Urbanism refers to a socio-spatial concept in which manufacturing is integrated into or adjacent to the city. It is based on the premise that technological evolution is altering fabrication's physical footprint, its distribution processes and innovation

networks, their need for access to transportation, and preference for geographical locations. It is shaping the approach to city planning through the renewed understanding that an urban location carries a competitive advantage thanks to access to skilled labour, educational institutions (centres of research and experimentation) and customers. New Industrial Urbanism emphasises the local economy, and aims to impact the social sphere by empowering small and medium-sized firms and individual entrepreneurs as a mean to buttress localism.

New Industrial Urbanism is linked to three overarching concepts of industrial development: Industry 4.0, industrial ecosystem and industrial ecology. Industry 4.0 refers to digitisation in manufacturing processes and consumer goods. It includes technological innovations ranging from artificial intelligence and autonomous machines to biotechnology, *inter alia*.[3] Industry 4.0 is viewed as a phase in industry that encourages and supports fusion, collaboration and crossovers in learning and knowledge transfer between different types of manufacturers. This type of technological development promises greater energy efficiency and cleaner, quieter industrial processes. An 'industrial ecosystem' encourages relationships and exchanges in the manufacturing sector and perceives it as consisting of one or more ecosystems. One spatial approach for achieving an ecosystem is developing geographical clusters, which may be grouped by product, and include firms that participate in its production at different points up and down the supply chain. This trend views the economy of a region and its manufacturers as a system, and aims to encourage innovation and, in turn, growth through the collaboration of manufacturers, educational institutions (especially universities) and governmental agencies/organisations.[4] In addition, it emphasises the relationships between high-tech and low-tech manufacturers, and considers manufacturer diversity as an important, if not central, component of the system. The third concept, 'industrial ecology', refers to environmental considerations, especially the goals of sustainability, energy efficiency and waste reduction when developing industrial areas. This concept aids economy by increasing efficiency (for example improving energy production and use, water production and use) and establishing more sustainable, closed systems that eliminate waste. Industrial ecology also benefits the environment by reducing industrial waste by establishing a loop in which one manufacturer uses the by-products of another, and so on. Spatially, eco-industry implies the use of green building technologies, generating solar power and using solar power for greater energy efficiency.

These concepts and ideas reconnect both society and space to industry. In terms of society, they depend on social capital and the societal sphere, encouraging (1) cross-sector relationships between academia and industry, government and academia, and government and industry; (2) cross-scale relationships between

Tali Hatuka,
Industrial revolution and development patterns

Planning practices respond to industrial revolutions, which influence societal progress and land-use allocation.

INDUSTRY 4.0 — Additive manufacturing, Digital fabrication, Automation, Artificial Intelligence

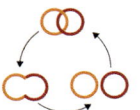

INDUSTRIAL ECOSYSTEM — Cross sectoral collaboration, Scaling up and down the supply chain; Clustering

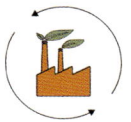

INDUSTRIAL ECOLOGY — Zero waste; By-product reuse; Sustainability

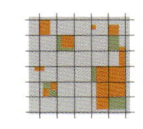

INDUSTRIAL URBANISM — Urban manufacturing; Cleaner, quieter industry in a small footprint; Live-work communities; Mixed-uses

entrepreneurs and established firms, or small and medium firms and large firms; and (3) up- and downstream relationships between suppliers and producers. In terms of space, these concepts emphasise the role of proximity, integration and improving access to the workplace for employees and nearby institutions that can support their work (universities and research centres), which is considered an advantage for the development of an ecological industrial system.

Integrating, Mixing and Synchronising
The current phase in the evolution of the city–industry relationship boosts the development of heterogeneous environments that include a variety of industrial activities. One planning approach to this dynamic has been the establishment of industrial urban districts and urban-edge hybrid areas.[5] In these hybrid districts, a mixture of uses (for example employment and commerce), varying both the type of activity (production, R&D) and the type of programme (the size of the lots and the relationships between them), are permitted and incentivised. The approach of combining and varying uses is seen as a response to the different professional abilities and aspirations of local residents, and a way to increase their occupational possibilities.

Mixed uses in industrial areas also increase the chances of them becoming active, lively places where public spaces are used by a broader segment of the population. These uses include, for example, education (vocational education and employee training), health (occupational health clinics) and the welfare of workers (sports centre, day-care centres). One example of an urban area of this type is the Kendall Square district in Cambridge, Massachusetts. Adjacent to the campus of the Massachusetts Institute of Technology (MIT), it has become the home of diverse commercial and retail activities, housing, educational/academic spaces and small incubators for startups, as well as many global technology players and key biotechnology and pharmaceutical companies. Another, more regional-rural example is the Wageningen Foodvalley in the Netherlands. A knowledge-intensive agri-food cluster, it spans eight municipalities in a 10-kilometre (6-mile) radius. Initiated and anchored by Wageningen University and Research, the area is home to a number of science, business and research institutes, all focused on food.

The architectural / urban design approach to the hybrid concept has led to 'synchronic typologies': areas or structures that simultaneously support residential and industrial/employment uses. Synchronisation – unlike mixed use – makes it possible for different uses to exist and function in parallel, in the same built space, without interfering with each other, and sharing resources management, particularly for land and infrastructure. The synchronic typology is based on several principles of integration: optimal management and use of land resources, integration of housing and work (not necessarily by the same users), reducing the daily commute and dependence on private vehicles, and using the built area at all hours of the day. Examples of synchronic typologies include Strathcona Village in Vancouver, Canada (2018), designed by GBL Architects. This project maintains the existing industrial area while increasing the local supply of housing by providing affordable housing necessary for a neighbourhood in which 30 per cent of the population works locally. Another example is 415 Wick Lane in London (due for completion 2022), designed by dRMM Architects. Located in a post-industrial landscape, this project preserves the local manufacturing heritage while promoting high-quality, affordable housing for residents of the area in order to create an employment-oriented place that combines light industry, retail, office and residential spaces, along with the adjacent 'heavy' industrial zone.

3D map of the Kendall Square area, Cambridge, Massachusetts, 2021

The site relies heavily on the human capital of the Massachusetts Institute of Technology (MIT) as an anchor resource, but the business district has grown beyond the university and forms a self-sustaining cluster of dynamic businesses.

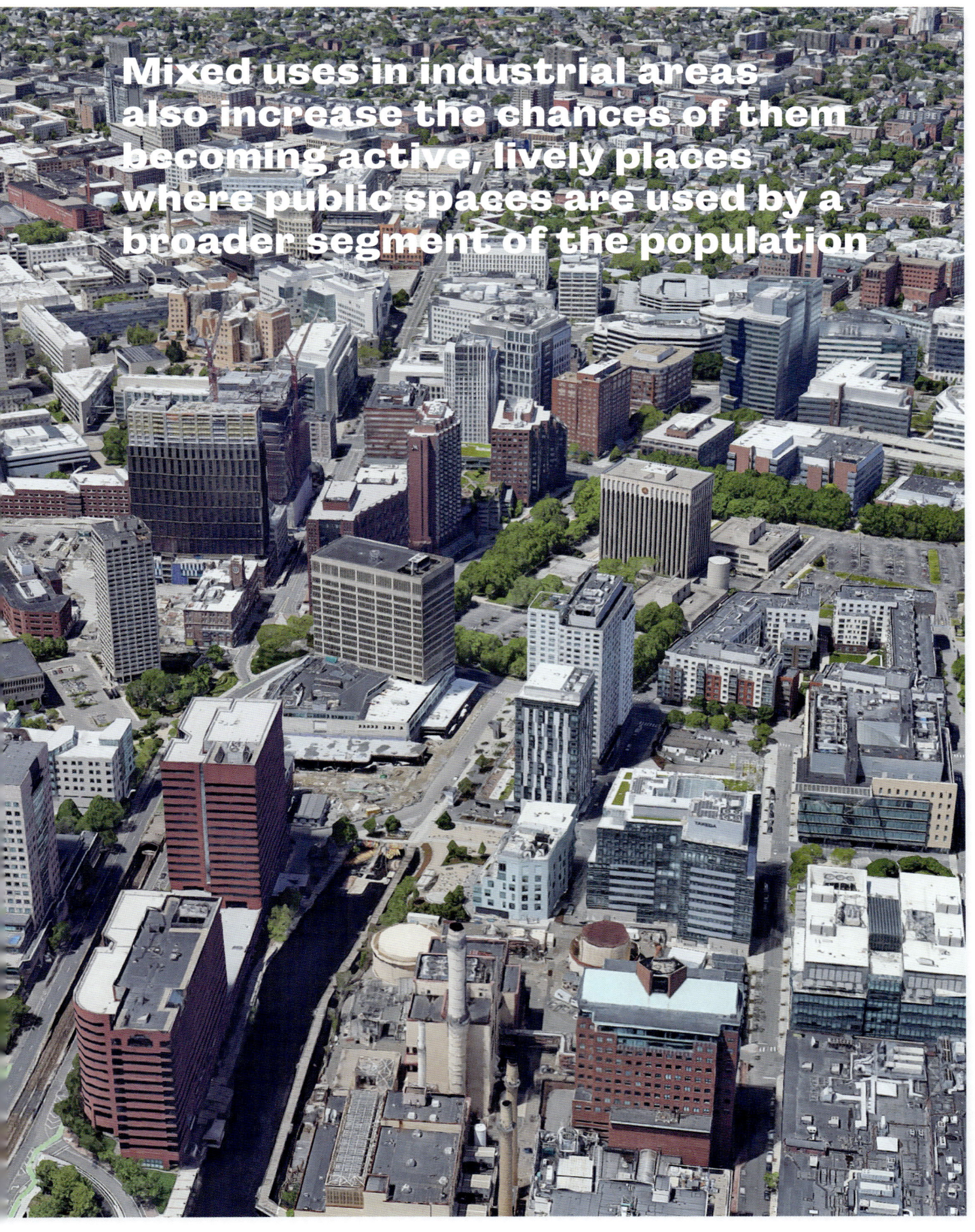

Mixed uses in industrial areas also increase the chances of them becoming active, lively places where public spaces are used by a broader segment of the population

GBL Architects,
Strathcona Village,
Vancouver, Canada,
2018

below: Podium and towers are built of a concrete structure with infill walls clad in corrugated metal panel, a material commonly used on industrial buildings.

opposite: A large loading area is located adjacent to the lane, which is one level below the front street. A freight elevator allows for the movement of goods between the two levels of light industrial flex spaces. The two levels of industrial uses are expressed on the east and lane elevations. Above the industrial uses there are 11 storeys of housing, a mix of market and low-income apartments.

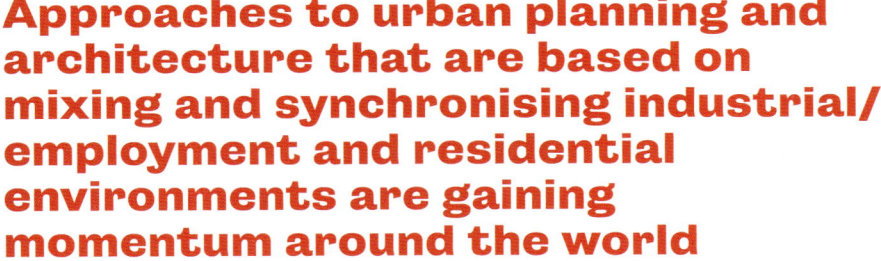

Approaches to urban planning and architecture that are based on mixing and synchronising industrial/employment and residential environments are gaining momentum around the world

dRMM Architects,
415 Wick Lane,
London,
due for completion 2022

The six separate residential buildings increase the penetration of daylight and landscape views. Public areas serve as leisure space and a transitional area joining the project to the neighbourhood.

The complex includes 175 residential units and approximately 2,500 square metres (27,000 square feet) of work areas. Work/commercial spaces are on the main street level.

Approaches to urban planning and architecture that are based on mixing and synchronising industrial/employment and residential environments are gaining momentum around the world. They are expected to further develop and expand as manufacturing regains its importance in our thinking about its presence in cities.

Cities in Transition

To be sure, New Industrial Urbanism is not new; the integration of residential and work areas existed prior to the First Industrial Revolution when most people worked in or near the area where they lived. However, the transition to mass production concentrated in factories and their attendant environmental consequences led to developing spatial divisions between residential and employment areas, and the concurrent trend towards commuting. Yet the rapid development of information technologies and accelerated use of digitisation create an unprecedented opportunity and demand for small, home offices and businesses.[6] Furthermore, the Covid-19 pandemic has brought home the realisation that globalisation has also hindered economic localisation. Shortages of critical products and goods exposed the vulnerabilities of the global supply chain and have made clear that to gain a strategic advantage, countries must readdress policies that target the manufacturing sector and supply-chain deficiencies. This renewed emphasis on localised industry demonstrates significant faith being placed in manufacturing as a crucial part in addressing global inequities and building a bridge towards economic recovery. The question, therefore, is not whether the city will be affected by Industry 4.0, but rather to what extent cities will embrace New Industrial Urbanism, and how it will affect society. History teaches us that every phase of industrial revolution has had a dramatic impact on architecture, planning and society as a whole. 𐐠

This renewed emphasis on localised industry demonstrates significant faith being placed in manufacturing as a crucial part in addressing global inequities

Notes
1. Tali Hatuka and Eran Ben-Joseph, 'Industrial Urbanism: Typologies, Concepts and Prospects', *Built Environment*, 43 (1), 2017, pp 10–24.
2. Tali Hatuka and Eran Ben Joseph, *New Industrial Urbanism: Designing Place of Production*, Routledge, forthcoming. For further reading and publications on the topic, see the website dedicated to the project: www.industrialurbanism.com.
3. Klaus Schwab, 'The Fourth Industrial Revolution: What It Means and How to Respond', *Foreign Affairs*, 12 December 2015: www.foreignaffairs.com/articles/2015-12-12/fourth-industrial-revolution; Elizabeth Reynolds, 'Innovation and Production: Advanced Manufacturing Technologies, Trends and Implications for US Cities and Regions', *Built Environment*, 43 (1), 2017, pp 25–43.
4. Henry Etzkowitz, 'Triple Helix Clusters: Boundary Permeability at University–Industry–Government Interfaces as a Regional Innovation Strategy', *Environment and Planning C*, 30, 2012, pp 766–79.
5. Timothy Love, 'A New Model for Hybrid Building as a Catalyst for the Redevelopment of Urban Industrial Districts', *Built Environment*, 43 (1), 2017, pp 44–57; Nina Rappaport, 'Hybrid Factory | Hybrid City', *Built Environment*, 43 (1), 2017, pp 72–86.
6. See Cutting Edge Planning & Design, *Does Live/Work? Problems and Issues Concerning Live/Work Development in London*, report for the London Borough of Hammersmith & Fulham, 2015: www.lbhf.gov.uk/sites/default/files/section_attachments/livework_final_lowres_tcm21-51146.pdf.

Text © 2021 John Wiley & Sons Ltd. Images: pp 14–15 Photo Van Gooien. Creative Commons Attribution-ShareAlike 4.0 International (CC BY-SA 4.0); pp 16–17 ©Tali Hatuka; pp 18–19 Google Earth / Landsat / Copernicus. Data SIO, NOAA, U.S. Navy, NGA, GEBCO; pp 20–1 Images courtesy of GBL Architects Inc. Photos Ema Peter; pp 22–3 Images courtesy of dRMM Architects Inc

Vicente Guallart

The Digital Reindustrialisation of Cities

The advanced technology of the early 21st century – digital fabrication, robots and global virtual connections – is giving us the opportunity to re-evaluate our modes and locations for industrial production. Equally these notions can enhance our ability to tackle climate change. **Vicente Guallart**, co-founder and former Director of the Institute for Advanced Architecture of Catalonia and principal of Guallart Architects, explains why.

Guallart Architects,
The Self-Sufficient City: designs for post-Covid housing for Xiong'an, China,
2020

Villas with small outdoor gardens are installed on the rooftops, offering a variant to suburban life that is inside the city.

We live in the eternal paradox by which we inhabit cities that were built in the past, following the cultural and productive models of their time, while there are already new methods of production, technologies and organisational principles of society that define a different human future and urban paradigm. In order for a change in urban models to take place, the opportunities and resources to implement them are needed. This is exactly what happened in 2020, from the overlap of the climate and life crises that have affected every country of the world.

While fighting in the short term to overcome the Covid-19 pandemic, the long-term challenge is to avoid planetary environmental catastrophe due to climate change and its effects on cities and human life. The accepted near-future aspect of the latter involves abandoning the use of fossil fuels and changing the energy model by using renewable energies in a structural way in our societies. Europe has set the year 2050 as the deadline to become a zero-emissions continent, while China has committed to doing so by 2060. Action is required at many levels for this to happen. The transformation of the global urban model and current production systems is one of the great challenges that can help meet the objectives set.

The urban models from the First Industrial Revolution, in the 19th century, prompted the creation of factories and productive areas inside cities, which at that time were expanding. New York, Barcelona and Paris are examples of this. The Second Industrial Revolution, associated with the modern urbanism of the 20th century, promoted the functional segregation of cities into industrial estates, residential areas and leisure areas, promoting the hyper-specialisation and hyper-concentration of production chains. With the arrival of the Third Industrial Revolution and the emergence of the digital world, we have seen in the first phase how industrialised countries focused on the development of digital technologies, design and services, while industrial production was concentrated in emerging countries, especially in Asia. However, this paradigm seems to be coming to an end because it generates great social inequalities, and advanced societies lose control of the production of a large quantity of essential products.

For this reason, a second phase of the city in the digital age, which will be especially appropriate after the pandemic and during the fight against climate change and social inequalities, could be based on new pragmatic principles guided by digitisation. To attest to these principles, Guallart Architects started developing the Self-Sufficient City in order to form the basis for this new holistic urban approach. The designs won the 2020 competition for post-Covid housing in Xiong'an, China, and it is hoped that the build will be completed in 2025.

Produce Locally, Connect Globally
Core to these principles is that the economy of the future should be based on producing locally while remaining connected globally. This is a new form of digital globalisation, not based on production in parts of the world where the cost of labour is lower and the subsequent shipment of products in containers around the world. Nor should it be based on the growing power of large digital platforms and a *Blade Runner*-type scenario in which society is controlled by large corporations. The new production model should be

Guallart Architects,
The Self-Sufficient City: designs for post-Covid housing for Xiong'an, China,
2020

The ecological city of the future will allow a mixing of activities and production of almost anything (food, energy, goods). The winning entry in a 2020 competition, this project is under negotiation at the time of writing, with the aim of completion in 2025.

based instead on the creation of networks of people and organisations that share, exchange and trade knowledge, while the material production of things (food, energy, products) is undertaken locally. We have already proven that global connectivity works, even with the increase in teleworking and video conferencing during the Covid-19 pandemic, but now we must invest in the local production of resources. In recent years, collaborative networks have been developed based on open-source design principles linked to technology centres and collaborative citizen platforms. Now, it is necessary to develop the physical infrastructures in cities so that this can happen in a systematic and massive way, using technologies such as digital printing, the production of electronic elements, the production of energy and food (in rural or urban environments) and the incorporation of new production systems in the city.

Empowerment of the Local

Global connectivity and local production is an ecological and social model, because it proposes to reduce the energy that is needed to run cities and countries, while empowering local communities to produce many of their products and resources locally. Relying less on external resources (such as oil or technological solutions) essentially tends to eliminate the political and economic dependencies of countries which, in many cases, do not hold the same values regarding personal freedoms as do Western countries. Reducing the global traffic of products implies reducing the amount of energy the global network of cities needs to function, which would contribute to the fight against climate change. The local production of resources should also contribute to reducing global migration for economic reasons and to fighting against social inequalities, which in the medium term produce global conflicts.

Produced and Connected Neighbourhoods

From an urban point of view, this means the opportunity to develop an urban model based not on the segregation of functions as is the modern city, which generates an obligatory basic mobility between residential, industrial and commercial districts. The opportunity is, on the contrary, to develop neighbourhoods where you live, work and rest, and in which there is access to all these functions of daily use within a radius of one kilometre (about two-thirds of a mile), with a relatively high density of between 15,000 and 30,000 people. They are productive neighbourhoods that operate at human speed, while connected regionally and globally, through digital networks and public and shared transportation systems. A walkable city where you can live, work and rest allows you to eliminate time from the daily trips of citizens and increases the quality of life. Logically, the city includes neighbourhood-scale equipment and services that must be distributed throughout the city, and other urban-, regional- or national-scale equipment such as hospitals, sports centres, convention centres and spaces for leisure, among others, which act as metropolitan attractors and that must have excellent access through public transport systems.

Self-Sufficient Buildings

Our cities must be radically transformed from places that import products and produce waste, to become places where goods are produced, consumed and recycled in a circular manner. People need to produce food, energy and products to live, drastically reducing material dependence on the global economy. In this way, by bringing the production of resources closer to neighbourhoods and to people, buildings have a functional mission in the immediate environment to incorporate new functions and activities in this

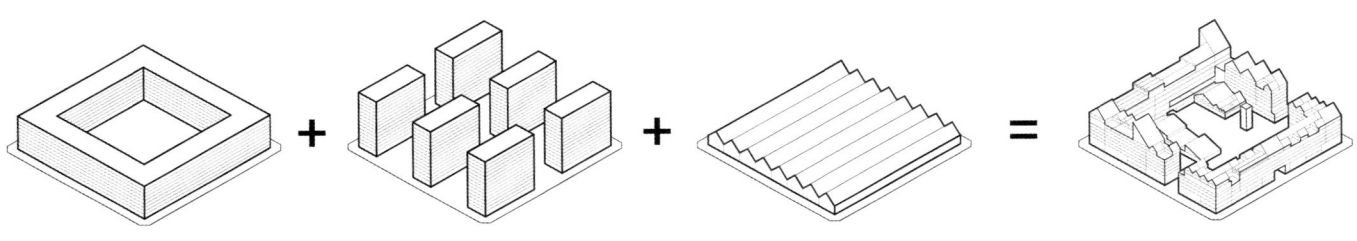

EUROPEAN URBAN BLOCK, 19TH CENTURY:

MIXED-USE CITY

CHINESE MODERN BLOCK, 20TH CENTURY:

HOUSING BLOCKS

PRODUCTIVE SOLAR GREENHOUSES:

PRODUCING FOOD AND ENERGY

THE NEW SELF-SUFFICIENT URBAN BLOCK

MIXED-USE COMPACT AND HUMAN WAY OF LIVING

A new model for a city district is produced through the combination of a courtyard block, housing block and production farming block, to produce a hybrid self-sufficient environment.

ecological-productive-connected world. This is the next challenge for buildings, blocks and communities in the coming years. If new requirements for buildings and architecture are produced every 50 years, the next goal is to build new or renovate existing buildings such that they are or become self-sufficient. For this to be possible, buildings must produce the energy they need to function, integrate local food production associated with the recycling of their water, and incorporate spaces for digital production as part of their urban structure. All of these initiatives should be based on new designs that transform the modern idea of buildings as 'machines for living in'[1] into buildings as organisms for life. Therefore, the basic materials for these new buildings should be materials of biological origin, such as wood, which is reproduced through natural cycles and, if forests are sustainably managed, can be an infinite resource.

Food production is present through greenhouses on the rooftops, fruit orchards in the courtyard and each balcony offering a potager – a kitchen garden.

The courtyard is intended to provide biodiversity and water management. All the ground surfaces are permeable. The water collected from the roofs is harvested to irrigate plants that have been selected to be nectar rich and provide a variety of food for butterflies.

Guallart Architects,
The Self-Sufficient City:
designs for post-Covid
housing for Xiong'an,
China,
2020

Urban metabolism at the scale of the neighbourhood guides the parameters for the self-sufficient city to rely on local treatment and production of resources. Renewable energy systems allow residents to store energy. Buildings made of wood promote renewable materials, zero waste and a circular economy.

- rainwater collection
- energy production
- food production (greenhouse, LED farming, aquaponics, agriculture)
- innovation and technology
- fablab-making
- community housing
- working, retail mixed use
- public space landscape self-sufficiency

Fresh food shops are arranged on the ground floor of the block, selling produce grown in the same district. The market also serves as a social meeting point for the various demographics.

The building has an intelligent system to manage energy, water and information, developing the principle of the Internet of Building.

Buildings must produce the energy they need to function, integrate local food production associated with the recycling of their water, and incorporate spaces for digital production as part of their urban structure

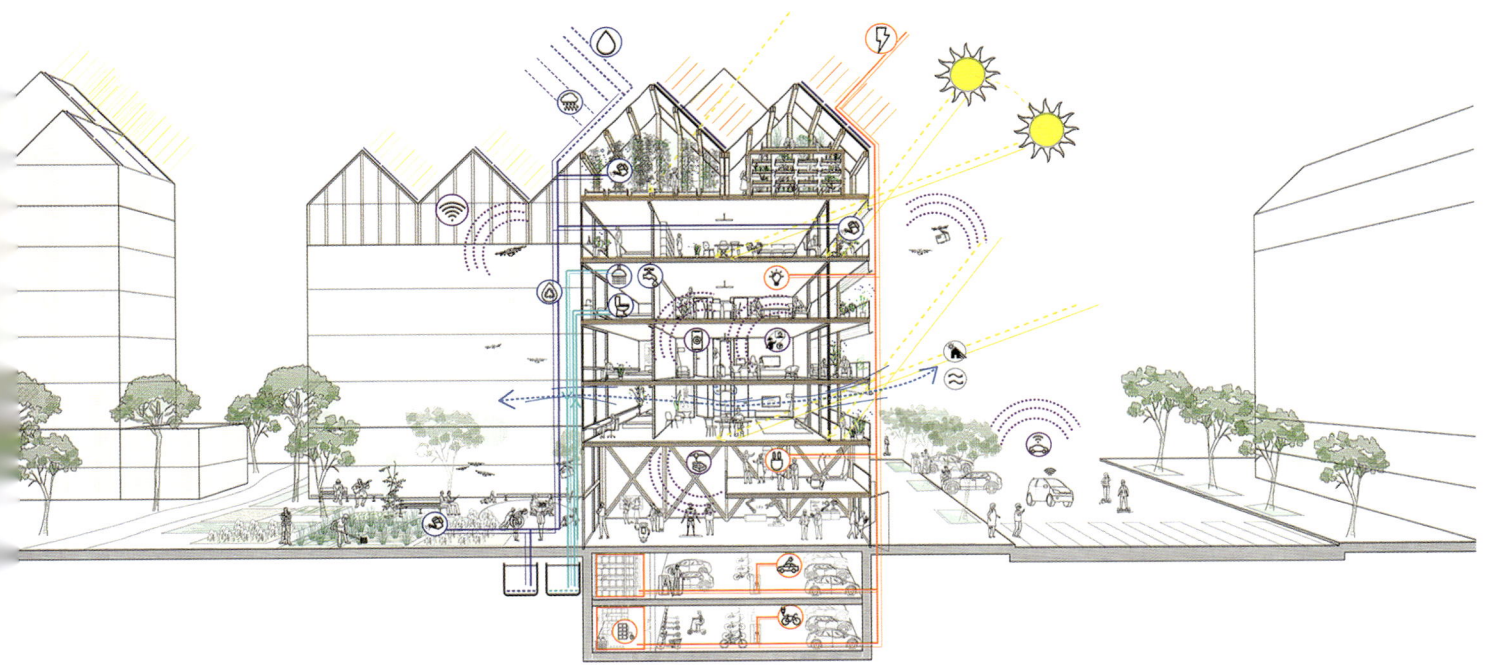

Guallart Architects, The Self-Sufficient City: designs for post-Covid housing for Xiong'an, China, 2020

Digital manufacturing will drive the ecological and distributed reindustrialisation of future cities. Fab labs as extensions of the home allow for residents to make or buy things made directly in the block with proper machinery and open-source knowledge networks.

It makes much more sense to bring the production of goods closer to the places where they are consumed, and to simultaneously boost thousands of local economies through distributed production

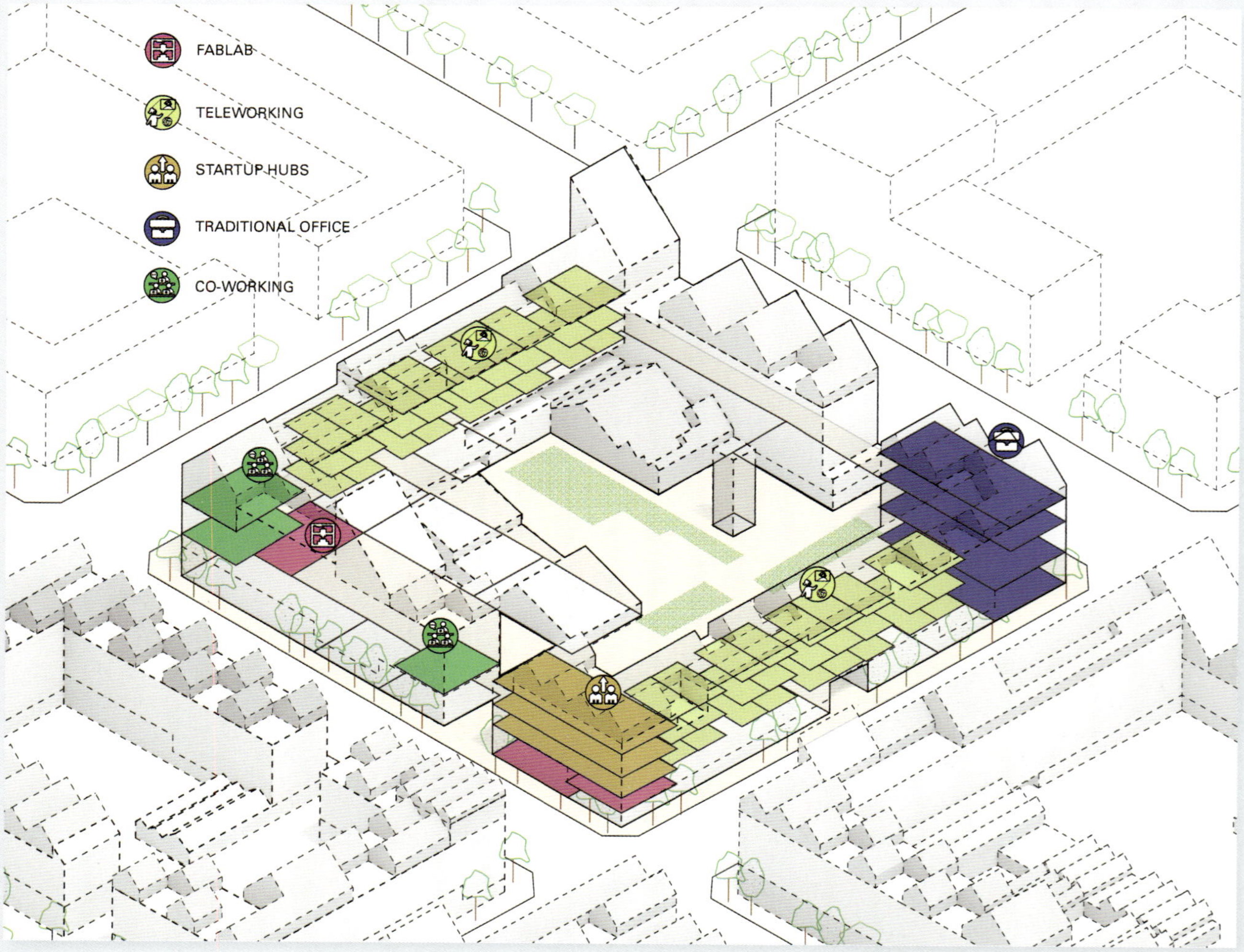

Local Digital Production
A new type of industry must be developed based on digital manufacturing, on site and on demand. The traditional industrial model has encouraged concentration in larger and larger factories, on the grounds that increasing the scale of production lowered the price of commodities. Over time, production has thus been concentrated in a few places around the world, where labour is cheaper. This circumstance has increased the widespread dependence on just a few places in the world and just a few companies for almost anything. If we analyse the state of industry up until the middle of the 20th century, a large number of products were produced inside cities, in workshops and medium-sized factories. The proposed return of the manufacture of industrial products to medium-sized factories and workshops in cities follows the same principles as organic food: it may be somewhat more expensive from a monetary point of view, but adds more value to society by empowering local communities, requires fewer resources, and is largely produced by those who will consume it. This production model is possible because a large portion of industrial production is now based on digital manufacturing, using 3D printing, or robots and advanced technologies that manipulate matter to make products. This type of industry, in general, has a very low impact in terms of noise or environmental pollution, which is why it can be integrated into the neighbourhoods of cities.

From Co-working to Co-factory
One of the phenomena that has begun to change the organisation of work, and with it the organisation of cities, is the relationship between people and the companies in which they work. In fact, the digital world has increased the proportion of freelancers compared to employed workers. Accordingly, facilities for co-working have been promoted where independent professionals share resources and spaces.
This principle of sharing can now be applied to industrial production. Indeed, digital manufacturing technologies are far more flexible than their analogue predecessors. The same machines can print a bicycle or a chair with equal ease. In some of the products that we buy today, the consumer must already participate in their final assembly. Digital production allows the development of parametric designs which are constantly adapting or can be customised by users. It no longer makes sense to concentrate repetitive production in a few places and in large industries, which in times of crisis prove ineffectively responsive. It makes much more sense to bring the production of goods closer to the places where they are consumed, and to simultaneously boost thousands of local economies through distributed production. This is the model of the digital age. Likewise, this urban industry model can allow the design, development, production and trade of these new-generation digital products to be integrated into the same building.

The City is a Mine
It is necessary to minimise the external contributions of raw materials needed for industrial development. In place of importation, these can be sought out within the cities themselves, which have huge existing concentrations of objects and products, called garbage when discarded. In the past, this has accumulated as mountains of waste on the outskirts of large cities, creating serious environmental problems. For decades, the burning of waste has been promoted to produce energy and heat networks in the cities themselves, also producing a significant environmental impact due to the associated carbon dioxide emissions. The recycling of urban waste, classified into various categories (plastics, cardboard, bio-waste, electronics, etc) can actually transform the city into a mine. Rather than burning matter to produce energy, which in turn is used to produce new materials and products, products can be directly recycled, their materials separated, and various techniques applied to re-incorporate obsolete objects into the matter cycle. It is this so-called circular economy that reduces the import of foreign matter to cities and therefore has important ecological benefits for them. For the circular economy to perform optimally, new products must be designed with their eventual recycling already in mind. The new productive city must be circular.

From the Industrial City to the Biocity
Circularity includes materials, resources and people from the regions around cities. Without the nature that exists around them, and that provides ecological services, cities would not be possible. This new model of a productive, ecological and connected city, in which buildings are organisms for life, can define a post-industrial urban paradigm, typical of a digital age in which humans are fighting against climate change that they themselves caused. These new cities, based on the circular bio-economy that tends towards connected self-sufficiency, could be called 'biocities'. Cities, rather than growing against nature, should be integral parts of nature. Therefore, if we analyse the organisation and functions of forests and natural ecosystems, we will discover how they can serve as ideal references for the local production of resources and the collaborative development of species.

Telecommuting and distributed work is already a reality. Therefore the block offers the flexibility to work from home, in co-working, small urban industries, office spaces, business incubators or spaces for traditional commerce through new distributed working models.

Note
1. As famously proposed by Le Corbusier in his *Vers Une Architecture* (*Towards an Architecture*), 1923.

Text © 2021 John Wiley & Sons Ltd. Images © Guallart Architects

Marina Otero Verzier

NOTHING IS AUTOMATIC

PRODUCING MORE-THAN-HUMAN RELATIONS IN THE PEARL RIVER DELTA

Het Nieuwe Instituut,
Ash Cloud factory (part of
Automated Landscapes project),
Shenzhen, China,
2018

Automation plays a key role in increasing efficiency and productivity in the Ash Cloud factory, yet here robots and AI have not replaced humans. Instead, they have reprogrammed them and become their managers.

In the light of rapid urbanisation, manufacturing processes in China's Pearl River Delta are undergoing extensive change. This is one of the regions where the collaborative research project Automated Landscapes has been exploring how automation affects the built environment. Among several international partners involved in the initiative is the Research and Development department at Rotterdam's Het Nieuwe Instituut, headed by **Marina Otero Verzier**. Here she charts how the area's industries are being rearticulated in line with shifting relationships between humans and machines, and how this is proving a double-edged sword for the evolution of the city.

While automated machines have captured humans' imagination throughout history, the architecture of full automation is no longer a distant project. Implemented today in places like the US, Germany, the Netherlands, Japan and Korea, autonomous machines maximise the performance of financial, logistical and production centres. Even the so-called 'factory of the world', the Chinese region of the Pearl River Delta, is transforming its production lines to become one of the main scenarios for the transition to automated systems.[1] And it is precisely in the region's manufacturing, logistics and supply chain infrastructures that the new architectures – buildings, spatial practices, technologies, protocols – for the interaction between humans and robots are being tested.

When in 2014 the Chinese government launched 'Made in China 2025' – a national plan aimed at redirecting the focus of its manufacturing industry from a quantity to a quality paradigm – mass production was giving way to so-called 'intelligent manufacturing'. At the core of this transition was the introduction of advanced robotics to increase labour productivity and competitiveness.[2] The national scheme triggered other regional and local programmes in areas of concentrated production.[3] One of these automation programmes, initiated by Guangdong province in 2015, has received more than 900 billion Chinese yuan in funding, with subsidies covering between 10 and 20 per cent of companies' investment in robotics upgrades. Its name evokes what many would consider a dreaded, dystopian future: 'Robots to Replace Human Workers'.[4]

If we are to take the name of this programme as equivalent to its ambition, it would seem that the Pearl River Delta is the ideal place to explore how these disruptive changes could affect the architectures of production and the labouring bodies that populate them. Yet while automation still seems, for many workers, to be leading to a future without work, machines are but the human fantasy of the working body par excellence. Or, as Michel Foucault put it, while 'men have dreamt of liberating machines, there are, by definition, no machines of freedom'.[5] In fact, modern conceptions of freedom and contemporary factories are both built upon the reproduction of industrial capital and the exploitation of human and non-human workforces. Their ideologies materialised into seemingly banal architectures.

Since 2017 the cultural centre Het Nieuwe Instituut in Rotterdam, the Netherlands, has been working on the initiative Automated Landscapes, a collaborative research project analysing precisely these unassuming architectures that are nevertheless emergent scenarios for the future of labour and production urbanism. Developed together with Marten Kuijpers, Ludo Groen, Victor Muñoz Sanz, Merve Bedir, the Future+ Aformal Academy in Shenzhen and Hong Kong, and a large number of supporters and collaborators, Automated Landscapes reflects on the implications of automation for the built environment and the bodies that inhabit it. In the Pearl River Delta, the research has focused primarily on the Build Your Dreams (BYD), Rapoo Technology and Ash Cloud factories – all located in Shenzhen – as case studies for the paradigms for the division of labour as socio-spatial relations between humans and non-humans.

Redistribution of Labour
Build Your Dreams is one of China's main manufacturers of cars, battery-powered bicycles, buses, trucks, forklifts, solar panels, and rechargeable and mobile-phone batteries. In its factory in Shenzhen's Pingshan District, humans and robots do not cross paths. Their domains are demarcated by a clear, straight, glass wall. Yet on both sides of the wall, bodies – human or otherwise – follow the same rhythm. That of the monotonous and predictable operations needed to keep the largest battery production in the world running.[6] A rhythm dictated and monitored by software systems that track the status of batteries.

This repetitive labour in the assembly lines is precisely what makes the use of automation cost-effective, as well as being the cause of the decrease of human workers employed in manufacturing processes. Robots maximise productivity and save space, while guaranteeing a working environment where lunch breaks, common spaces and human comfort are becoming obsolete. Where workers' unions have no place. With the exception of a handful of engineers and managers – who rarely make incursions into the domain of machines – the presence of the human body and the architecture designed around it becomes more irrelevant. The glass wall might soon be so too.

However, automation does not only imply the replacement of human activities by machines, but also a redistribution of labour. The bodies of those who previously populated the human domain are not necessarily liberated from the bondage of labour, but instead pushed to relocate. Workers disappearing from the Build Your Dreams production line may appear elsewhere – notably in places where the precision of their human fingers' movements is still in demand. The factories of the Shenzhen-based electronics manufacturer Rapoo Technology are such a space.

Rapoo started to introduce automation within its assembly lines in 2005. The measure was meant to be a solution to labour shortages in peak-demand seasons. It took the company four years to complete automation of one of its production lines. Paradoxically, the product for which the technology had been implemented was already outdated by then. Robotic solutions, they learned, needed to be constantly adjusted in order to respond to changes in market cycles.

To avoid a repeat of such complications the company designed a flexible manufacturing system based around collaboration between humans and robots, instead of the replacement of the former. Robots carry out the repetitive tasks needed for the production of standardised components, in addition to the more dangerous and heavy activities. Human labour is, in turn, focused on adding the plasticity that market changes demand.[7] Yet there is always trouble in paradise, and Rapoo's human–machine collaborative strategy also resulted in the reduction of its human workforce from about 3,000 to 700 employees.

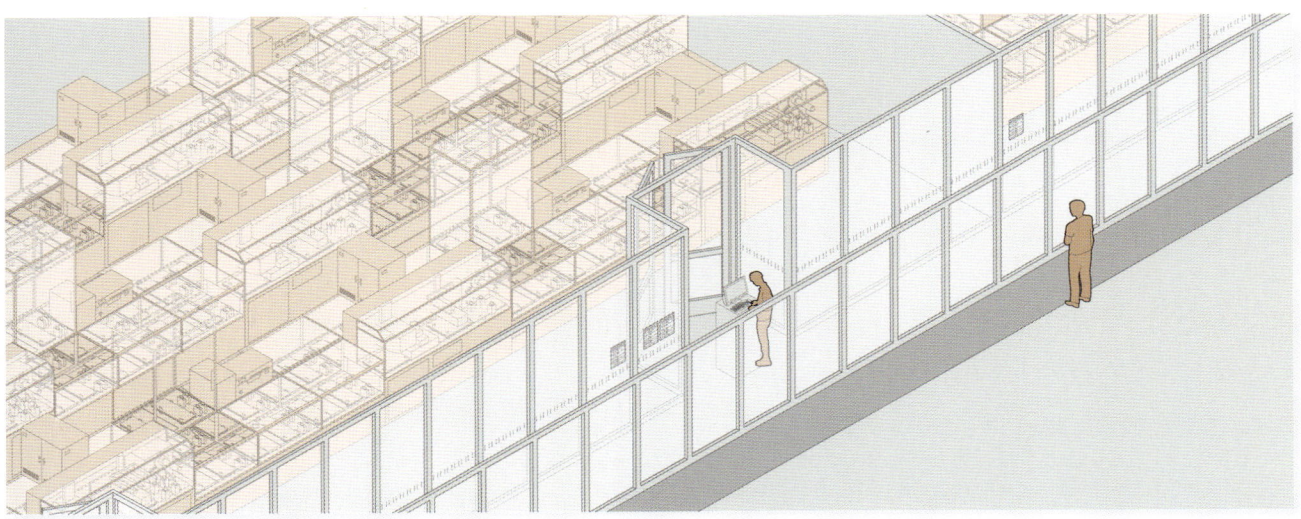

Het Nieuwe Instituut,
Build Your Dreams factory
(part of Automated Landscapes project),
Pingshan District,
Shenzhen, China,
2018

Founded in 1995, Build Your Dreams is a major manufacturer of various vehicles as well as solar panels, and rechargeable and mobile-phone batteries. The company has transitioned to automated technologies for efficiency. As humans disappear in favour of robotic labourers, assembly lines and storage areas are reorganised to maximise productivity. Engineers and managers do not venture into the domain of machines here unless absolutely necessary.

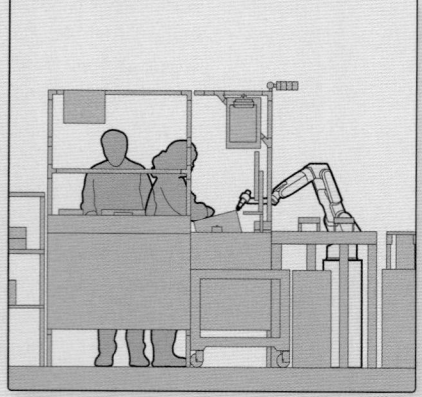
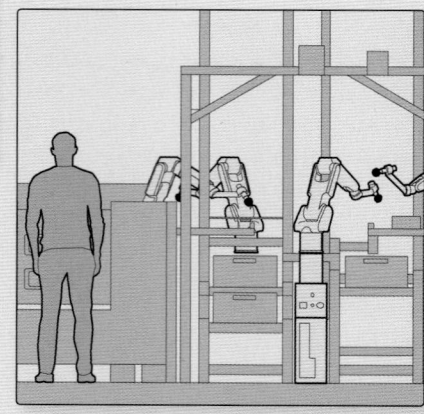

Rapoo Technology is a Shenzhen-based electronics manufacturer that has introduced automation in its assembly lines since 2015. Rapoo's strategy is based on collaboration between humans and robots, and the factory's architectural solutions reflect the various scales and formats for these human and non-human interactions.

Het Nieuwe Instituut,
Rapoo Factory (part of Automated Landscapes project),
Shenzhen,
China,
2018

The work and maintenance of the robots, as well as the training of human employees to achieve maximum efficiency, is controlled by AI

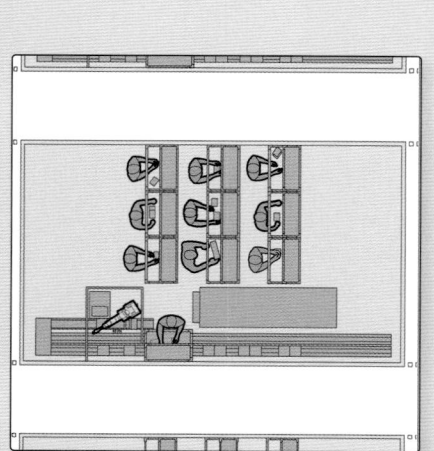
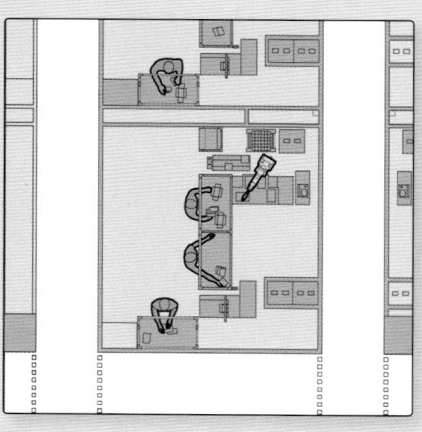
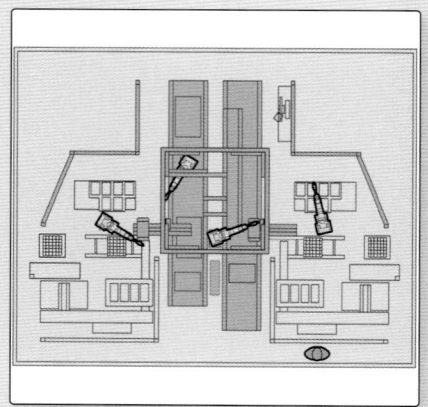

The spatial configurations of human–machine relations inside the Rapoo factory are organised into rectangular work islands, where the levels of automation range from manual to fully automated manufacturing. Robot arms work alongside human operators assembling computer keyboards, mice, and their sub-components.

Human workers are still in demand at Ash Cloud, a company also located in Shenzhen that produces accessories for mobile phones and tablets. There, robots and AI have not replaced humans. Instead, they have reprogrammed them and become their managers. The enterprise resource planning (ERP) system manages the factory internally and remotely to the point that the figure of the middle manager has been rendered redundant.

The ERP monitors supply and demand, product stocks, employee tasks, shifts, hours and vacations, resource usage, waste produced, currency exchange and stock market activity in real time. Easily accessed through an IOS application, the system quantifies performance and efficiency and makes results intelligible through the screens of computers, tablets and mobile phones. It in fact channels all communication between the management team and human and machinic employees.

The work and maintenance of the robots, as well as the training of human employees to achieve maximum efficiency, is controlled by AI. In this way, the productivity of each assembly line is measured against objectives and cost. Productivity is also enhanced by digital avatars of a sad turtle or a happy rabbit that emerge and preside over the assembly lines to either push or motivate the human teams' work. Nothing is fully automatic. It is designed for subjecting bodies to the crude pace dictated by production needs. As architect and filmmaker Liam Young puts it, human bodies are optimised and trained to perform as components of an efficient planetary-scale production line.[8]

New Paradigms
The examples of Build Your Dreams, Rapoo Technology and Ash Cloud demonstrate how automation does not necessarily lead to a utopian human society organised around leisure, nor to one of rampant unemployment due to the total replacement of the human workforce. They show, instead, how under the relentless scrutiny of AI, employees are pressured to perform at their limits to contribute to an infinite supply of cheap labour at the expense of resting time, one-to-one communication, welfare and safety issues. Their bodies are in fact abstracted into numbers and graphs displayed on smooth surfaces. They are data on a screen where forms of empathy and solidarity towards the worker are rendered irrelevant to the AI or humans who coordinate, recalibrate and control them. A perfected Cartesian regime designed for maximum profit through the full exploitation of bodies, and unbothered by changing social dynamics and working conditions.

These infrastructures and dynamics have a profound impact on the environment. As some human bodies and their capacities become dispensable (or exhausted), so do the spaces that they inhabit even beyond the assembly lines and production centres. Automation does not mean replacement, but displacement and differential distribution of the social, ecological and economic effects of these regimes.[9] What happens in the factories in Shenzhen has an impact on the city's landscape and economy and in its neighbouring cities and regions where workers made redundant may need relocate. It is also felt in more distant territories, where the changes in the pace of production and the supply chain that automation is instilling in the Pearl River

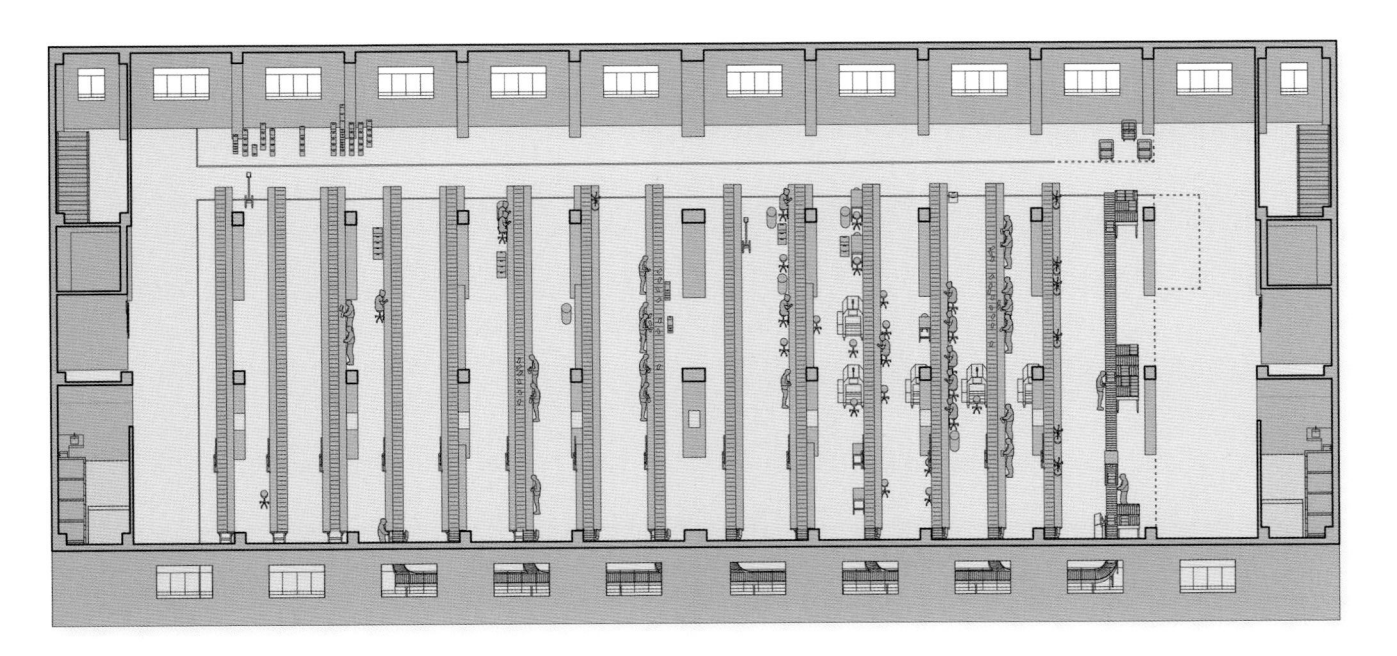

Het Nieuwe Instituut,
Ash Cloud factory (part of
Automated Landscapes project),
Shenzhen, China,
2018

The Ash Cloud factory, focused on the manufacturing of mobile phone polyurethane cases, still depends on human labour and maintains a spatial organisation based on assembly lines that operate during fixed hours.

Rather than aiming for enhancing productivity, a post-anthropocentric and non-Cartesian architecture could instead serve to challenge the inevitability of unequal relations between humans and the planet

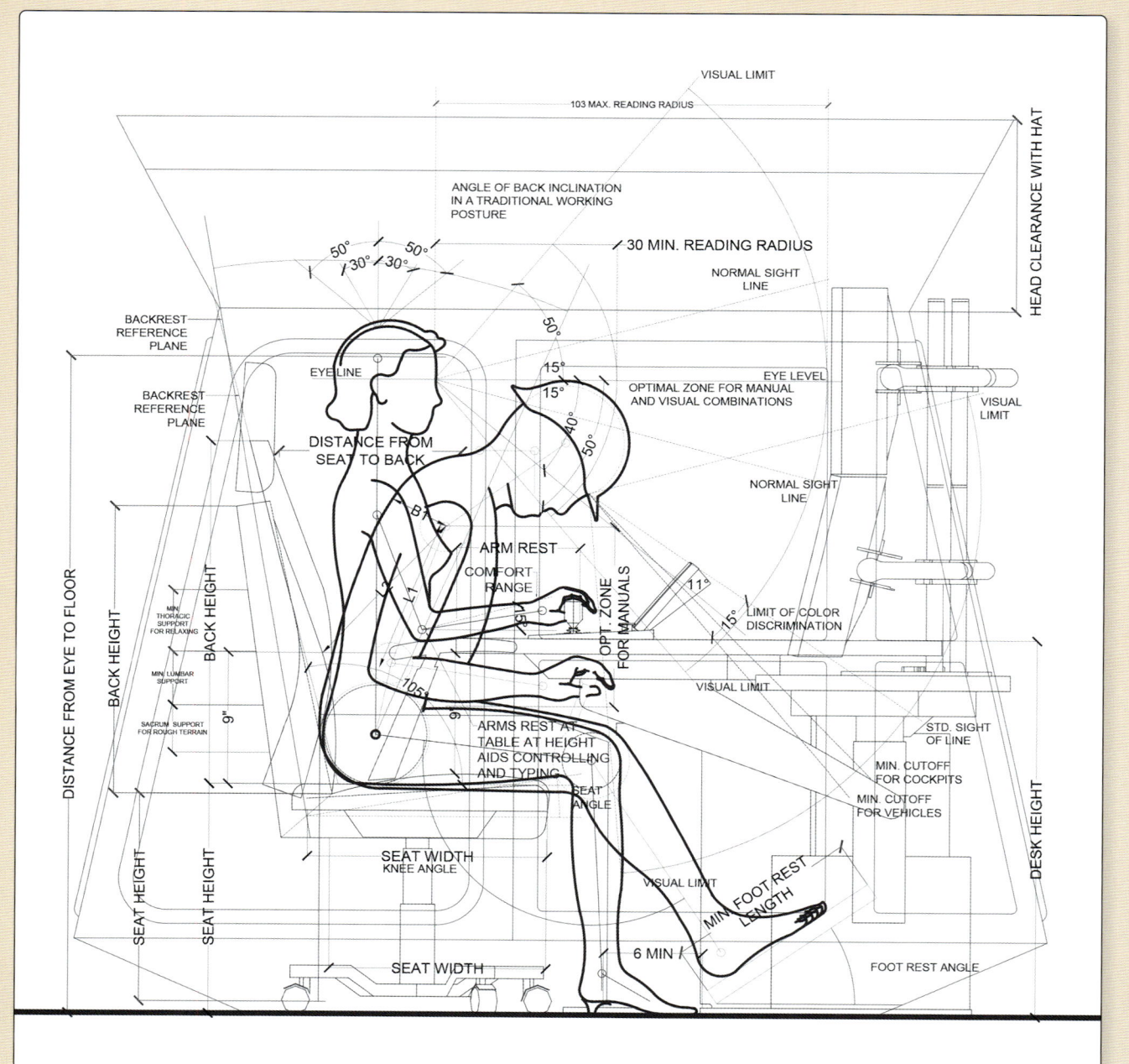

Het Nieuwe Instituut, Anthropometric graphical study of crane cabin operator versus remote control operator, Automated Landscapes project, 2018

The Automated Landscapes project initiated in 2017 had as a hypothesis the substitution of humans by robots in production centres due to the introduction of emergent automation technologies. Yet the research demonstrated that blue-collar human workers are not disappearing from production sites, but being displaced to other markets and territories and/or replaced by white-collar workers who control operations remotely from their laptops and iPads.

Delta translate as even more pressure on the already strained manual labourers to remain competitive.

What to do with the replaceable, displaced humans has been the focus of educational programmes to develop workers' skills and competencies or proposals for a universal basic income. Yet perhaps the most important question to address is how these new paradigms of work could bring the seed of an alternative organisation of society and its accompanying architectures. After all, the fascination and anxiety produced by an automated world can be redeployed towards the actual prospect of social, economic or ecological collapse in the face of climate crisis – a crisis brought about by this quest for relentless production based on the exploitation and invisibility of labouring bodies.

Future Speculations

If there is something to glean from the architecture of the Build Your Dreams, Rapoo Technology or Ash Cloud factories it is that, unlike contemporary cities, they do not have humans at their centre. Perhaps the de-centring of the human that we are witnessing in the productive architectures of the Pearl Delta River could be taken further, to the de-centring of the notion of humankind as a universal, rational subject. However, rather than aiming for enhancing productivity, a post-anthropocentric and non-Cartesian architecture could instead serve to challenge the inevitability of unequal relations between humans and the planet. For nothing is fully automatic. Humans, their time, their labour and behaviours are managed by technologies, protocols, legal documents and social conventions. The product of automation is not only commodities but, perhaps more importantly, the technologically enabled biopolitical production, reproduction and extraction of forms of life.

Yes, human bodies are subject to programming. We could, therefore, be willingly self-reprogrammed not for the pursuit of profit and privilege for some humans, but instead to unleash ecological practices and networks of ethics and responsibility. To combat climate injustice. To conceive and enact an architecture not based on systems of exploitation of bodies, on the depletion of resources, on the dictates of the market and the rationality of economic efficiency. An architecture for the future that is not confined to managerial disciplinary boundaries or technological industrial progress. ⌂

Notes
1. International Federation of Robotics (IFR), *Executive Summary World Robotics 2017 Industrial Robots*, 2017: https://ifr.org/downloads/press/Executive_Summary_WR_2017_Industrial_Robots.pdf.
2. Made in China 2025: http://english.www.gov.cn/2016special/madeinchina2025.
3. Huang Yu and Naubahar Sharif, 'From "Labour Dividend" to "Robot Dividend": Technological Change and Workers' Power in South China', *Agrarian South: Journal of Political Economy*, 6 (1), p 55.
4. Dongguan City Government Office, 'Management Measures for Special Funds for "Machine Substitution" in Dongguan' (in Chinese), 25 March 2016: www.dg.gov.cn/gkmlpt/content/0/591/post_591399.html#684; Dongguan City Government Office, 'Dongguan City Promotion Enterprise "Machine Substitution" Action Plan (2014-2016)' (in Chinese), 11 August 2014: www.dg.gov.cn/zwgk/zfgb/szfbgswj/content/post_353845.html; Huang Yu, 'Can Robots Save Dongguan?', HKUST Seminar, 16 March 2017: https://iems.ust.hk/events/academic-seminar/2017/can-robots-save-dongguan-huang-yu.
5. Michel Foucault in conversation with Paul Rabinow, 'Space, Power, and Knowledge', in Sylvère Lotringer (ed), *Foucault Live: Interviews, 1961–84*, trans Lysa Hochroth and John Johnston, Semiotext(e) (New York), 1996, pp 340–41.
6. Jiang Shan in conversation with Merve Bedir (member of the research team), Pingshan, China, 25 January 2018.
7. Steven Lee in conversation with Merve Bedir and Marten Kuijpers (members of the research team), Shenzhen, China, 25 October 2017.
8. Liam Young in conversation with Simone Niquille and Arif Kornweitz, 'Useful Life Podcasts', part of *Work, Body, Leisure*, Dutch Pavilion at the 2018 Venice Architecture Biennale, curated by Marina Otero Verzier: https://work-body-leisure.hetnieuweinstituut.nl/audio.
9. Dieter Ernst, 'Advanced Manufacturing and China's Future for Jobs', *East-West Center Working Papers: Innovation and Economic Growth Series*, 8, 2018, p 20.

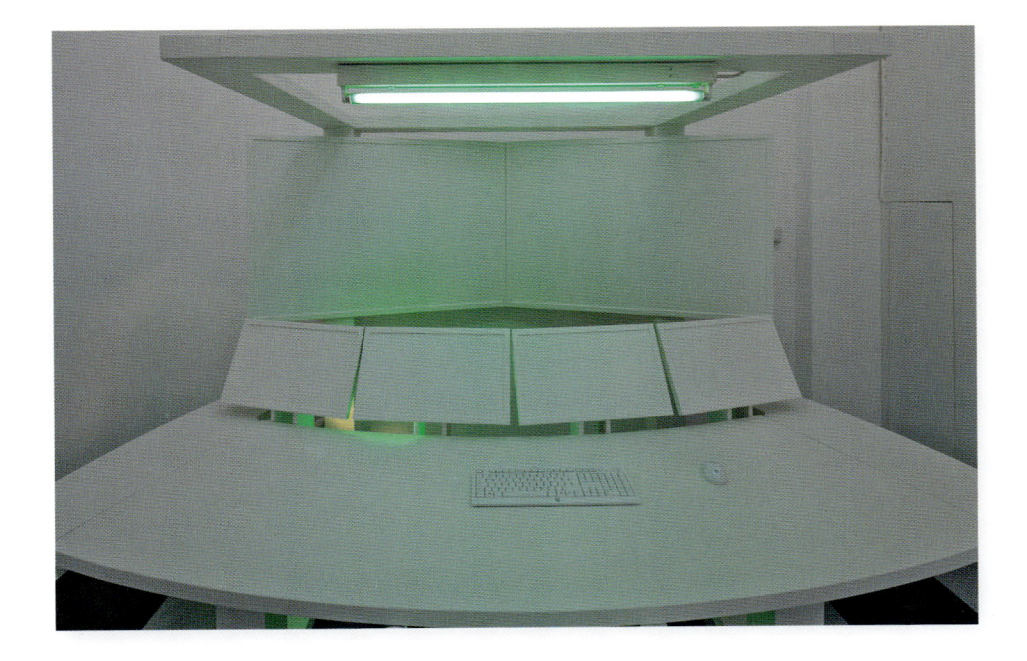

Marina Otero Verzier (curator),
Work, Body, Leisure,
Dutch Pavilion,
Venice Architecture Biennale,
2018

This work, by Marien Kuijpers and Victor Muñoz Sanz, and included in the OFFICE Room in the Dutch Pavilion at the 2018 Venice Architecture Biennale, looked into the transition to automation production and the effect it has on territories and labouring bodies. Shown here is a replica of the operator's remote work area inside the fully automated container terminal in Rotterdam (APM).

Text © 2021 John Wiley & Sons Ltd. Images: © pp 32–8 © Het Nieuwe Instituut; p 39 © Het Nieuwe Instituut, photo Daria Scagliola

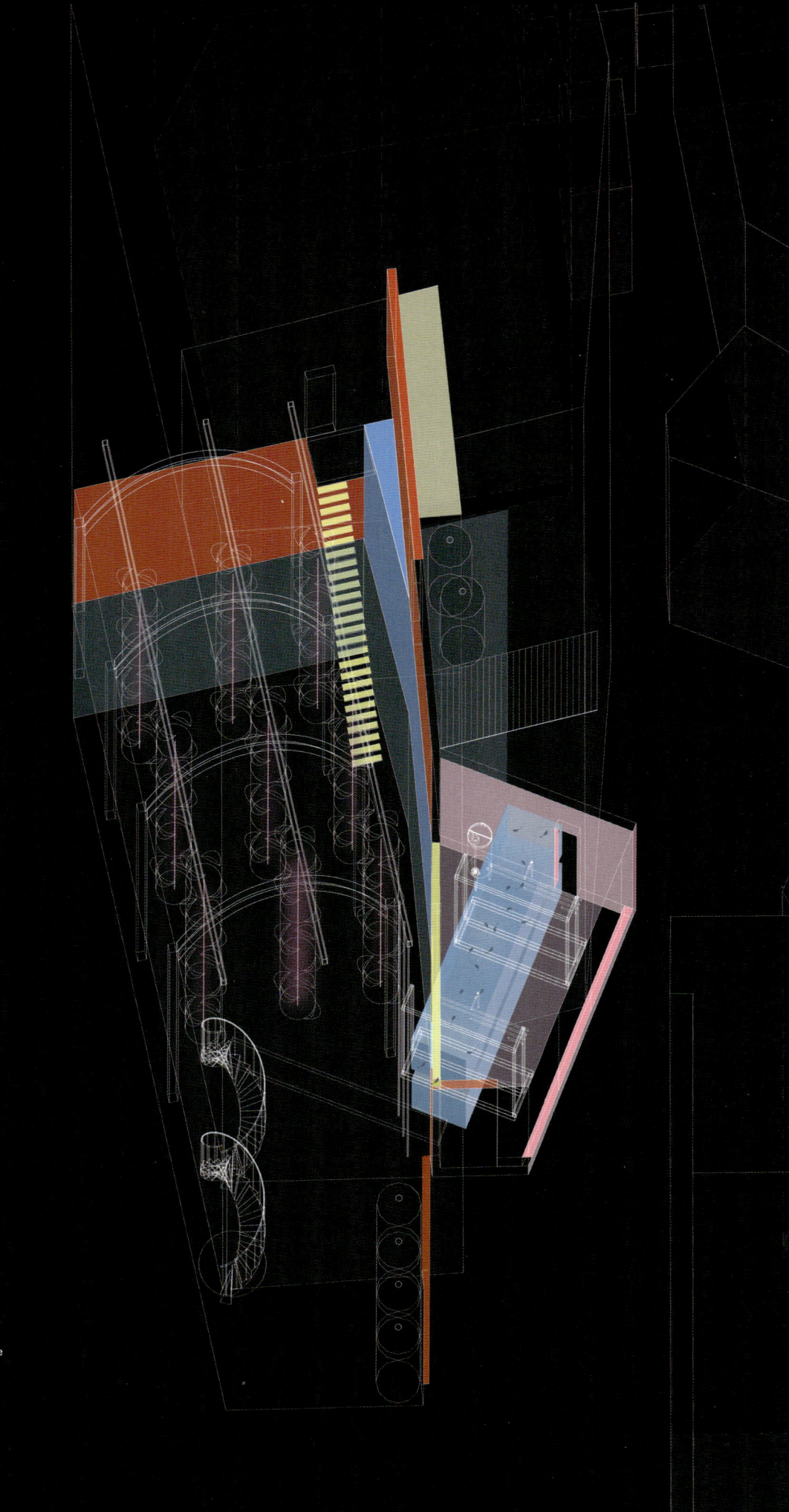

Scott Lloyd and Alexis Kalagas,
No vacancy,
2021

Cloud-connected modular aeroponic arrays transform empty storefronts into high-precision growing environments, incorporating the surreal theatre of automated agriculture into the ritual of the late-night flâneur.

Scott Lloyd and Alexis Kalagas

SALAD DAYS

URBAN FOOD FUTURES

Food production has never been entirely absent from our cities. While the coronavirus pandemic has imposed and inspired new forms of localism in urban environments, a confluence of technological, societal and ecological forces was already driving a shift towards more distributed and circular food systems. **Scott Lloyd**, architect and director of the design research group TEN, and **Alexis Kalagas**, strategic designer and leader of an advanced architecture research unit at Monash University in Melbourne, navigate and speculate on these intersecting dynamics in relation to nascent models of urban food production.

Seventy per cent of food produced globally is destined to feed urban areas.[1] Invisible to the city dweller, industrial agriculture – and the sprawling infrastructural networks and complex supply chains it entails – lies at the heart of urban life. Yet as accelerating processes of 'logistification' and digitisation deliver fresh food on-demand to our door, we often fail to 'see' food for what it is: our most vital shared resource.[2] With food production re-entering the urban environment, driven by the same confluence of technological, societal and ecological forces transforming industries like manufacturing, the distinction between a consumptive city and productive hinterland is beginning to collapse. Meanwhile, the fast/slow shocks of the pandemic and climate emergency have exposed the fragility of wider food systems, compelling a re-examination of how we produce, process, prepare, consume and recapture food in a context of enveloping planetary urbanism.

Despite the fiction of an urban-rural divide, cities and agriculture co-evolved, and food production has never been banished entirely from urban settings.[3] Even with the advent of industrialised economies, allotment gardens – a product of the 19th-century British enclosure acts and German Schreber movement – were central to both Ebenezer Howard's Garden City movement and Le Corbusier's early Modernist 'Contemporary City' proposal (1922).[4] Allotments flourished in the interwar period, culminating in Allied 'Dig for Victory' campaigns during the Second World War, which transformed parks and spaces of leisure into 'victory gardens', as citizens were urged to grow their own food to supplement rations.[5] While food security imperatives were abandoned in the postwar consumer society, supplanted by the rise of intensive farming practices, the urban crisis of the 1970s and concurrent birth of the environmental movement saw urban agriculture reframed as grassroots community activism.

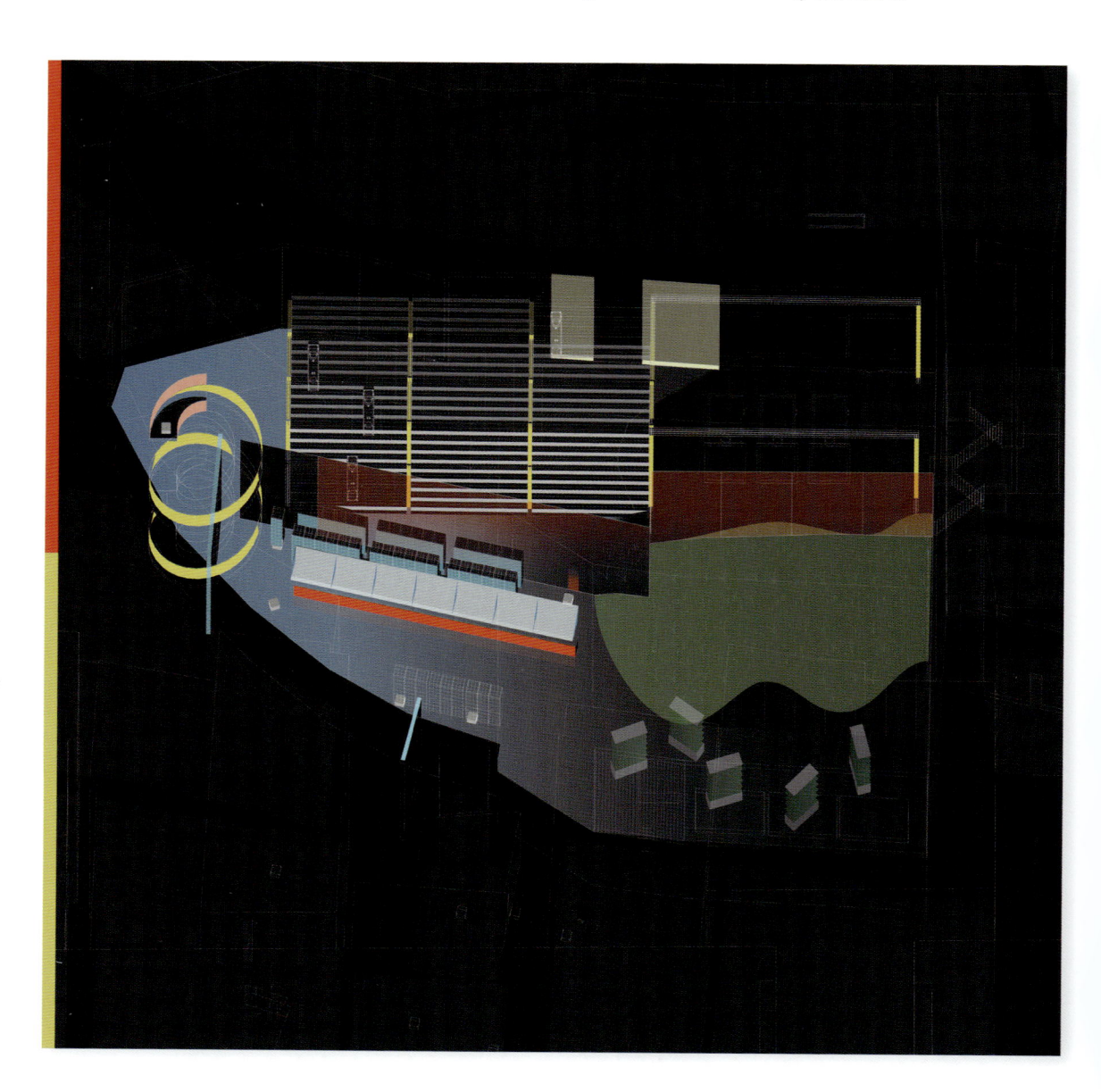

Scott Lloyd and Alexis Kalagas, Growing environments, 2021

A hybrid digital/physical grocery store is part-automated fulfilment centre for on-demand delivery, and part-synthetic nature experience, spatialising the distinction between fresh and processed foods.

Bio-Design and the Metabolic City

Linking sustainability advocates – 'AgTech' evangelists, hyper-local gastronomes, social justice campaigners, venture capitalists, spatial designers and real-estate developers – contemporary urban food production is fast evolving beyond the performative lifestyle signifiers of boutique rooftop farms and edible gardens. As real-time algorithmic precision enables increasingly compact, low-energy and automated forms of high-yield indoor cultivation without soil or natural light, parallel advances in lab-grown 'cultured meat' and designer plant-based proteins suggest a future where cities could soon become productive hubs positioned within more circular and localised food systems. These developments would not only significantly reduce the 21 to 37 per cent of anthropogenic carbon emissions attributed to the inefficiencies of the existing agro-industrial complex, but also contribute through surface planting to a range of associated 'ecosystem services', including decreasing stormwater runoff, mitigation of the heat-island effect, nitrogen fixation and biological pest control.[6]

AeroFarms, which employs a closed-loop aeroponics growing system augmented by predictive analytics and machine learning, harvests almost 1,000 tonnes of salad greens annually across its modular vertical farms in post-industrial Newark, New Jersey: repurposing a steel mill, laser-tag facility and shuttered nightclub. The cloud-connected network of Berlin-based Infarm is expected to expand to 5 million square feet (465,000 square metres) of distributed productive space across Europe, North America and Asia by 2025, including controlled in-store growing environments in major supermarkets and grocery stores. Late last year, San Francisco start-up Eat Just announced plans to build a new facility in Singapore, shortly before its cell-cultured chicken was the first lab-grown meat product worldwide to gain regulatory approval, consistent with the '30 by 30' initiative led by the Singapore Food Agency to produce 30 per cent of the country's food supply locally by 2030 (the city-state currently imports more than 90 per cent of its food).[7]

The diversity and density of urban resource flows can also subvert territorial-scale processes of extraction. Food waste is responsible for 10 per cent of global emissions.[8] Within cities, less than 2 per cent of nutrients in discarded organic resources (food waste at the point of distribution or consumption, processed food byproducts, human sewage) are captured for reuse – a focus for closed-loop experiments as far back as Graham Caine's Eco-House (1972). Built with the anarchist collective Street Farm, Architectural Association (AA) student Caine lived in the off-grid prototype with his family in South London for three years.[9] More recently, Bubbly Dynamics has adapted an industrial meatpacking facility in Chicago as a food start-up incubator and living laboratory. The Plant recovers more than 40 per cent of byproducts through integrated aquaponics, algae bioreactors and anaerobic digestion. These metabolic processes, supported by collaborative platforms like NYSP2I's Organic Resource Locator that identify symbiotic adjacencies at an urban scale, can reduce resource inputs in more circular systems and feed the cultivation of composite biomaterials.

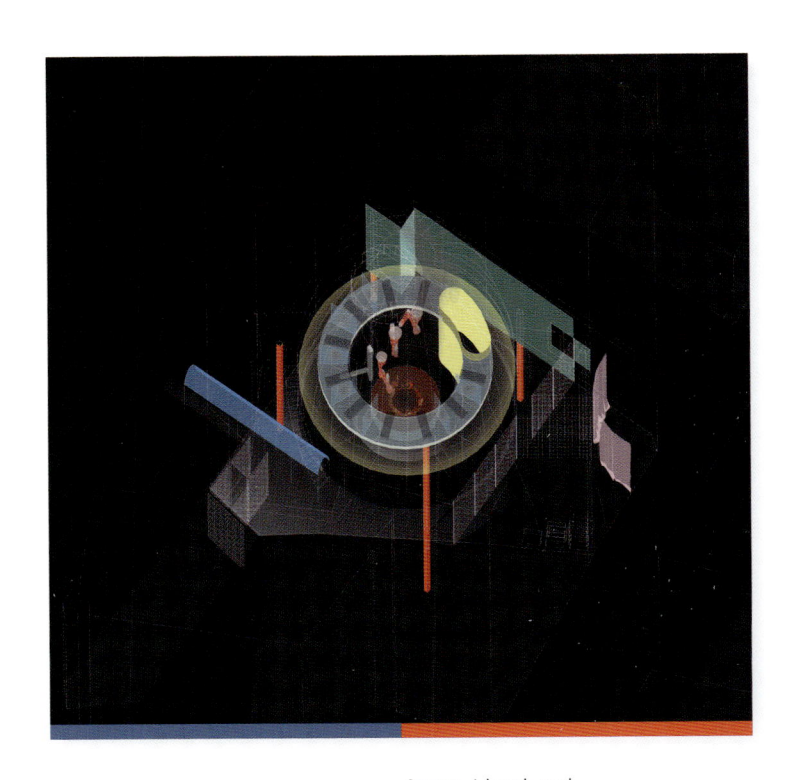

Scott Lloyd and Alexis Kalagas, The cathedral of eating, 2021

Separated by glass, guests flock to experience dining as a performance in the round, with their meals meticulously assembled by agile industrial robots in a simulacrum of elemental food practices.

The Choreography of Consumption

Supply-side innovations are matched by transforming practices of urban food consumption, shaped by a pervasive sense of time, energy and labour in flux: an accelerated cultural progression from farm-to-table to 'ghost-kitchen-to-sofa'.[10] Amazon (Deliveroo) and Google (Kitchen United) are investing heavily in plug-and-play dark kitchen infrastructure optimised for delivery. The Neighborhood Kitchens Food Hall exists only as a virtual storefront in Uber Eats, with 'last block' fulfilment handled by Reef Technologies via its network of off-grid kitchen pods located in 4,500 parking lots across the US. In California, Zume Pizza orders are half-cooked by robots in a sterile production facility and finished in constantly circulating food-truck ovens, seamlessly integrating food preparation into the choreography of logistics flows. In China, Hema – a chain backed by Alibaba – has reimagined the supermarket as fulfilment centre, and restaurant dining as automated theatre, channelled through a single app interface linked to the Alipay e-payment platform.

Even before enforced social distancing and stay-at-home orders laid waste to the hospitality sector in countless cities, more than half of restaurant spending in the US was already projected to be 'off premises' in 2020.¹¹ As operators worldwide pivoted abruptly amid the pandemic to cling to revenue lifelines, the improvised assembly of entirely new supply chains – connecting small-scale food producers directly to urban customers via a web of hybrid food service and retail models – suggests the future potential for digital channels and distributed physical spaces to challenge the monopolistic control of supermarket conglomerates, while reinstating the social rituals and community resilience once present at the intersection of food production and consumption. The alternative is evident in the cold logic of an unbound global food system, which recently saw India's locked-down coastal states opting to buy soybean oil shipped from Argentina rather than trucking it from inland producers.¹²

In the face of continuing Covid-19 disruption, the agile, adaptive capacity of urban food systems has also produced instructive examples of care and mutual aid: from the repurposing of municipal buses by groups of private volunteers in Wuhan to create mobile food hubs supporting communities in lockdown, to the conversion of Toronto libraries into distribution centres, Lagos schools into decentralised, physically distanced markets, time-share food lockers in Milan and 'mobile markets' in Manila. Beyond a concern for those most vulnerable to shocks and contagion, these initiatives demonstrate how designers can think creatively beyond the singular spaces and functions conventionally associated with food in cities, embedding accessible, flexible micro-infrastructures throughout the urban landscape and harnessing the capacity for local self-organisation – an entanglement of uses evoked in the image of the city as simultaneously a 'dining room, market, and farm'.¹³

TEN Studio and Alexis Kalagas, The Distributed Cooperative, 2019

The short-stay suite, self-contained accommodation that forms part of an 'extended home', allowing cooperative members to temporarily expand their domestic footprint to host friends and family.

The collective showroom, a flexible shared space that introduces a social quality to omnichannel retail experiences in a discreet 'future storefront' elevated above the ground plane.

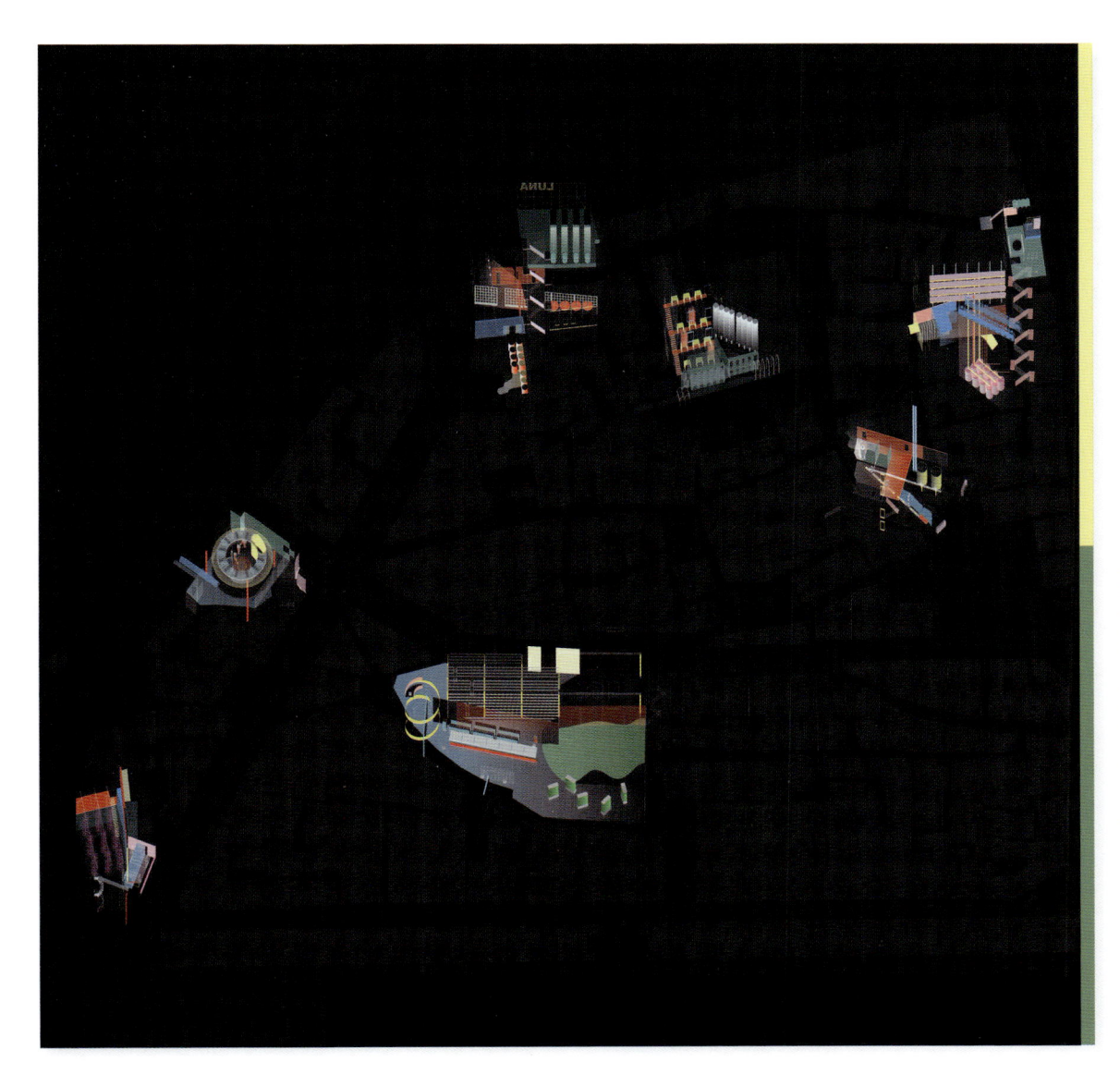

Scott Lloyd,
Alexis Kalagas and
Belen Ruiz Arenas,
Localised, networked,
hybrid,
2021

A speculative foodscape overlaid on an existing urban neighbourhood, uniting compact, circular and automated processes of production and consumption across a series of interlinked sites.

Localised, networked, and hybrid, distributed models mirror the complexity of the city itself, enabling regenerative zones of activity within the hollowed-out spaces of a dematerialised capitalist landscape

(More) Stories About Buildings and Food

The revolution in urban food systems underway may position food at the centre of an expanded field of production urbanism. Localised, networked, and hybrid, distributed models mirror the complexity of the city itself, enabling regenerative zones of activity within the hollowed-out spaces of a dematerialised capitalist landscape. Through our ongoing design research project The Distributed Cooperative, we are exploring strategies to reimagine mixed-use cooperative housing at a neighbourhood scale: automating the search for undiscovered spatial potential embedded within a city's existing urban fabric and exploding the diverse functions usually consolidated within a single development across a cluster of sites. Beyond opportunities for infill housing, the strategy also begins to trace the contours of an alternative approach to adaptive reuse – reprogramming and retrofitting multiple spaces to perform as an integrated foodscape uniting future modes of production and consumption.

In the new kind of city, emerging, hyper-local, digitally traceable supply chains will deliver bio-engineered food to our tables, laboured over round-the-clock by loving machines in airless laboratory settings. It is a city where seamless last-mile logistics infrastructures maintain an optimal flow of just-in-time fresh produce for assisted home preparation, circulated by a non-stop fleet of autonomous refrigerated smart lockers. Certified 'organic', the a-seasonal fruit and vegetables arrive direct-to-consumer as a perpetual harvest, fulfilled by a shifting network of compact aeroponic arrays optimised by machine-learning growing systems, casting a pink night-time glow in vacant storefronts. The same produce is purchased, via AI-driven inventory management, by a ghost-kitchen hospitality incubator renting shared space by the hour. In a vertically integrated platform model, fledgling virtual restaurants nimbly execute dynamic menus responding to neighbourhood-scale predictive analytics, operating out of off-grid modules nestled into unseen urban interstices.

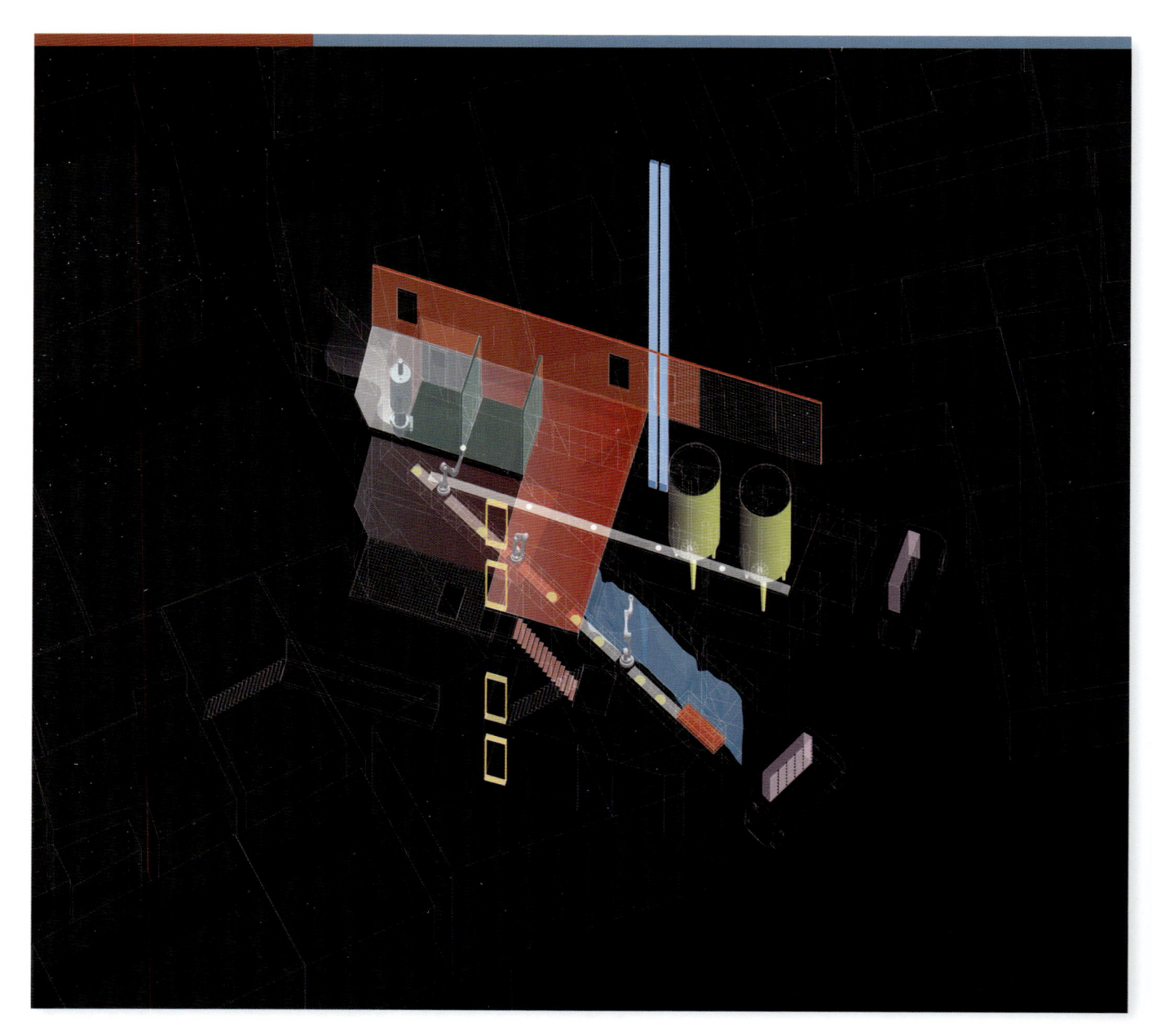

Scott Lloyd and Alexis Kalagas,
Last-mile logistics,
2021

An automated pizza production line feeds a constantly circulating fleet of hybrid mobile ovens, allowing an intricate orchestrated flow of just-in-time deliveries that merges food preparation and logistics.

Scott Lloyd and Alexis Kalagas, Fermentation to fabrication, 2021

A local brewery's microalgae bioreactor is fuelled by the carbon-dioxide byproduct captured during fermentation, supporting the in-house cultivation of an alternative protein concentrate.

Whether hi- or low-tech, the future of food in our cities depends on the same resistance to monocultures that has driven the revival of localised food systems worldwide

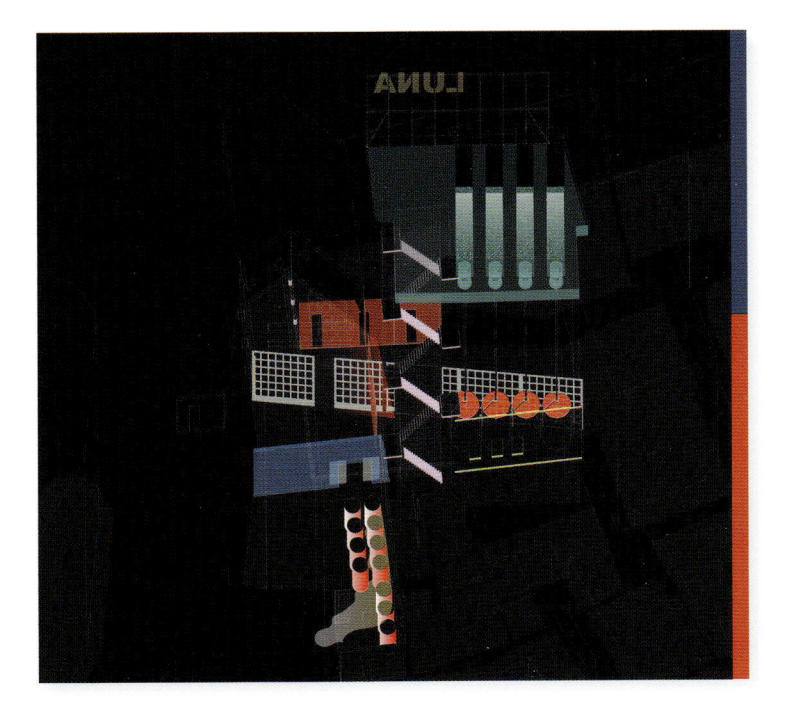

It is a city where the organic waste generated across the network is monitored and traded through a booming digital marketplace, including to a nearby warehouse as pasteurised substrate destined to be seeded with spores of mycelium to fabricate fire-resistant insulation for low-carbon construction. Across the street, a new 'fast casual takeaway' concept has launched, where industrial robots 3D-print finish-at-home meals from nutrient-rich food concentrates, catering to personalised diet plans informed by nutrigenomics and a constant stream of real-time data from ubiquitous wearable bio-monitors. On 'cheat' days, locals flock to the popular neighbourhood microbrewery. Perusing the menu, they choose between 'fried cultured chicken' or supersized vegan burgers, oblivious to how the protein substitute is produced from a basement microalgae farm fed by carbon dioxide released during a beer fermentation process practised unchanged by humans for more than 5,000 years.

These technologies already exist. As our built environments transition to accommodate new realities and new possibilities, food's dual role as both sustenance and fetish object can obscure larger questions of food insecurity and labour precarity – issues the pandemic has brought into stark relief. In designing more efficient, resilient and circular models that enable food to reclaim distributed spaces of production in the meta-industrial city, challenging our understanding of *terroir*, it will be essential to preserve diversity and complexity. Despite the active role of grassroots movements and organisations, platform logic and venture-backed growth reward industry consolidation and the scale necessary to capture network effects: a countervailing force to the power of 'small pieces, loosely joined'.[14] Whether hi- or low-tech, the future of food in our cities depends on the same resistance to monocultures that has driven the revival of localised food systems worldwide. ⌂

Notes
1. FAO, *FAO Framework for the Urban Food Agenda*, FAO (Rome), 2019, p 6.
2. Carolyn Steel, 'Hungry for Change: Cities Don't Feed Themselves', *The Architectural Review*, 1455, October 2018: www.architectural-review.com/essays/hungry-for-change-cities-dont-feed-themselves. For an explanation of 'logistification', see Jesse LeCavalier, *The Rule of Logistics: Walmart and the Architecture of Fulfillment*, University of Minnesota Press (Minneapolis, MN), 2016, p 6.
3. See Jane Jacobs, *The Economy of Cities*, Random House (New York), vintage edition, 1970.
4. Ebenezer Howard, *Garden Cities of To-morrow* [1902], MIT Press (Cambridge, MA), 1965; Le Corbusier, *The City of Tomorrow and its* Planning [1929], Dover Publications (New York), 8th edn, 1987, p 204.
5. See Twigs Way, *Allotments*, Shire Publications (Oxford), 2008.
6. Intergovernmental Panel on Climate Change, *Climate Change and Land: Summary for Policymakers*, 2019, p 7: www.ipcc.ch/srccl/chapter/summary-for-policymakers; Nicholas Clinton et al, 'A Global Geospatial Ecosystem Services Estimate of Urban Agriculture', *Earth's Future*, 6 (1), 2018, pp 40–60.
7. Catherine Shu, 'Eat Just to Sell Lab-Grown Meat in Singapore After Gaining "World First" Regulatory Approval', *Tech Crunch*, 2 December 2020: https://techcrunch.com/2020/12/01/eat-just-to-sell-lab-grown-meat-in-singapore-after-gaining-world-first-regulatory-approval.
8. Intergovernmental Panel on Climate Change, op cit, p 24.
9. Lydia Kallipoliti, 'From Shit to Food: Graham Caine's Eco-House in South London, 1972–1975', *Buildings & Landscapes: Journal of the Vernacular Architecture Forum*, 19 (1), 2012, p 87; Ellen MacArthur Foundation, *Cities and Circular Economy for Food*, Ellen MacArthur Foundation (Isle of Wight), 2019, p 19.
10. Jonah Engel Bromwich, 'Farm to Table? More Like Ghost Kitchen to Sofa', *New York Times*, 24 December 2019: www.nytimes.com/2019/12/24/style/ghost-kitchen-food-delivery.
11. Derek Thompson, 'The Booming, Ethically Dubious Business of Food Delivery', *The Atlantic*, 2 August 2019: www.theatlantic.com/ideas/archive/2019/08/all-food-will-be-delivered/595222.
12. 'The World Food System Has So Far Weathered the Challenge of Covid-19', *The Economist*, 9 May 2020: www.economist.com/briefing/2020/05/09/the-worlds-food-system-has-so-far-weathered-the-challenge-of-covid-19.
13. See Karen A Franck, 'The City as Dining Room, Market, and Farm', in Karen A Franck (ed), ⌂ *Food + The City*, May/June (no 3), 2005, p 10.
14. Dan Hill, 'Small Pieces Loosely Joined: Practices for Super-Local Participative Urbanism', in Mark Burry (ed), ⌂ *Urban Futures: Designing the Digitalised City*, May/June (no 3), 2020, pp 66–71.

Text © 2021 John Wiley & Sons Ltd. Images © Scott Lloyd, Alexis Kalagas and Belen Ruiz Arenas

Nina Rappaport

The New Industrial Commons

Brooklyn Stone & Tile factory, Brooklyn, New York, 2021

Miguel, a cooperative worker, returns to work as the factory reopened following the safety protocols mandated by the US Center for Disease Control and Prevention for Covid-19.

Sleeping quarters for striking auto-workers at the General Motors Fisher Body Plant factory number three, Flint, Michigan, 1937

The workers used the car seats to sleep in quiet zones in the factory.

Worker-Owners and Factory Space

Strikes are no longer the only way for workers to put their case. Writer, curator, consultant and educator **Nina Rappaport** charts the continuing rise of worker empowerment, whether through 'expropriation', workers' collectives or similar employee-owned businesses, giving varied examples of where such approaches have occurred around the world. The catalyst for these moves has often been where the prevailing capitalist model has left spaces vacant and derelict, due to its relentless search for efficiency and economies of scale.

Linda said that she 'took a deep breath, almost hyperventilating,' when she agreed she could take on the factory's general management.[1] Today, as she surveys the factory space, her factory space, she and her co-owner workers clean up the shop, carefully placing cutting tools away and closing out the order log for the day before they leave for home in the city.

Over the past decade, manufacturing has been returning to cities in multiple ways – smaller, local, greener, cleaner, flexible, hybrid, vertical and visible. The organisation of manufacturing technologies and methods, and thus their spaces and design for production, have also shifted, in tandem with economic, environmental, political and social flux.[2] As cities have become increasingly global, dense and vibrant, and as the Covid-19 crisis has demonstrated that factory workers are 'essential', their increasing empowerment has imbued the factory system with a new relevance. In turn, the current economic crisis and protest in response to racial injustice has shown that workers can engage more holistically with production systems. Factory workers are empowering themselves in a new industrial commons, not only striking or occupying the production spaces and organisations in camaraderie, but also through commoning as cooperatives that are entrepreneurial, share goals and pool resources, while also contributing to productive cities.

Industrial cooperatives took hold in the mid-20th century from workers' movements that engaged in the ideas of 'Occupy, Resist, Produce', and succeeded in forming democratic workplaces. With shared workspace and industrial knowledge, workers are deeply invested in financial and social equity. As cooperatives, these worker-owned companies provide alternatives to the top-down, hierarchical system of capitalist hegemony. Factory cooperatives have relevance for shared economies and envisioning the factory space as a new working commons that can address today's crises relating to worker control and liveable wages. They pose a new socially and economically equitable paradigm as we reweave manufacturing into cities in future imaginaries.

Around the globe, for example in Italy, Spain and Argentina, new movements to embrace cooperative organisation are catalysing workers, owners and investors to create worker-controlled factories

Brooklyn Stone & Tile factory,
Brooklyn, New York,
2021

Joey operates stone-cutting machinery. Large machines make up the majority of the space, which intrinsically keeps the workers separated on the factory floor.

Aside from the power tools and heavy machinery, the factory shares common spaces such as a lunchroom. The cooperative environment allows for the domestication of the industrial space.

Brooklyn Stone & Tile factory,
Brooklyn, New York,
2021

The team of Linda, Joey, Miguel and Jay distance themselves in the workspace.

A Factory Transforms Today

Around the globe, for example in Italy, Spain and Argentina, new movements to embrace cooperative organisation are catalysing workers, owners and investors to create worker-controlled factories. This has been seen most recently in declining economies such as in Argentina where factories have been shuttered and machinery idled. In 2000, workers decided to 'expropriate' the production process and space at Zanon Ceramics, a tile manufacturer in the country's Neuquen province, which they renamed FaSinPat ('Factories without Bosses'). Similarly, at Brukman, a 'recovered' textile company in Buenos Aires, workers organised as the '18 de Diciembre' cooperative in order to improve wages and save the factory.[3]

In 2018, the former owner of Brooklyn Stone & Tile in New York wanted to retire from his business, which makes countertops and porcelain slabs, among other stone-based products. A business broker contacted The Working World, a financial organisation that assists companies to restructure using non-extractive financing rather than go into debt. The first deal fell through, meaning the company would have to close. However, Brendan Martin, the founder of The Working World, still had the financing on hand, so he asked Linda Díaz, Brooklyn Stone & Tile's Vice President of Operations, if she would like to create a worker-owned business.[4] The 20 employees wanted to keep their jobs as well as improve working conditions. In the original factory the air quality was horrendous – the dust residue collected by the pound on the inventory. There was no place to sit; workers ate their lunches on the open shop-floor. Their morale was low, as they could never express their opinions for improvements or voice grievances.

Linda realised that they could save their jobs; she closed the Manhattan showroom, and with The Working World structured a new business model. In April 2018 the new cooperative moved into a 4,500-square-foot (420-square-metres) former shipbuilding factory space in Building 12 at the Brooklyn Navy Yard, which they share with IceStone, producers of recycled glass countertops, and then expanded by another 2,500 square feet (230 square metres). By September the same year, the floodgates opened and they made a profit. By February 2019, Brooklyn Stone & Tile was in the workers' hands. Linda encouraged them to think like owners and take on new responsibilities. Ventilation systems now clean the air to reduce the dust, and they share a lunchroom and a basketball hoop. The profit-sharing is the opposite of a hierarchical system, and the atmosphere makes this clear: they request equipment and receive it in a timely manner, listen to their own music, and joke and fight like a family.

The worker-owners' dedication continued through the first wave of the Covid-19 pandemic in 2020 when the company shut down for two months before safety protocols were put in place. After receiving government loans they reopened with the required safety precautions. They now wear masks and can maintain distance even as their community thrives.

Strikes as Occupying

Historically, one demonstrative means of worker control was the act of occupying factories and striking, even at the risk of losing jobs. Until social reforms in the mid-19th century curtailed abuse, company owners often treated workers as part of the 'mass' in mass production, not as individuals who each have an important role to play. As an example, in the early 20th century, Italian philosopher Antonio Gramsci advanced Marxist ideals, as did the workers themselves, in order to achieve workplace democracy. To Gramsci, labour power as part of what he called *operaismo* (workerism) recognised worker estrangement and alienation and promoted internal committees of workers, called 'workers' councils', to organise production.[5] In Northern Italy between 1919 and 1920, in sympathy with the Russians who were striking for better working conditions, half a million dissatisfied workers occupied factories in protest during a period of intense social conflict called the Biennio Rosso. Through workers' councils they self-managed the production processes and distribution. As a result of their protests, the government reduced work hours to an eight-hour day and initiated a national minimum wage.

In the US, the renowned 'sit-down' strike at General Motors in Flint, Michigan, in 1936–37, became one of the longest strikes in history when workers occupied the factory for 44 days to protest against being overworked and underpaid, as well as the fast pace, overtime and precarious working conditions in the quarter-mile-long plant. When the workers heard that General Motors was transferring out machinery and steel dies to other factories, they moved into the plant, dividing the factory floor into spaces for eating, sleeping and hygiene needs, and taking care of one another in a civil and organised fashion. With the production line silent, they camped out in different sections of the factory floor, used the car seats as couches, coordinated activities including meals in the cafeteria, recreation, bathing, rumour control, press relations, security and fire safety.[6] While the women workers and family members were not allowed to stay inside, they donated meals and supplies. The union leveraged its new power to negotiate a victory that included an increase in pay among other benefits.

By the 1960s, workers rose again in Italy with support from philosophers, including Antonio Negri and Mario Tronti who promoted Marxist ideals.[7] The 1962 strike at the Fiat Mirafiori factory in Turin spread to other factories, as workers crowded together to listen to speakers inside and outside numerous plants. They gathered in a new commons – the factory floor – normally an active assembly line. They disregarded the yellow lines delineating the work aisles and crossed the space so that the factory itself became a place of occupation and protest as they fought against the capitalist hegemony and harnessed a new autonomy.

Strikes are thus a spatial act – the taking-over of private property as workers occupy a space that

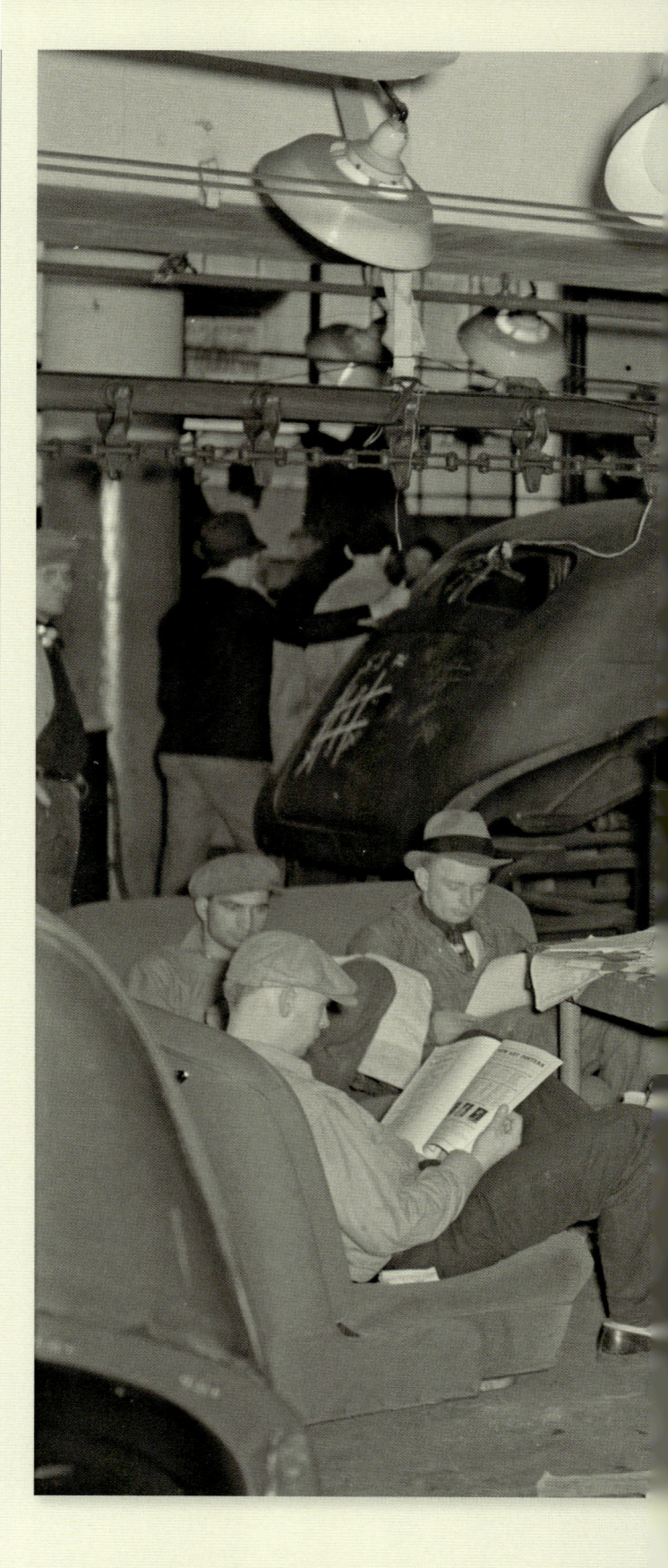

Living quarters for striking auto-workers at the General Motors Fisher Body Plant factory number three, Flint, Michigan, 1937

As the strike took hold, car seats were moved inside the plant to form social living spaces among the machinery.

Workers occupied the factory for 44 days to protest against being overworked and underpaid, as well as the fast pace, overtime and precarious working conditions

Striking workers demonstrating in Piazza San Carlo, Turin, Italy, 25 September 1969

below: During the *Autunno caldo* (Hot Autumn) of 1969–70, factory workers in Northern Italy's industrial centres organised large strikes demanding better work hours, conditions and pay. Northern Italy had largely grown its workforce population due to immigration from the south.

bottom: Workers protested against industrialists such as Giovanni Agnelli, founder of the Fiat motor company, and grandson Gianni Agnelli, who headed Fiat during this period.

The Italian constitution encourages cooperatives, stating in Article 45 that 'the Republic recognises the social function of cooperation with mutual character and without private speculation purposes'

they physically command by remaining in place, not moving the production line or their bodies. Their actions of occupation signalled an operation of territorial ownership, like squatting, even if temporarily. Gradually, the companies met workers' needs with more amenities, including nurseries and break rooms, which influenced factory designs. Layouts in the 1970s removed physical and organisational hierarchies by placing research and development adjacent to the factory floor, increasing common areas and integrating spaces for more social interactions.

Cooperative Production Space

The most direct worker control of the factory floor has always been ownership: cooperatives and profit-sharing. These go beyond the reach of unions and internal workers' councils to give workers financial share in the company, as is occurring at Brooklyn Stone & Tile. The idea of combining capital, machinery, skills and common ideologies fosters cooperative businesses from diverse ownership models and financing for the common benefit of working members – all enhancing workers' physical, mental and economic well-being. The origins of cooperatives in both manufacturing and agriculture go as far back as the beginning of the Industrial Revolution. For example, when French industrialist Jean-Baptiste Godin retired in 1858, he ceded control of his cast-iron manufacturing business with its utopian Fourier Familistère, in Guise, France, to his workers, and it remained in cooperative ownership until 1968.[8]

In Italy, the 1919–20 strikes, followed by massive unemployment, inspired workers to start factory cooperatives. Among them were nine young mechanics who used social capital to found the Società Anonima Cooperativa Meccanici Imola (SACMI) in Imola. This industrial hub of the Emilia-Romagna region became a cooperative centre boasting over 75,000 cooperatives in the services and manufacturing sectors. The regional networks of small family-based factories support each other financially and technologically. They have an advantage in that the Italian constitution encourages cooperatives, stating in Article 45 that 'the Republic recognises the social function of cooperation with mutual character and without private speculation purposes'.[9] The profits are not taxed if they are reinvested, and the government subsidises companies that wish to convert to a worker-owned cooperative and can prove that it can raise additional funds both internally and externally.

SACMI began as a repair shop and then produced agricultural equipment, and in the 1920s was raided by Mussolini's men. In the 1940s it produced wartime machinery, and in 1945 the workers reorganised as a ceramic tile cooperative (Cooperativa Ceramica) that still exists today. Cooperativa Ceramica expanded to produce full production-line machinery and today has 4,600 member/employees. Production has increased in scope and includes food and beverage packaging as well as Industry 4.0 technologies. It focuses on worker well-being through its democratic operations, such as a Code of Ethics that includes good practices that apply not only to internal and external business relationships, but also to social causes in their communities. To become a member and representative on the 'assembly', there are hefty financial requirements to own shares in the company. This worker investment means that the funds come from within the company, rather than from outside investors or even banks, and reinforce the shared goals.[10]

Some cooperatives have grown even more dramatically, such as the Mondragon Cooperative Corporation founded in 1956 by a priest and five workers. The largest cooperative in Europe, centred in the Basque region of Spain, it grew to 92 companies in 1980 with 18,000 worker-members. By 2009 they employed over 90,000 workers and now are the seventh largest business in the country.[11] Mondragon has numerous subsidiaries that manufacture all sorts of goods, from electronics to furniture, semiconductors, construction systems, electronic cars, railway lines, food production and tools. It also has a self-reliant financial infrastructural system and rarely borrows funds, allowing the corporation to move capital and labour within its own system so that it reinvests as it spins off new cooperatives and maintains a stable workforce.[12]

Similar to SACMI, Mondragon workers invest in the company as owners, pool profits, share risks and manage wages, thus determining their own compensation. This worker-owned, socially based economic enterprise allows them to adapt to changes on demand and, even in recessions or times of crisis such as Covid-19, to maintain full employment (while receiving a temporary cut in pay during the pandemic). Mondragon's upper-echelon managers are for the most part underpaid by choice, earning only eight times that of the lowest-paid worker. The company is run by a member-based board of directors called a Cooperative Congress, whose motto is 'Humanity at Work'. Its mission includes fostering employee participation through democratic organisation, continual training, education, social transformation and innovation, in contrast to the top-down control of the hegemonic global factory focused on shareholder profits.

Factory Commoning
The idea of what can now be called 'factory commoning' through cooperatives thus incorporates the actions of both occupying and organising. Members of a community take on responsibilities of shared production, whether through the act of making things, quality control of the production process, or management. This was foregrounded in the dedication of workers during the early days of the Covid-19 pandemic when workers at the Braskem America petrochemical factory in Pennsylvania lived in the factory for 28 days in April 2020. In that case, while the workers were not owners, they occupied the factory to produce millions of pounds of polypropylene used to make nonwoven fabrics for medical facemasks, disinfectant wipes and gowns. Inside they cooked, set up an on-site gym, turned offices into sleeping areas and organised games and chores as a 'live-in' – a more relaxed atmosphere than the 1936–7 General Motors 'sit-down' strike.

The Braskem workers' primary concern was making raw materials for first responders and keeping themselves and their families safe from the coronavirus while the factory remained open.[13] After the work marathon, they received wage increases and vacations. As examples such as this illustrate, beyond traditional ideas of capitalist ownership, the factory instead can become a common both organisationally and spatially – a place of sharing and invested engagement in a supportive community. ⌁

> **The idea of what can now be called 'factory commoning' through cooperatives ... incorporates the actions of both occupying and organising. Members of a community take on responsibilities of shared production**

Notes
1. Author in discussion with Linda Díaz, worker-owner of Brooklyn Stone & Tile, in 2020.
2. See Nina Rappaport, *Vertical Urban Factory*, Actar (Barcelona), 2015/2020, and *Design of Urban Manufacturing*, Routledge (New York), 2020.
3. The Lavaca Collective, *Sin Patron*, Haymarket Books (Chicago, IL), 2007, and *The Take*, directed by Avi Lewis and Naomi Klein, Canadian Broadcasting Corporation, 2004.
4. Author in discussion with Brendan Martin, founder of The Working World, in 2020.
5. See Antonio Gramsci, *Prison Notebooks* [1925–1935], Columbia University Press (New York), 2011.
6. Described in Sidney Fine, *Sit-Down: The General Motors Strike of 1936–37*, University of Michigan Press (Ann Arbor, MI), 1969.
7. See Steve Wright, *Storming Heaven: Class Composition and Struggle in Italian Autonomist Marxism*, 2nd edn, Pluto Press (London), 2018.
8. Leonardo Benevolo, *The Origins of Modern City Planning*, MIT Press (Cambridge, MA), 1971, p 56.
9. The Constitution of the Italian Republic, 22 December 1947.
10. See Matt Hancock, 'The Cooperative District of Imola: Forging the High Road to Globalization', Progress Report, Research Project on the Cooperative District of Imola, prepared for MUEC, 2004–05: https://base.socioeco.org/docs/imola_0.pdf.
11. See John Curl, 'The Cooperative Movement in Century 21', *Affinities: A Journal of Radical Theory, Culture, and Action*, 4 (1), Summer 2010, pp 12–29.
12. Davydd J Greenwood, 'The Fagor Group of Mondragon', in Frances Abrahamer Rothstein and Michael L Blim (eds), *Anthropology and the Global Factory*, Bergin & Garvey (New York), 1992, pp 177–90.
13. Meagan Flynn, 'They Lived in a Factory for 28 days', *The Washington Post*, 23 April 2020: www.washingtonpost.com/nation/2020/04/23/factory-masks-coronavirus-ppe/.

Text © 2021 John Wiley & Sons Ltd. Images: pp 48, 50–1 © Nina Rappaport; pp 49, 52–3 Library of Congress Prints and Photographs Division Washington, D.C. Photographs by Dick Shelton; p 54(t) © Bettmann / Getty Images; p 54(b) Photo by Mario De Biasi/Mondadori via Getty Images

Rafael Luna and Dongwoo Yim

From Food Hub

What is architecture's role within the agenda of food as a catalyst for urban production and development? Having completed a commissioned study in 2015 for the West Louisville Food Port in Kentucky, along with a research studio at the Graduate School of Design at Harvard University, **Shohei Shigematsu**, partner at OMA, shares his insights on the subject with Guest-Editors **Rafael Luna and Dongwoo Yim**.

to Food Port

OMA,
West Louisville Food Port,
Louisville, Kentucky,
2015

The linear massing has the potential of forming a barrier between two sides of the site. In order to avoid this, the massing is perforated with a canopy entrance that forms a transition between the logistic parking and the public plazas.

In Conversation with OMA's Shohei Shigematsu

When discussing urban production, food is an inevitable topic as it represents the most essential requirement for our survival. Urban farming has ushered in many of the contemporary discussions on urban production and manufacturing. The food industry already presents sophisticated networks for a much-sought circular economy encompassing production, consumption and recycling within the city, from which other industries – including architecture – can learn.

Invited by Harvard University's Graduate School of Design (GSD) to develop a continuous three-year research project that could become a body of knowledge for the school, Shohei Shigematsu explained why he chose food as a theme that could be highly specific yet diverse enough to offer a new lens for architecture and urbanism.[1] Out of the three fundamental human needs – food, clothing and shelter – food has not been globalised at the same scale that fashion and architecture have. The latter two have experienced standardisation and homogenisation at a greater rate; conversely, while food is being produced globally, it still benefits from the phenomenon of *terroir*, whereby it can be infused with the local climate, local soil and local culture. 'Like Champagne, its super-local specific regional quality also becomes super-global. Through the lens of food, we could see architecture and urbanism in a different way, beyond the generic, and present new typologies,' says Shigematsu.

Integral Dispersion
Despite urban agriculture being a subject of study for reintroducing the food supply chain within the city, the reality is that the global urbanisation process has propelled the need for a decentralised network as cities sprawl towards rural fields, rendering the term 'rural' extinct. Retrospectively, this led Shigematsu to re-inspect visionary projects like Frank Lloyd Wright's Broadacre City (1932). The plan recommends that each residence own a certain amount of agricultural land, merging food production as part of the vastly expanded and distanced city: 'While the several sketches showed a radical proposal, the physical model exhibited at MoMA in 1934 underwhelmed the vision compared to the sketches. Yet, when I saw images of what is happening in Zhejiang province in China now, the Broadacre City model looked almost as if it had predicted the future. In Zhejiang, the city is growing exponentially into an intense agricultural suburban condition, merging the dispersal of the city and the agricultural land.'

Shigematsu discusses this phenomenon as an example of the current state of urbanism, and its imminent expansion towards the agricultural fields. It offers the potential of reintegrating a connection between producer and consumer. Becoming distanced from food production has deteriorated people's general knowledge of where food comes from. This is not just

The aerial view shows the linear form contorting on the site in order to create an urban connection to the neighbouring grid, and a series of public spaces.

A Food Hub is a typology established by the United States Department of Agriculture (USDA) that is composed of aggregation, distribution, storage and marketing spaces. By mixing socially conscious programmes, a typical Food Hub is transformed into a Food Port as an urban anchor.

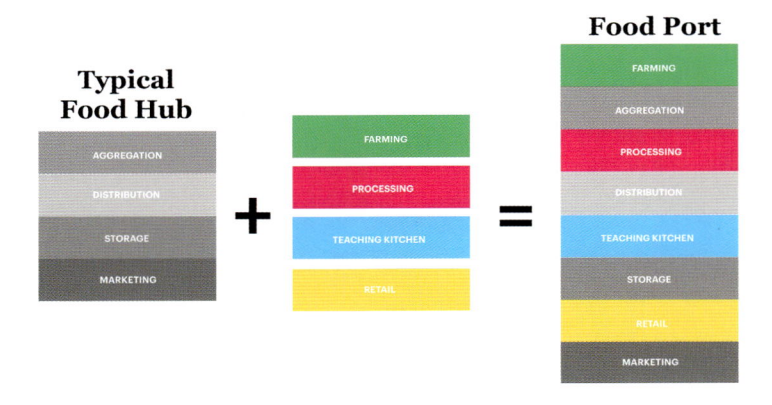

OMA,
West Louisville Food Port,
Louisville, Kentucky,
2015

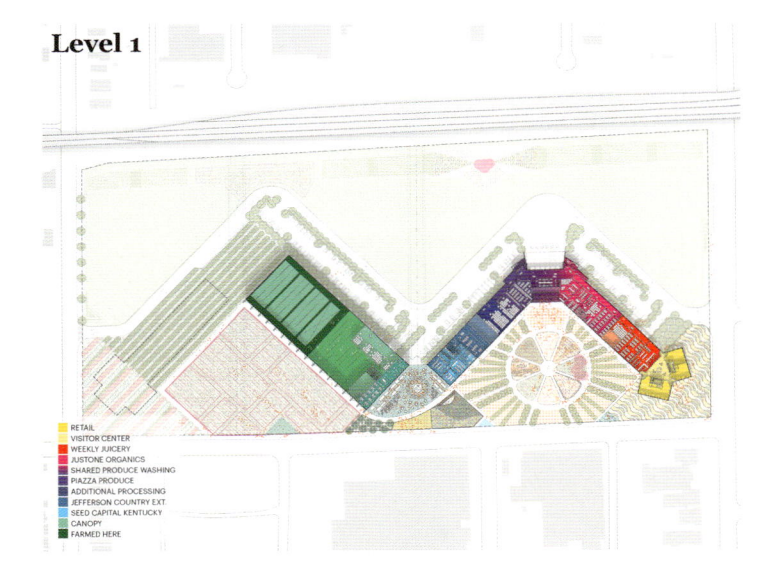

The site plan shows the integration between logistics and social programmes within a linear bar. The colouring represents the mixing and diffusion between the programmes.

an educational issue, but an indication of the transition from being producers (farmers) to consumers.

Urban expansion in China also hints at a scarcity of land that forces either the reintegration of farming and city, or a redirection to another source of expansion: the ocean. Dietary habits dominated by beef consumption have led to the deforestation and reappropriation of fertile land for grazing pastures, yet since 2011 farmed fish production has surpassed beef production.[2] This paradigm shift could pose an interesting reconceptualisation of architectural visions, such as adding an element of food production to the man-made islands and platforms of the Tokyo Bay expansion (1960) by Kenzo Tange. Shigematsu calls to mind the vernacular floating villages in Hainan, China, where fishermen live on the water, working and dwelling in the same setting. With regard to Tange's project, he observes: 'I believe these types of models could become more convincing if the floating city could relate to the production of food as the oceans become the ultimate resource.'

Food and Mobility, and Proximities
Decentralisation and urban expansion heavily rely on mobility, which has a long-standing relationship with architectural typologies, urban morphologies and ultimately food production logistics. Drive-in, drive-thru and drive-to typologies drastically transformed the architectural experience for the food industry. This was challenged again through the development of smart delivery systems, and ultimately will transform once more through autonomous delivery: 'The biggest investments are going towards food tech startups that are developing new ways to move food. During the Covid pandemic Uber Eats has surpassed Uber transportation services, for example, showing this new dynamic. Regardless of the pandemic, this is a new reality. Amazon started distributing books, and Uber started distributing people, but now both have ended up distributing food.'

Based on these new mobility trends, logistically charged market typologies have increasingly become a target for disruption. As food mobility becomes more efficient and decentralised, markets represent real-estate urban voids that are replaced with larger developments. For OMA, the West Louisville Food Port (2015) represented an opportunity for urban regeneration, by transforming an industrial site in Louisville, Kentucky that sits within 4 kilometres (2.5 miles) of the downtown area, in the middle of a food desert within an underserved community. In contrast to mobility and decentralisation, by producing a central node of food production, distribution and consumption, a variant market typology can serve as a new anchor for development.

Farmers' markets have become popular in an attempt to support local farmers due to their perceived connection between producer and consumer. This is actually a misconception as farmers' markets have a business-to-consumer model. Instead, Shigematsu argues that we need to rethink the model in order to

OMA,
West Louisville Food Port,
Louisville, Kentucky,
2015

In order to break the paradigm of a logistics centre as inaccessible to the public, the image of the Food Port is represented as a comprehensive destination.

As one of the intents of the project is to establish a connection with the neighbourhood, a plaza for food trucks forms a transformable collective space.

support the farmers by changing from a business-to-consumer to a business-to-business model. There is a large demand for local food from much larger consumers such as hospitals, airlines and schools. The problem is that local farmers do not have infrastructure to distribute to larger businesses. The Food Port idea came from that.

Production as a Social Anchor

The social agenda for the project began by looking at the historical makeup of the city. A flood map of the Ohio River showed how there was a natural divide in Louisville between the high-income residents that lived in the East side, and the low-income residents from the West. This site would become an intersection for both on a 24-acre (10-hectare) plot designated by the city. A 'Food Hub' is a facility type established by the United States Department of Agriculture (USDA) that deals with aggregation, distribution, storage and marketing. The West Louisville Food Port adds functions beyond the system of a typical food chain to support the local communities themed through this shared facility. It aims to be a local food education point for the area, targeting food education as a new part of the circular economy. Although designed as a singular mono-space bar, it aims to produce a simple gesture that is also meaningful to the local community. The form is contorted to fit the site, separating specific productive programmes while infilling with community-driven programmes at each turn.

Although Shigematsu's research focused specifically on the food industry as a generator of typologies, it serves as an example of how other means of urban production, such as energy or manufacturing, could also take an architectural lead. The socio-economic chain between production and consumption that the Food Port is trying to enhance is something that an architectural typology in the meta-industrial city should pursue. Local means of production are transforming the ways that cities are boosting their economy, producing local jobs and resources. Through incentives for production-driven development, architects are enabled to propose a new generation of production typologies. ⌀

This article is based on a Zoom interview on 18 June 2020 between Rafael Luna and Dongwoo Yim in Seoul, and OMA partner Shohei Shigematsu in Tokyo.

Notes
1. The resulting work can be seen in Shohei Shigematsu and Christy Chen, 'Alimentary Design', in Leire Asensio Villoria (ed), *GSD Platform 7*, Actar (New York), 2015, pp 210–12, and in Tomonari Cotani, 'What's Alimentary Design'?, *WIRED*, 17, 2015, pp 48–50.
2. Janet Larsen and J Matthew Roney, 'Plan B Updates: Farmed Fish Production Overtakes Beef', Earth Policy Institute, 12 June 2013: www.earth-policy.org/plan_b_updates/2013/update114.

Local means of production are transforming the ways that cities are boosting their economy, producing local jobs and resources

Text © 2021 John Wiley & Sons Ltd. Images: pp 56–7 © OMA, Robota; pp 57(r), 58–61 © OMA

DK Osseo-Asare and Yasmine Abbas

OCCUPYING AFRICA

PROTOTYPING A TRANSFORMAL MAKERSPACE NETWORK

Experimenting with the varied contexts of work, living, education and making/producing throughout Africa, **DK Osseo-Asare and Yasmine Abbas** – both members of the Architecture and Engineering Design Faculty at Pennsylvania State University – have co-founded and developed the Agbogbloshie Makerspace Platform (AMP). They outline the background and functioning of this enabling system that encourages participants to use the low-tech resources around them to build their skills and change their environments.

Agbogbloshie Makerspace Platform,
Spacecraft_ZKM,
Accra, Ghana,
2018

Members of the AMP makers collective conduct quality-control exercises and evaluate a design decision during the launch of the third-generation AMP spacecraft prototype in the Agbogbloshie scrapyard. The kiosk architecture is a form of para-structure or occupiable scaffolding that serves as an open design framework with polyvalent affordances to support makerspace tools, equipment and interactive manu-digital co-creation.

The continent and islands of contemporary Africa have the youngest human population and fastest rate of urbanisation on Earth. Current projections anticipate billions of new African urban dwellers in decades, and more than one in three people alive being African by the end of the 21st century. This shift towards an emergent pan-African eperopolis[1] intensifies anthropogenic pressure on transcontinental society, economy and climate-ecology systems. According to the United Nations, whereas all other world regions will decline from all-time peak populations, becoming increasingly aged, Africa alone will sustain demographic growth over the same period, providing a supermajority of the worldwide human workforce.[2] Such unprecedented growth demands scalable climate-conscious models for providing quality education and regenerative livelihood opportunities for hundreds of millions of African youth.

Across Africa, binate pedagogical paradigms frame disparate worlds-cum-trajectories of work life. Some youth learn a 'trade' through apprenticeship: experiencing shared heuristic situations with peers, making and doing together 'in the field' via imitation and trial-and-error. Others spend more time in(side) bounded school environments, learning within structured spaces delineated by books and classroom practices that privilege recitation, memorisation, examination and written assignments. Members of the latter fledgling 'professional' class risk acquiring technical knowledge with limited chance of applying it to solve unbounded, undefined, open-ended and complex problems, or to 'build with their hands'. Soft know-how and hard knowledge dichotomies parallel Yona Friedman's call to integrate 'prenticeable disciplines' (arts and crafts, architecture and planning) whose practitioners operate by subjective 'tricks of the trade', with objective 'teachable disciplines' that are rule-based and 'scientific'.[3] This view offers that design best supports democratic functioning within society when professionals and laypersons engage with their environment and each other, in tandem. Bi-channel information architectures ('twofold instruction')[4] enable novice and expert to co-construct intercommunication using 'the same rules, but on different levels', providing both open access and the option to contribute to a common repertoire of material procedures for transforming spatiality.

Explicating the quadratic nature of pan-African urban dynamics, the dual-sector model in development economics bifurcates early-stage economies, such as those of newly independent countries or post-colonial states, into the 'subsistence sector' (consisting of communal agriculture, petty trading and domestic workers) and the 'capitalist sector' (primarily manufacturing, corporate agribusiness and extractive industries).[5] Augmented textility[6] of economically advantaged countries, enshrined by convention as the 'formal sector', juxtaposes the 'informal sector', a misnomer that describes interwoven conditions and procedures defining resilient life and work communities performed out of convivial relations[7] and ways of dwelling (for example, self-building, collective farming, barter, economies of affection). Not unlike how ekistics pivots regional planning from fixed mapping to dynamic modelling, Rahul Mehrotra reframes the colonialist archetype of formal and informal classes of spatial colonisation as an urban conservation model of static and kinetic city[8] layers, an architectonic view of occupation that extends three-dimensional space into a fourth dimension of temporality, freeing from fixity the architecture of Global South urbanism and its attendant mobility rites.

African states, tribes and nations navigate simultaneous nonaligned systems of jurisprudence: customary law, based on traditional rulership models and indigenous systems of land-, resource- and cultural custodianship, alongside statutory law, designed per international legal precedent to sync with global networks, standards and commerce. This ambient duality corresponds to how denizens of African towns and cities transit a syncretic realm that straddles these competing worlds in resonance with *oikonomia* – management of the place of dwelling (*oikos*). Everywhere occurrent across everyday Africa – but only at ground

Agbogbloshie Makerspace Platform,
AMP spacecraft prototype,
Agbogbloshie scrapyard,
Accra, Ghana,
2015

Elements of the AMP spacecraft-like modular hanging furniture and bifold hangar doors open to provide both shade and shelving, operating as a form of kinetic, multifunctional and polyvalent 'para-structure'. Its components and subassemblies adhere to an open or adaptive standard whereby standardised product families make provision for the incorporation of irregular sub-parts. Examples include repurposing offcut steel-reinforcement bars sourced from construction sites, and non-conventional infill partition and finish materials upcycled out of the Agbogbloshie scrapyard's waste stream (for example, condemned tyres and rubber conveyor belts from scrap mining equipment).

Map of the Agbogbloshie scrapyard,
Accra, Ghana,
2017

AMP community agents conducted a community mapping of the scrapyard site using GPS-enabled mobile phones to determine its emergent organisation. Geospatial layout of the waste ecosystem and its operations indicate advantageous interlacing between quasi-formal (e-)scrap industry, recycling activities, cottage industry and repair workshops.

- MOSQUE
- MOSQUE TERRITORY
- WEIGH STATION
- DISASSEMBLY AREA
- BURN AREA
- STOCKPILE — scrap metals, plastics
- STOCKPILE — glass circa 2013
- SALES & REPAIR
- MAKER WORKSHOP
- BATHROOMS / WATER
- FOOD & ENTERTAINMENT — chop bar, foosball, drinking spot, cinema
- UMBRELLA POS
- VEHICLES
- TREE
- RUBBLE / DUMP
- MANGROVES circa 2000
- WATER POND 2008-2016 / ORIGINAL ODAW RIVER

Prototyping a smart toolbox,
Accra Timber Market,
Ghana,
2018

opposite: An AMP-trained welder fabricates a third-generation toolbox based on the spacecraft's cuboctahedron module. This folded metal housing serves as an equipment pod armature for the initial prototyping work for the 'scanopy' environmental sensing kit, which collects air quality, temperature, atmospheric pressure and humidity data in real-time and streams to the AMP digital platform.

level – 'kiosk culture'[9] denotes the network of tiny- and small-scale makers and entrepreneurs working out of kiosks, sheds, shanties and metal containers, roofed with tarpaulins and corrugated metal sheeting, or temporarily installed under trees, by roadsides, in vacant lots and buildings still under construction, as well as adaptive workspaces housed in more 'formal' edifices, that constitute a broad belt of indigenous pan-African innovation. Kiosk culture is a highly responsive phenomenon, experimenting relentlessly with old and new strategies and tactics for creating alternative futures, and implicates architecture because it is the non-contiguous arena shaping the building industry in this context: no construction project in Africa exists solely within the so-called formal sector, even though the majority of infrastructure under development does not directly involve architects.

Stellate Design: Making Architecture Participatory

In 2012 Low Design Office (LowDO) and Paris-based strategic design consultancy Panurban launched the Agbogbloshie Makerspace Platform (AMP). AMP is a youth-driven initiative to promote maker ecosystems geared to interface Ghana's Agbogbloshie scrapyard.[10] The project seeks to amplify grassroots maker potentials and to empower cooperative entrepreneurship through open architecture, distributed co-production and materials life-cycling (multi-site fabrication, assembly, disassembly and recycling).[11] It utilises a stellate design process to apply participatory methods for inducing inclusive innovation: mining what already works for models and methods, and deploying co-creation across class, religious and tribal strata within existing communities of makers.[12] As a general protocol for making architecture participatory in the pan-African plane – a multi-modal interactive scaffold for 'spacecrafting' Afronautics – AMP is a transdisciplinary project that bridges the fields of design and futures.[13] The systems framework and artefacts of the platform integrate landscape, building and computer architecture, technology development, social innovation and engineering. This inclusive approach to distributed manufacturing contributes to emerging models of commons-based peer production.[14]

Agbogbloshie scrapyard circulates the Old Fadama community, a slum 'district'[15] in central Accra where tens of thousands of men, women and children live and work. A small but hugely contested territory, Agbogbloshie is a quasi-formal urban alternator: a space that generates economic power from human material, determination, hard work and ingenuity. The site is infamous across the globe for being 'the world's largest e-waste dump'. This is a false narrative; it is in fact an example of urban agglomeration – a cluster of allied industries collocated in the vicinity of the scrapyard in order to capture value out of the waste stream. Agbogbloshie scrap dealers operate locally, nationally and across the West African subregion, travelling as far afield as Côte d'Ivoire, Nigeria and Benin to purchase end-of-life equipment for dismantling, materials recovery and resale. At Agbogbloshie, grassroots makers work hard to increase their visibility by leveraging both their social networks and spatialised opportunity-finding, such as proximate location to high-traffic zones and corridors. Referrals play a significant role in the flow of information, as well as mobile phone-powered communications via video, voice and text messaging. Furthermore, most engage in various informal, peer-to-peer lending and investment practices (both digitally enabled via mobile money, cash transfers or by proxy of non-financial currency) ranging over periods of time from short to long duration (hours to years).

However, in most instances, such actions remain decoupled: individual constellations of resources, know-how, kit and can-do momentum do not necessarily stellate wider spheres of influence and interoperation. Lessons learnt, insights and micro-innovations may not transfer from one maker to others outside of their personal social network. Despite the best efforts of artisans and craftspeople, engineering technicians, recyclers and micro-entrepreneurs active in the informal sector, their scenarios of opportunity remain highly constrained not only by limited financial capital, but also by poor access to tools, equipment, materials, information (about how to make or do something, where to find customers, materials or a specific part), skill and expertise. In response, LowDO and Panurban developed AMP as an experimental demonstration of stellate design principles centred on amplifying peer-to-peer collaboration via 4D hyperlocal[16] design templates.

Spacecraft: Remaking Collective Environment

The AMP makers collective comprises over a thousand young people – scrap dealers and grassroots makers working together with students and young professionals in science, technology, engineering, arts and mathematics (STEAM) fields from universities in West Africa, Europe and the US – who have participated in both community mapping exercises and over 50 design and maker workshops exploring the Agbogbloshie e-waste ecosystem for opportunities for innovation in informal sector e-waste processing, as well as collaboration to conceptualise and

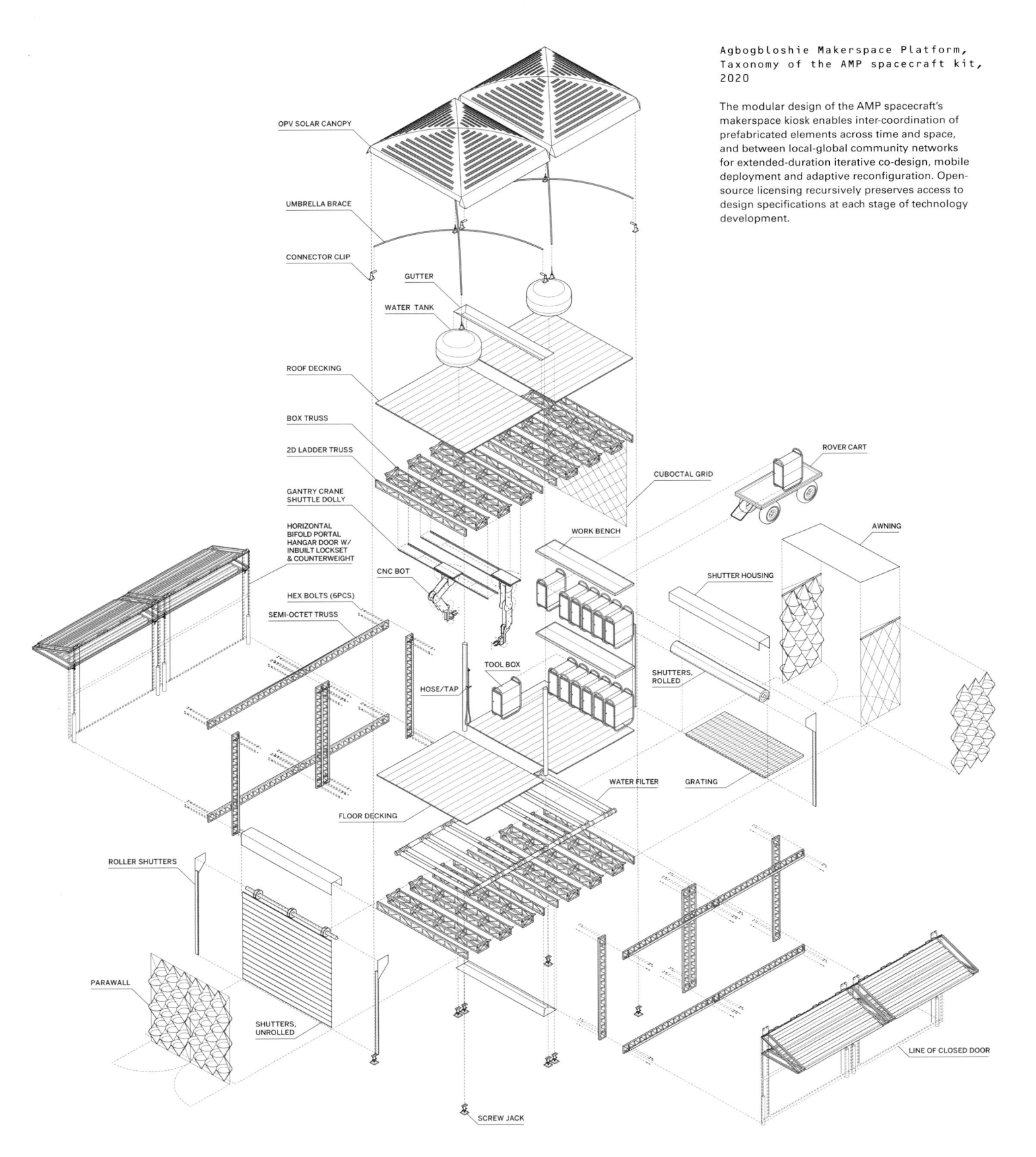

Agbogbloshie Makerspace Platform,
Taxonomy of the AMP spacecraft kit,
2020

The modular design of the AMP spacecraft's makerspace kiosk enables inter-coordination of prefabricated elements across time and space, and between local-global community networks for extended-duration iterative co-design, mobile deployment and adaptive reconfiguration. Open-source licensing recursively preserves access to design specifications at each stage of technology development.

Agbogbloshie Makerspace Platform,
Spacecraft_AGB,
Accra, Ghana,
2017

opposite: A member of the AMP makers collective moves a second-generation toolbox inside the first-generation makerspace prototyped and installed at the Agbogbloshie scrapyard. This set of toolboxes stack together with table tops to create mobile workbenches with modular storage lockers. Toolboxes are designed for easy transport via 'push truck' hand carts, a major conveyance vehicle within informal-sector transportation networks.

Agbogbloshie Makerspace Platform,
Spacecraft_ZKM,
Accra, Ghana,
2018

Working together, Agbogbloshie scrap dealers complete the subassembly of a shuttle dolly for the overhead gantry crane system of the AMP spacecraft kiosk. This version, which followed several previous prototypes, serves to enable the overhead suspension of workpieces and equipment mounted to the chassis frame, including an additional set of workbenches, storage pallets and multi-axis CNC robotic-control mechanisms under development.

Agbogbloshie Makerspace Platform,
Spacecraft_KT,
'Afropixel #6: Non-Aligned Utopias'
festival, Kër Thiossane,
Dakar, Senegal,
2018

Led by Migrating Culture, a nonprofit design services firm, members of the AMP makers collective collaborated with youth from the Defko Ak Niëp Fab Lab and the artisanal engineering workshop BASS Design to build and customise a second-generation AMP spacecraft for Kër Thiossane, a community-based digital arts and culture organisation. This unit, which prototyped a number of new features and operates jointly as a makerspace, pop-up shop, cinema and performance stage, moved around the city during the Dak'art Contemporary African Art Biennale, before travelling to Mauritania and back hosting youth-led maker workshops on digital design and fabrication.

Key to this alternative approach is interlinking formal and informal worlds through 'transformal' methods of collaborative making

Agbogbloshie Makerspace Platform,
Spacecraft_ZKM,
'Digital Imaginaries: Africas in Production' exhibition,
ZKM | Center for Arts and Media,
Karlsruhe, Germany,
2019

opposite: AMP spacecraft is a hyperportal between local-global makerspaces. Here, members of the AMP makers collective in Ghana were digitally projected from the Spacecraft_ZKM during installation in Karlsruhe. The live demonstration, recorded as a video tutorial, of how to solder AMP's custom-printed circuit board and program the open-source Arduino controls to 'make your own scanopy' (an open-source environmental sensing kit, suspended in the middle of the image), linked real-time climate data from user communities in Ghana and Germany.

prototype open-access tools for recycling-driven micro-industries and digital manufactories. Agbogbloshie Makerspace Platform is a collective effort to co-develop a practical approach to transforming the Agbogbloshie scrapyard, recycling network and maker ecosystem into a hybrid physical-digital platform for cooperative design, fabrication and recycling of the built environment.

AMP spacecraft is an open architecture, or collaborative design and development framework, that combines a maker kiosk building system with a customisable equipment toolset and digital platform for interlinking 'soft know-how' and 'hard knowledge' manifolds to generate iterative building versioning that incorporates parallel inputs from professional, academic and vernacular maker constituencies: community-based architecture that prototypes the architecture that follows. This approach draws on standard models of appropriate technology to cross-optimise prototypical kiosk architecture that is modular, deployable and robust, but also buildable by grassroots makers facing intermittent and unreliable resource supply and non-standard material stock. AMP's Rockefeller Foundation-funded pilot project phase (2013–17) seeded this open-source maker technology development trajectory with online digital publication of version 1.0 of the AMP spacecraft maker-kiosk design kernel (with hundreds of downloads to date), and a mobile phone application for the Android operating system. Content generated as part of this process included environmental, health and safety resources (videos narrated in the local language, and downloadable manuals) for handling e-waste in grassroots maker contexts, as well as how to pirate parts and components from end-of-life electronics for re-utilisation in new projects.

AMP has since conducted technology transfer from Ghana to Senegal, building and customising a second-generation AMP spacecraft with a community-based fab lab in Dakar, and trans-shipping spacecraft internationally, both by land (Senegal to Mauritania) and by sea (Ghana to Germany). The AMP makers collective has expanded to a second workshop in Accra's Timber Market, where the community offers on-demand production of third-generation AMP spacecraft. Members of the collective participate in co-developing the open-source catalogue of demountable kiosks and intercoordinated parts, making use of digital fabrication tools. The latest prototype, known as 'fufuzela', is a species of deployable bamboo para-structure ('bambot') for actuating bio-digital pan-African futures. Given the explosive urban growth in Sub-Saharan Africa, AMP probes how open design can help transition architecture from a service industry complicit in regimes oriented around economic growth – that are extractive, non-regenerative and correlate with ecocide – to commons-based provision of technology for metabolic planetary wellbeing.
Key to this alternative approach is interlinking formal and informal worlds through 'transformal' methods of collaborative making. Blending the dynamics of open technology start-up culture with West Africa's artisanal belt of material production supports new forms of cooperative occupation – in the sense of networked vocational opportunities – and builds pathways to inclusive architecture. ⌂

Notes
1. Constantinos A Doxiadis, 'Economics and the Ekistic Grid', *Ekistics*, 40 (236), 1975, pp 1–4.
2. United Nations Department of Economic and Social Affairs, *World Population Prospects 2019: Highlights*, United Nations (New York), 2019: https://population.un.org/wpp/Publications/Files/WPP2019_Highlights.pdf.
3. Yona Friedman, *Toward a Scientific Architecture* [1975], MIT Press (Cambridge, MA), 1980, pp 11–12.
4. *Ibid*, pp 13–14.
5. W Arthur Lewis, 'Economic Development with Unlimited Supplies of Labor', *The Manchester School*, 22, May 1954, pp 139–91.
6. Tim Ingold, 'The Textility of Making', *Cambridge Journal of Economics*, 34 (1), January 2010, pp 91–102.
7. Ivan Illich, *Tools for Conviviality* [1974], Marion Boyars (London and New York), 2009.
8. Rahul Mehrotra, 'Conservation and Change: Questions for Conservation Education in Urban India', *Built Environment*, 33 (3), 2007, pp 342–56.
9. DK Osseo-Asare, 'Kiosk Culture', *MONU*, 32, Spring 2020, pp 105–9.
10. DK Osseo-Asare and Yasmine Abbas, 'Waste', *AA Files*, 76, 2019, pp 179–83.
11. DK Osseo-Asare, 'Lowness', *FOLIO: Journal of Contemporary African Architecture*, 2, 2020, pp 283–98.
12. DK Osseo-Asare and Yasmine Abbas, 'Investigating 3E-materials at Agbogbloshie in Accra, Ghana', *Raising Awareness for the Societal and Environmental Role of Engineering and (Re)Training Engineers for Participatory Design Conference Proceedings*, IEEE Engineering4Society, 2015, pp 41–50.
13. Cher Potter, DK Osseo-Asare and Mugendi K M'Rithaa. 'Crafting Spaces Between Design and Futures: The Case of the Agbogbloshie Makerspace Platform', *Journal of Futures Studies*, 23 (3), 2019, pp 39–56.
14. Michael Bauwens, Vasilis Kostakis and Alex Pazaitis, *Peer to Peer: The Commons Manifesto*, University of Westminster Press (London), 2019.
15. AbdouMaliq Simone, *Improvised Lives*, Polity (Cambridge), 2018, pp 15–19.
16. Lucy Bullivant (ed), ⌂ *4D Hyperlocal: A Cultural Toolkit for the Open-Source City*, January/February (no 1), 2017.

Text © 2021 John Wiley & Sons Ltd. Images: pp 62–3, 64(b), 65–9 © AMP / LowDO; p 64(t) © Julien Lanoo

Barkow Leibinger,
Trumpf Smart Factory Chicago, Hoffman Estates,
Chicago, Illinois,
2017

Vast glazing and timber accents confer an organic quality on the ultra-modern factory interiors. These natural elements do not undermine but instead complete the symbolic function of the steel trusses, which mark the structure and its machines as models of technology at its apex.

A NEW PARADIGM FOR THE PERIPHERY
THE CASE AGAINST REUNITING CITY AND FACTORY

Frank Barkow

Amid all the hype about bringing factories back from the periphery and reintegrating them into the city centre, are some of the downsides of central location being ignored? **Frank Barkow**, co-founder of architectural practice Barkow Leibinger with offices in Berlin and New York, argues for a continuation of the industrial edge condition on the grounds of scale, flexibility and adaptability as well as in terms of transport infrastructure.

An homage to Corbusier's Green Factory, the Smart Factory is woven into a patchwork of wetlands and grasses, naturalising industry in the process.

In the post-Second World War period, factories moved from the centres of Western industrial cities to the peripheries. To mitigate overcrowding, preserve property values, and economise the structure and arrangement of cities, limits on building size, density and separate incompatible activities had to be set. Zoning regulations and taxation were the principle means for achieving these goals. Housing, manufacturing and retail activities, formerly intermixed, now took place in different parts of the city. Recently, some architects and planners have broached the idea of re-joining industry and the city. But *should* the factory return to the city? On the contrary. Through the practice's work, Barkow Leibinger has observed an urbanisation of the peripheral spaces between cities and countryside where large-scale factories are currently located. As a result of the categorical transformation in the design typology, function and identity of these factories during recent decades, they seem to be particularly well-suited to the suburbs.

Urban real estate is now too expensive for all but small-scale industry. Suburbs, on the other hand, offer low tax bases, zoning flexibility, possibilities for high-density growth, and cheaper land. This has allowed factory sites – particularly in Europe and the US – to evolve into expansive and programmatically diverse 'campuses', conceived to attract a workforce in search of a work-life balance. But the imperative for factories to remain on the periphery transcends financial pragmatism. The dynamic and adaptable design typology crucial for today's factories is more easily supported by peripheral space, where there is room for expansion as well as existing building stock that can be acquired and reused. This landscape allows for a building typology that remains in flux. Today's factory is designed to respond to changes in use, in masterplanning strategies, supporting technologies, and available land. Large-scale factories (20,000+ square metres/215,000+ square feet) are especially suited to spaces able to accommodate unanticipated expansion and transformations over time.

The effects of this programmatic expansion are significant; the factory has effectively urbanised its suburban surroundings. Suburban factories are adjacent both to the necessary transport infrastructure and to residential areas, agriculture and nature reserves. They are becoming independent centres that combine desirable aspects of urban living such as housing, entertainment and cultural activities with the factory. To this end, the increasingly popular 'industrial campus' is programmatically inclusive: a place to live, work and learn, and to enjoy leisure activities.

The discourse surrounding models of the factory and labour-centred city appropriate for today's social landscape has an especially illustrious forefather. Le Corbusier posited that functionally specialised spaces, generated by adjacent factory and residential areas (with all of their amenities), could be situated together along green belts parallel to infrastructure channels to form what he called the Linear Industrial City (designed 1935). These peripheral cities would join living and working spaces in a continuous, non-hierarchical geographic swathe of development with the potential for continued growth and both high- and low-density housing typologies. The Linear Industrial City contains all the fundamentals: infrastructure, factories, housing, social programming, educational facilities and governance, out of which a new city model can grow.

Embedded in these cities is a distinct model for a factory: organised as a patchwork, the Green Factory (1947) integrates saw-tooth roofed sheds with skylit interiors interspersed with open and green spaces. Workspaces, gardens, sky and water are all woven together, signifying the naturalised productivity of industry. This organisational patchwork concept is highly flexible; factories grow in symbiosis with the

Barkow Leibinger,
Trumpf Campus, Ditzingen,
Germany,
1998–

The campus sits between the Autobahn and agriculture on the one side, and residential, commercial and industrial development on the other. Thoughtfully set apart from the broader community infrastructure, the factory nevertheless exists as a life-source for the community, co-determining the physical and social architecture of this linear city.

lands available and spaces can be infilled and grow in multiple directions as necessary.

Le Corbusier's models shaped the spatial paradigm of labour/leisure life that characterises the Barkow Leibinger factories catalogued below.[1] His designs anticipate most of Barkow Leibinger's industrial projects: factories following a linear growth pattern are interwoven with nearby or adjacent living areas, schools, and spaces for leisure, commerce and sport. These factories and their adjacent spaces constitute 'meta-industrial cities' in their dedication to incorporating co-living and production in a single realm. However, instead of returning to the space of the city, such factories organise a new model of urban life, distanced and distinct from that of the metropolis.

Barkow Leibinger's factories upend the historical model of a mono-functional factory located within the space of an urban centre. They are based on a paradigm that grows out of a radically changed, 21st-century model of working/living, and is a force that in turn shapes the relationship between these dimensions of life.

Factory as City
Over the last two decades and through a series of successive interventions, Barkow Leibinger has transformed a mono-functional factory for the machine tool and laser manufacturing company Trumpf, in Ditzingen, Germany, into an expansive campus. The practice has completed, in turn, the Laser Machine Tool Factory (begun in 2000 and ongoing), a Customer and Administration Building (2003), Service Training Centre (2007), Gate House (2007), Campus Restaurant (2008), Logistics Centre (2017), Carpark (2018), Daycare Centre (2019) and a Fitness Centre (2020). By 2020, long distances between various factory divisions had become problematic for Trumpf's 2,000 workers and as workforces expanded, exchange and team-identity became increasingly difficult to maintain. Yet the industrial campus had reached its limit for horizontal expansion. Because it is located next to an Autobahn and bounded by neighbouring properties and the town of Ditzingen, vertical growth was the only option. In deference to the concepts of Le Corbusier's Green Factory, Barkow Leibinger took cues from the surrounding landscape. Embedded in a patchwork of agricultural fields, new areas of factory space were organized *around* the land, built upwards, and linked together to form an aggregate.

Trumpf-Ditzingen is a story of soft planning; the firm's initial masterplans were initiated as a framework that could later be adapted in response to the shifting needs of company and labourers. In its original 1972 iteration, Trumpf-Ditzingen was simply a workplace – a factory and office tower. White-collar workers managed blue-collar workers, and both lived elsewhere. During the 50 years since its conception, Trumpf-Ditzingen has grown parallel to infrastructure: what was once a production factory on the outskirts of Stuttgart is now a fully fledged campus that offers work, education, childcare, spaces for exercise, meeting, training, inventing, gardening – and even play.[2] Barkow Leibinger designed a factory that was initially loyal to the historical model, but which had the flexibility

Barkow Leibinger's factories upend the historical model of a mono-functional factory located within the space of an urban centre

to transcend its original paradigm and capitalise on the advantages conferred by its peripheral location. The social inclusivity of the urban city has been adopted and updated in the peripheral city model, and the expanses of available land provide the basis for welding together these heterogeneous fragments into a collective. In the urban city, the convenience of an aggregate cluster of such spaces and structures would not be possible.

Suburbia 4.0: Industry at its Apex
The Trumpf Smart Factory Chicago (2017) is a factory/showroom where machines are constructed and displayed to clients on the one hand and, via a showroom window, to travellers along the I-90 interstate-highway on the other. The building site was purchased as an abandoned business park. The opportunity to reuse such sites is integral to understanding the periphery as the most prudent home for industry. The site's neighbours include a forest preserve, strip malls for shopping and dining, a community church, high school, and single-family housing community. This is a self-contained, urbanised community in which industrial/tech companies coexist in a symbiotic relationship with residential areas, leisure facilities, educational hubs and swathes of natural countryside – emphatically in-line with the Corbusian model.

The adjectival qualification 'smart' refers to the factory as an exemplar of Industry 4.0 – the fourth phase of industry in a lineage beginning with the first Industrial Revolution. Interconnected, digitally controlled, increasingly robotic machines require negligible human interaction and operate without pause. Visitors to the Smart Factory can thread through steel trusses on catwalks and exhibition spaces to peer down at the machines in operation below. The building is, itself, a machine for looking into and for viewing from within. Through this optimisation of transparency, the conceptual underpinnings of the Green Factory are once again embodied.

Creative Production: An Ecumenical Factory
Harvard ArtLab (2019) is a recent addition to Harvard's modern Allston campus in Boston, Massachusetts, located across the Charles River from the university's

main Cambridge campus centred on Harvard Yard. The Allston campus's silhouette, implications and relationship to the main campus remain ambiguous. Best characterised by its sprawl, its geography is far less cohesive than that of the main campus, but is nevertheless significant for its adjacent residential neighbourhoods.

Barkow Leibinger conceived of the ArtLab as a platform that would meet the Harvard-wide programming mandate for flexible 'maker spaces'. In response, the practice designed an industrial workshop: a hub space for performance and exhibition ringed by film-editing spaces, studio space, a cafe and an office. As a pilot project, it is both net-zero, generating its own power, and transient, in that it can be demounted and erected elsewhere. These dimensions of sustainability and flexibility are in keeping with Le Corbusier's Green Factory model.

Though the name ArtLab evokes a scientific laboratory – a site of experimentation – the design and structure emphatically evoke a factory – a site of production. The design references a long history of appropriating and reusing industrial spaces for art exhibitions and pays homage to the factory-turned-art-space model. It is constructed of lightweight, open-web steel trusses, plywood, polycarbonate cladding and raw concrete floors. The resonances between Le Corbusier's Linear Industrial City and the Allston campus are overt; the ArtLab factory is a locus for production, joined on this peripheral site by residential structures, natural areas, transportation infrastructure and sites for leisure and learning. But ArtLab as factory also pushes this paradigm towards a radical model of inclusivity on the periphery, inviting and instigating interaction between Harvard students and the wider community.

Separated Symbiosis
As Barkow Leibinger originally conceived it, the HAWE Hydraulics factory (2014) peripheral to Kaufbeuren, Bavaria, drew explicitly from the Green Factory model. The idea was to coax the agricultural landscape into a symbiotic relationship with factory spaces that would then be incorporated into an expanding patchwork scheme. Its picturesque location ensured workers would have access to the nearby Alps and the adjacent medieval village of Kaufbeuren.

North-facing shed-roofed production halls are constructed of prefabricated concrete and can be added to over time, forming green courtyard spaces for the workers. Its location, within agricultural fields, allows the factory to grow in three directions along the highway. This allowance for horizontal growth is critical to the success of an ever-growing company and is only possible because of the site's adaptability. Because HAWE is programmatically limited to production, office work and canteen dining, the factory benefits from its direct adjacency to Kaufbeuren, with all of its community assets. Like Barkow Leibinger's other factory models, HAWE benefits from its proximity to infrastructure which affords a degree of separation between town and factory, but which also joins the two as extensions of one another.

Barkow Leibingers,
Harvard ArtLab,
Allston, Cambridge, Massachusetts,
2019

An assemblage of multipurpose spaces within, the ArtLab factory nevertheless projects a complete and inviting image outward to the community. A factory aesthetic marks the space as a site of creation and production that is distinct from the singularly programmatic academic halls of historical Harvard.

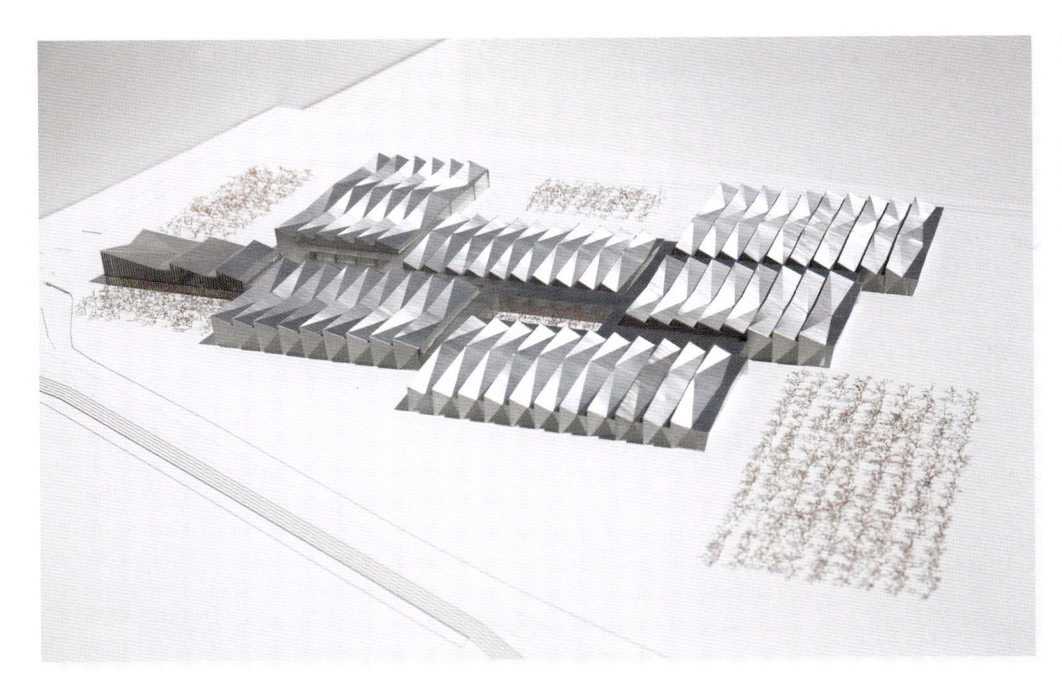

Barkow Leibinger,
HAWE Hydraulics factory,
Kaufbeuren, Germany,
2014

Homogeneous component elements of the factory are joined to form a compound on an expansive swathe of land afforded by the factory's location on the periphery.

North-facing shed-roofed production halls are constructed of prefabricated concrete and can be added to over time, forming green courtyard spaces for the workers

Light-flooded interiors naturalise this model of modern industry. An ultra-sleek take on Le Corbusier's Green Factory, HAWE Hydraulics nevertheless heeds the Green Factory's mandate for visibility and transparency.

The division of town and factory by the freeway affords opportunities for physical industrial expansion that would be unimaginable in the context of an urban setting.

In the spaces of self-contained, urbanised peripheries, the factory is afforded the opportunity to grow, and becomes integrated with the existing structures and geographies that surround it

Barkow Leibinger,
Industrial models: Chicago,
Ditzingen, Boston and Kaufbeuren,
2021

The integration of industrial factories within the spaces peripheral to urban centres can take place in four different ways: symbiosis with residential zones, creation of a denser, more diverse industrial urban landscape, engagement with the broader community, and formation of a new industrial nucleus.

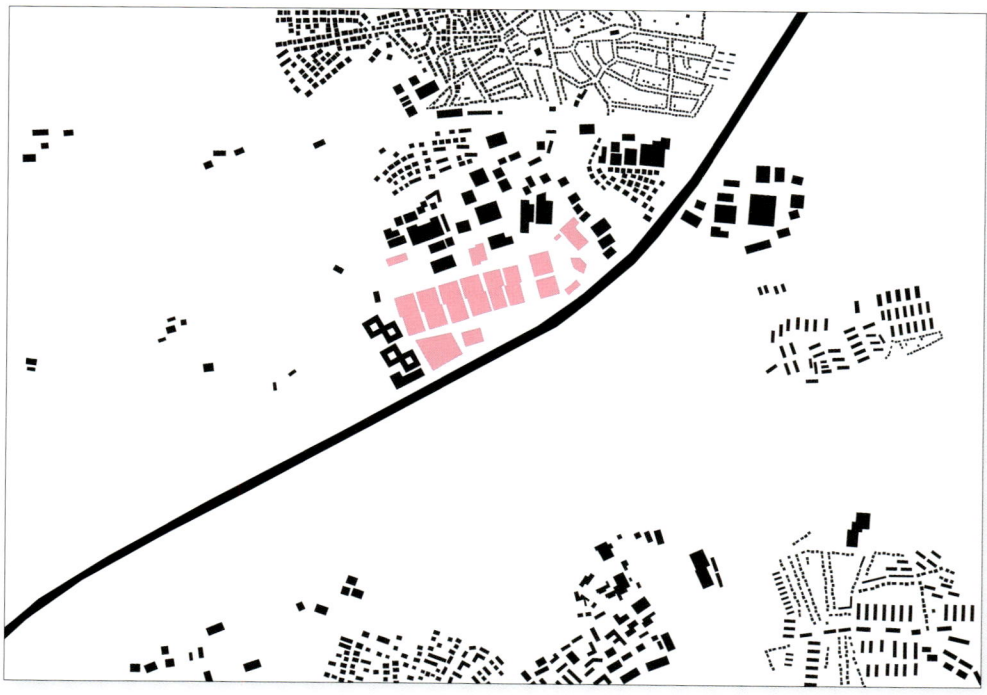

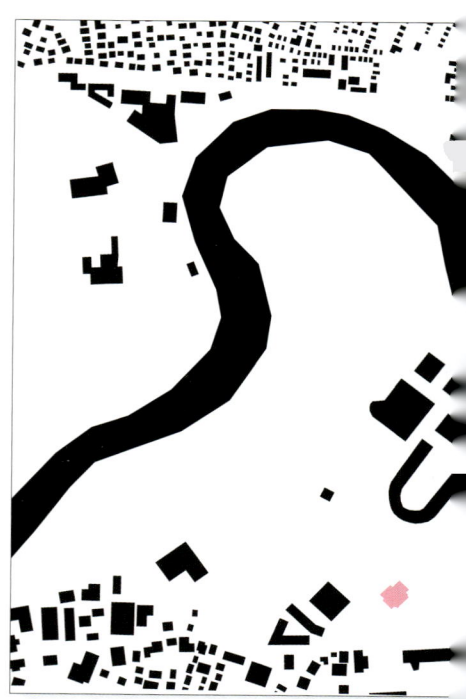

Industrial Landscapes: Factory Towns

Urban factories, conceived as the *raison d'être* of the contemporary meta-industrial city, function well enough as craft spaces or local production centres within the limits of urban scale and economy. But space is congested, flexibility is limited and real-estate expensive. Urban factories therefore remain stunted, fragmentary and without opportunity for growth. The impulse to 'bring the factory back to the city' seems based on little more than a sentimental return to light manufacturing or urban farming. The impetus behind industry's flight from the cities – namely, the lack of financial and functional flexibility they afford – remains a forceful argument against their return. Large-scale manufacturing at the level of the Tesla Gigafactory, Apple, Amazon or Daimler/ Mercedes Benz demands peripheral, suburban sites and their attendant expansiveness and low costs.

Although the machine-tool and hydraulics companies, or even the academic institutions for which Barkow Leibinger works, are mid-scale in size, they nonetheless remain functionally incompatible with high-density urban centres. And though these industrial campuses, as private entities, do not generate public space in the mode of traditional cities, there is nevertheless an impulse and wish to open parts of these spaces to a wider public, insisting on an animated relationship between the labourers or creatives of production spaces and the wider community.

Four Sites (Chicago, Ditzingen, Boston, Kaufbeuren)

In Chicago, the Trumpf Smart Factory exists in a balanced, symbiotic relationship with the residential zone. The Trumpf Campus outside Ditzingen infills the industrial area, producing a denser, more programmatically diverse industrial urban fabric.
In Boston, the Harvard ArtLab serves as a catalyst for development in Allston, inviting a broader community and supporting an interdisciplinary practice that is distinct from the pedagogical modes shaped by main-campus architectures. The HAWE Hydraulics factory outside Kaufbeuren forms a new industrial nucleus.

In the spaces of self-contained, urbanised peripheries, the factory is afforded the opportunity to grow, and becomes integrated with the existing structures and geographies that surround it. Within the space of a city, the middle- to large-scale factory cannot exist as anything other than an intrusive body. This is the reality with which planners, architects and designers must contend. In response, we would do well to adopt and adapt the Linear Industrial City model, designed to facilitate movement and adaptability, as a vital and valid typology for the peripheral city.

This model has informed much of Barkow Leibinger's work. As the practice imagines a future symbiosis of work and leisure, it seems clear that the appropriate factory typology for our age will – and must – remain in the space of the periphery. ⌂

Notes
1. See WD Darden, 'City Planning Theories of Le Corbusier', Master's thesis, The Rice Institute, Houston, Texas, May 1956: https://scholarship.rice.edu/bitstream/handle/1911/89323/RICE0361.pdf?sequence=1, and 'Les Couleurs® Le Corbusier, 'Architectural promenades: discover Le Corbusier's architecture while travelling': www.lescouleurs.ch/en/journal/posts/architectural-promenades/.
2. Henri Lefebvre, 'The Right to the City', in Eleonore Kofman and Elizabeth Lebas (eds), *Writings on Cities*, Blackwell (Oxford), 1996, pp 147–59.

Text © 2021 John Wiley & Sons Ltd. Images: p 70 © Simon Menges; p 71 Photo Steve Hall © Hall + Merrick Photographers; pp 72, 74 © Iwan Baan; pp 75(t), 76–7 © Barkow Leibinger Architects; p 75(bl) © David Franck; p 75(br) © Ina Reinecke

Kengo Kuma

Architecture for Plateaus and Valleys

The Marketability of Industrial Mixing

Kengo Kuma & Associates,
Starbucks Reserve Roastery,
Tokyo,
2019

The balconies produce an exterior collective
space that connects the surrounding scenery
with the industrial machines inside, creating
the scene of a factory as a spectacle.

Tokyo-based international practice Kengo Kuma & Associates has in recent years been commissioned for two projects that mix the uses of café/roastery/shop on the one hand and printworks/museum on the other. **Kengo Kuma** tells the story of how these innovative projects have evolved – a mixture of cultural and social drift, planning zoning in the city of Tokyo and the architectural joy of combining functionally disparate building typologies.

Tokyo is a composite metropolis that consists of two cities with different characters. One is a hilltop city, the other a valley-bottom city. Japan's capital was moved from Kyoto to Tokyo – then called Edo – in 1602. During the Edo Period (1603–1868), people were divided into four classes, from highest to lowest: samurai, farmers, craftsmen and merchants – all ruled over by the shogun. Edo's complex topography of many hills and valleys – in contrast to the flatness of Kyoto – was used to perform zoning to separate the places where people lived way before modern zoning was invented in the 20th century. The shogun had his office at the location where the Imperial Palace is now. The samurai class who served the shogun had their homes on the hilltops. This was the city of the samurai. The low valley area, on the other hand, was a city of farmland, craft and trade.

Even after the name was changed from Edo to Tokyo in 1868, the plateaus where samurai previously lived were used by white-collar workers, and while the volume of farmland decreased, the valleys were still a place for farmers, craftsmen and merchants. The complicated topography was effectively used for residential and industrial areas. They coexisted in extremely close proximity, complementing each other. Rather than being a product of modern city planning, the structure of Tokyo was created by a combination of the natural terrain, a historical class system and industrial ingenuity.

However, after the Second World War, the power of the valleys was considerably weakened. Industry was transferred to reclaimed land along the waterfront and to regional cities outside of Tokyo, and the small factories that were in the valleys vanished one by one. Shops on the lively human-scale shopping streets in the valleys disappeared, replaced by large supermarkets. The decline of the valleys was robbing Tokyo of the allure of a great city. The contrast between the high towns and low towns is necessary for the true Tokyo to thrive and shine.

A REBIRTH OF THE VALLEY
After the recession of the 1990s, which has been called 'the lost decade', people began to return to the valleys, marking a shift away from their previous trend of decline. The areas along the rivers became particularly vibrant. These are areas where small factories were located side by side, using the river for water transport. Their appeal can be illustrated through two projects by Kengo Kuma & Associates, which have formed part of the valleys' rediscovery.

One of these areas is the valley along the Meguro River. The original catalyst here was the development of the Daikanyama area, on a northern plateau very close to the valley. The Hillside Terrace (1992) designed by the architect Fumihiko Maki over three decades became the impetus for a fashionable, quiet, high-end residential district, starting the Daikanyama boom. However, despite acquiring expensive tastes, younger generations wanted to settle somewhere 'cool' rather than high-end, and they began to flow down into the area by the small Meguro River at the foot of the hill, which was once awash with many small factories. This association of industrial areas with 'coolness' has been a common trend since the bubble economy of the 1990s, and had now come to Daikanyama.

The opening of Starbucks Reserve Roastery (2019), a flagship Starbucks store, along the Meguro River in Tokyo was the result of some serendipitous circumstances. Initially, Starbucks was looking for land in the central business districts of Ginza and Ometesando in Tokyo. However, the roaster which is at the heart of the Roastery, in the centre of its atrium, is defined as a 'factory' according to Japan's Building Standards Law – which means that this type of store cannot be built in Ginza or Ometesando. The Starbucks Roastery stores in New York, Seattle and Chicago are all located in the central business districts, but the strict law in Tokyo does not permit this. Instead, building of a roastery here is limited to locations that are zoned as factory or semi-factory areas. Many stakeholders wondered whether or not a roastery that was also a restaurant would be successful as a business in this type of location. Fortunately an offer was received for a piece of land along the Meguro River in a district which, having been a town of factories in the past, had been designated as a semi-factory area.

Therefore, a series of random factors led to the creation of a roastery which is a combination of store and factory in a light industrial area that is a little bit different than the Starbucks Reserve Roastery stores in New York, Chicago, Milan and Shanghai. A large terrace was built to allow people to feel the special ambience of a town of light industry, looking out over the river while drinking their coffee. The terrace is decorated with cast-iron planter boxes with exposed water supply pipes that exude the atmosphere of small factories.

Kengo Kuma & Associates,
Starbucks Reserve Roastery,
Tokyo,
2019

right: The first-floor roaster becomes a central focus for the visitor, shifting the view of industry as a cultural attraction.

below: The pipes throughout the Roastery are both ornamental and functional, serving as ways to transport beans to storage in the coffee cask at the centre of the building.

opposite top: The roastery faces the Meguro River, opening up with a series of balconies that resemble a more residential scale within this semi-industrial neighbourhood.

opposite bottom: The building turns its back on the surrounding parking lots, creating a tension between high-end retail and the semi-industrial site.

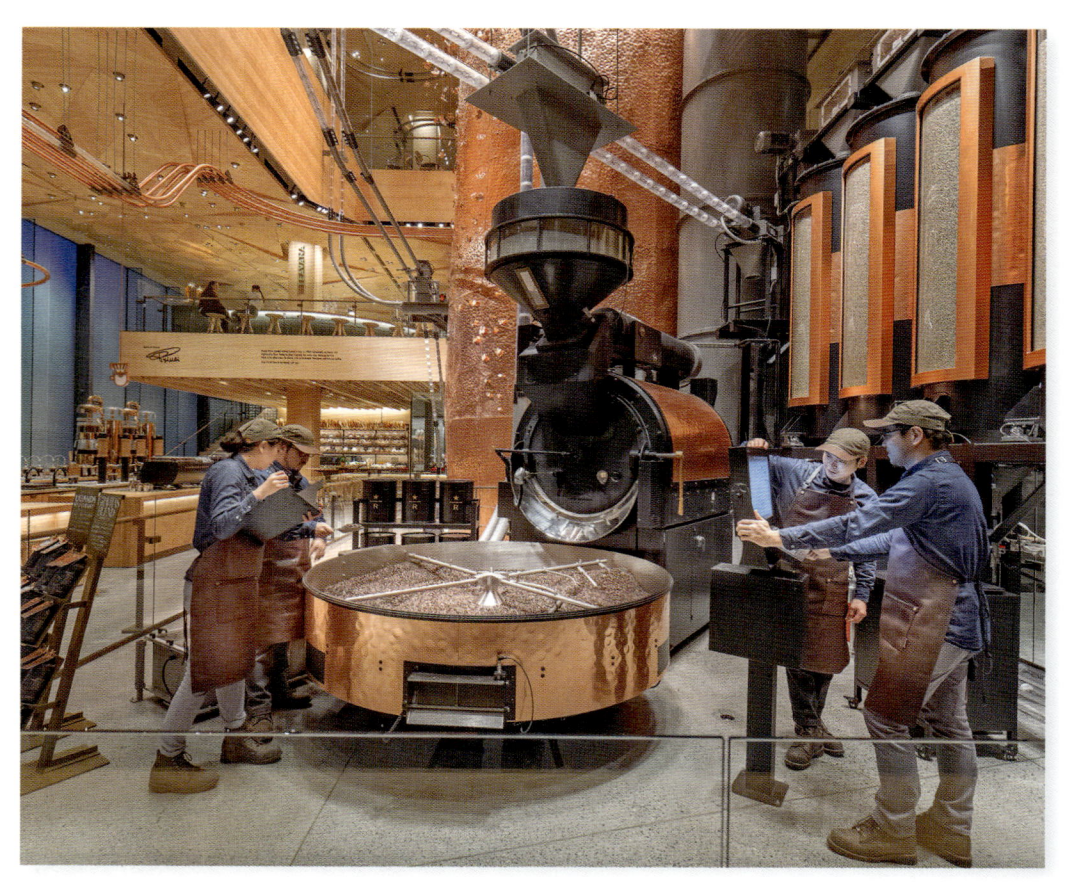

81

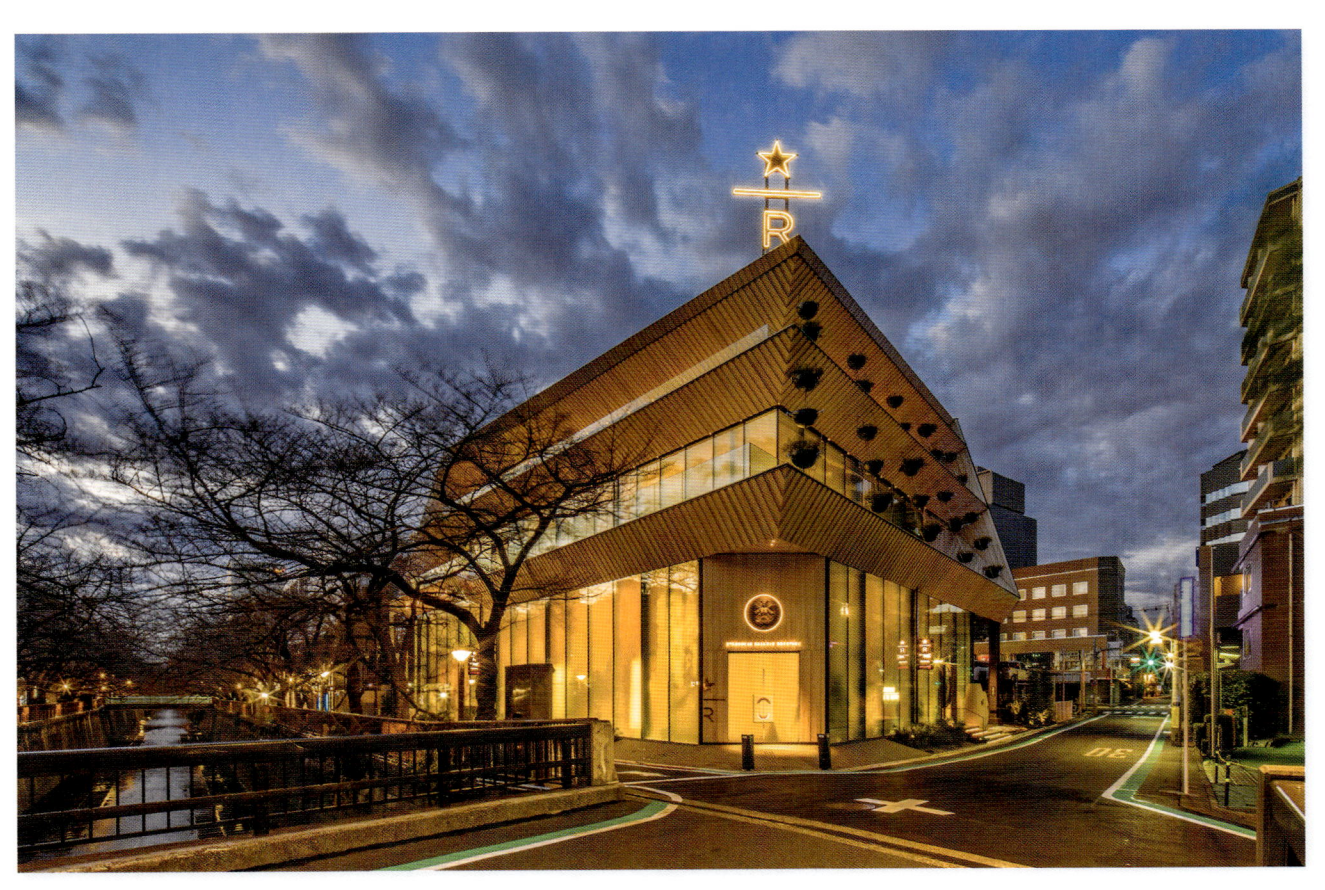

The combination of a hill and plateau is representative of this mixture of high and low cultures

VALLEY AS MIXER

The second valley project for the practice was Kadokawa Sakura Town (2020), situated in the valley along the Azuma River in Tokorozawa, northwest of Tokyo. Kadokawa Shoten, one of the largest publishers in Japan, was looking for a site for a new type of printing factory that combined the functions of an on-demand printer, digital print shop, museum, retail store and hotel. The key element for this location was that it was zoned as a semi-factory area. Tokorozawa is the location where an army airfield was built in 1911, the first airport in Japan, and a few small aircraft-related town factories remain along the river. Kadokawa focused on the light-industry ambience as an interesting attraction, and planned a new 'factory' for this location.

Differing from other publishers, Kadokawa devotes considerable effort to anime and other 'low' cultures. It is interesting that Kadokawa, which covers both high culture and low culture, focused on this location. The combination of a hill and plateau is representative of this mixture of high and low cultures, and it has been an important part of the specific character of Edo since the advent of ukiyo-e painting. This composite facility needed to be different from a conventional museum or commercial setup as it strove to transcend 20th-century categories such as those of the 'cultural' or 'industrial' facility. As a tectonic quality the project combines wire netting used in town factories, the coarse surface of stone and the soft texture of wood in a mystical manner.

HIGH AND LOW

The mixing of high and low culture is an important architectural theme. The tension that is created by the combination of high plateau and low valley area, reflecting this cultural range, produces a discourse for a new direction towards an architecture of mixing. While at one point industry was driven out of the city, perhaps as low culture, it is now becoming the attractor for commercial viability, producing this low/high duality in new typologies: museum/factory, cafe/factory. ⌂

Kengo Kuma & Associates,
Kadokawa Sakura Town,
Tokorozawa, Saitama,
Japan,
2020

above: The Kadokawa Culture Museum serves as an anchor to the complex, pairing high and low culture through museum and industry.

right: The complex was exhibited as a model at the Kadokawa Culture Museum. The display shows the integration between cultural spaces, social spaces and industrial productive spaces as one singular experience.

Text © 2021 John Wiley & Sons Ltd. Images: pp 78, 81(b) © Masao Nishikawa; pp 80, 81(t) © Starbucks Coffee Company; pp 82–3(t) © Kenshu Shintsubo; p 83(b) © James Lambiasi

Wesley Leeman

Floating Farms

Feeding Rotterdam from Within

As consumers become ever more engaged with the ethics of where and how their food is grown, businesses have developed that are totally transparent and sustainable in their production processes. **Wesley Leeman**, partner at Goldsmith.Company, an architectural firm operating out of Rotterdam, documents his practice's design for floating factories that cater to these criteria.

Goldsmith.Company,
Floating Farm Dairy,
M4H district,
Rotterdam,
2019

The view along the public gallery around the cow garden shows the interesting combination of two environments. The cows are fed by a fully automated system that drops their food from above, from a series of conveyer belts. This operation brings a new contrast to the area, but also has strong similarities to the port context of barges, boats and cranes dropping bulk goods in the background.

The Floating Farm Dairy (2019), designed by Goldsmith. Company, produces, processes and distributes a wide range of dairy products in the city, close to consumers. For a city like Rotterdam, the project has become significant for a quest to reinvent the relationship between the inner-city ports and the urban fabric around them. It is a food-producing facility with a highly transparent and educational character. By introducing urban farming, it contributes to the city economically, ecologically and socially through a series of networks. This 'added value' transcends into the price of a single dairy product, compensating for the project's lack of scale in order to be economically viable from mere dairy production alone – making it a relevant project for the current debate on the revaluation of agricultural tradition. As a highly compact dairy farm for 40 cows it not only combines know-how from the fields of agriculture and nautical trade, but gives a hint towards a possible future for both sectors. This future has become even more relevant during the period of the Covid-19 pandemic.

Agri-Culture
In the Netherlands, agricultural production has evolved from a relatively small-scale, diverse, soil- and hand-based industry that was always physically and socially attached to cities towards an ever larger export-oriented, monofunctional, machine-based industry that exists only outside of cities. The Dutch agricultural 'landscape' is monotonously repetitive and standardised to such an extent that it logically had its effects on our climate and environment, the loss of biodiversity, living conditions of animals and consumer awareness. It has thrived on dulled consumers that are totally uninterested in where their food comes from. Correspondingly, all 'food-producing' buildings that accompany the Dutch countryside (mostly large, monofunctional, horizontal structures) are the result of the same quest for economic efficiency and, consequently, lack a need for architecture that does anything besides covering the industrially efficient processes inside.

The export-oriented food production system for which the Netherlands is so renowned has come into question even more during the Covid-19 pandemic. As logistical restrictions were imposed and food supply chains suddenly broke, the push towards food security, food safety and locality has only grown even larger. Subsequently, the neglected small scale is the centre of attention and food self-sufficiency is back at the heart of the debate, giving ample reasons to address urban agriculture as relevant, and to re-evaluate the co-existence of food production and urban culture entirely.

The Floating Farm Dairy contradicts current agricultural dogmas in several ways and, in so doing, brings various benefits. Producing, processing and packaging food inside the city drastically shortens the supply chain, adds a certain social value and a certain level of food security, contributes to new forms of urban circularity and (logically) promotes an efficient use of scarce space due to the lack of it. Unlike the production of food in the countryside, producing food in the city requires a transparent process that interacts

Goldsmith.Company,
Floating Farm Dairy,
M4H district,
Rotterdam,
2019

The dairy processing chamber, one of the spaces of the factory floor that is completely transparent. Employees enter via a separate sluice before dressing into their hygienic gear. The setup is relatively small and simple, fitting to the daily output of 40 dairy cows.

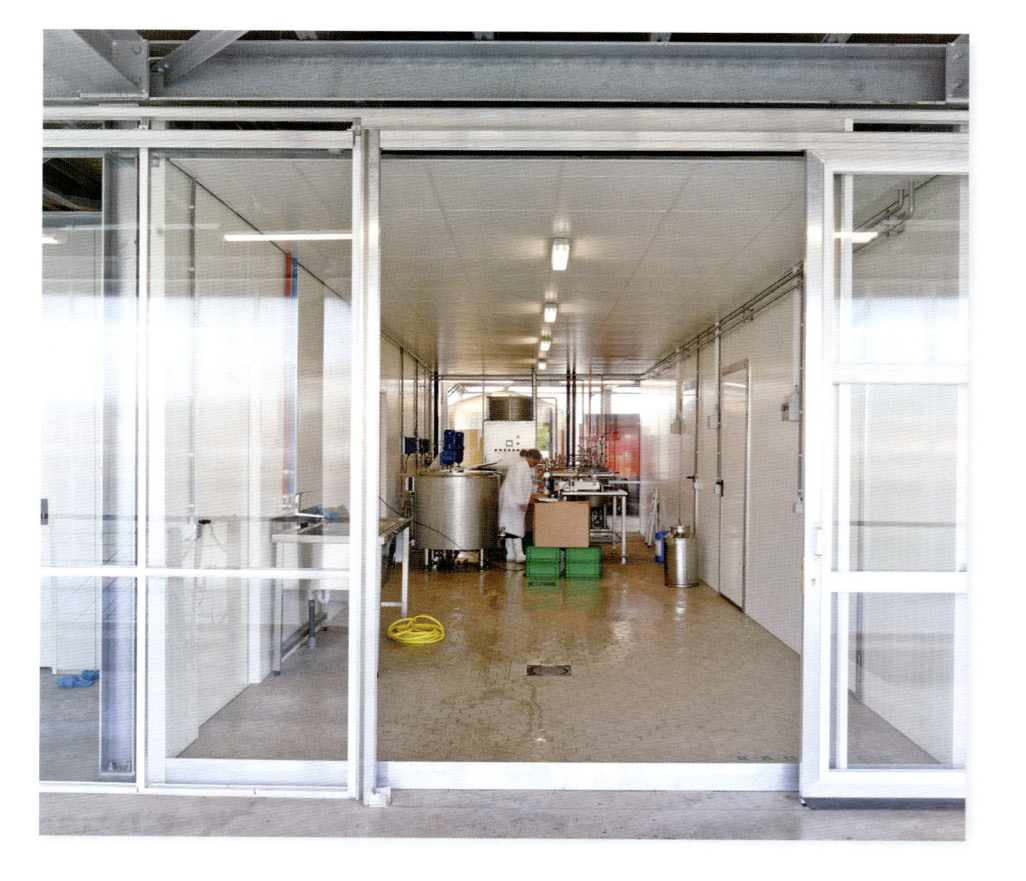

The Floating Farm Dairy contradicts current agricultural dogmas in several ways and, in so doing, brings various benefits

with inquisitive consumers. Next to that, urban farms can play an important part in city culture as they are physically attached to the urban fabric and city life. For the Floating Farm Dairy, Goldsmith.Company never looked at these initial complex conditions as a burden, but used them to create additional value for the dairy products. This creation of value (by incorporation of the production process and exchanging product and waste flows within the city) should compensate for the lack of space in an urban environment. As consumers are willing to pay more for a local brand that they understand and connect with, transparency is very important, even becoming part of 'the brand'. Because a building for food production in the city deals with all these additional aspects, the building itself becomes important, and its architecture becomes equally relevant.

Urban Dairy Farm

The Floating Farm Dairy is a compact and efficiently stacked urban farm with a strong public and educational character. The building combines technical installations, storage, production and processing of dairy on board. The floating body of the structure consists of three connected concrete pontoons. As they are almost completely submerged, they maintain a constant temperature all year round, making them ideal spaces for LED-based fruit production (ingredients for dairy products). Storage and filtration of rainwater, toilets and additional installations are also organised here.

The factory floor above combines milk and yogurt processing, cow feeding system, manure handling, dairy product packaging and a small retail space.

roof structure

free range cow barn

factory floor

floating body

Isometric drawing of the various floor levels. The aim of the farm was to use the available floor space as efficiently as possible, and optimally include a 'food producing' programme on each level.

A view into the 'feeding kitchen'. The food for the cows is stored and mixed here, while allowing just enough space for manoeuvring the vehicle. In the same space, the manure is collected and (pre-)processed. Dairy processing spaces are behind the glass walls on the left.

The Floating Farm Dairy is, in essence, an agricultural building based on nautical principles

Goldsmith.Company,
Floating Farm Dairy,
M4H district,
Rotterdam,
2019

opposite: Every time the cows are allowed to graze in the pasture on the quay, they seem completely at ease, and unfazed by the surrounding smells and sounds of the M4H district.

below: The three layers that comprise the farm, ranging from concrete to translucent to entirely open. The use of materials in this fashion made the separate levels explicit architecturally, while also tackling the nautical conditions of buoyancy and stability.

This involves the storage of raw milk, pasteurising of dairy products and various additional storage- and hygiene-related programmes. From a basic office, employees can monitor everything via screen, from the amount of raw milk produced to the complete health condition of each cow, thanks to a digital chip system.

The covered cow barn on top is in fact a free-range stall for 40 dairy cows. It provides a single cow with roughly twice the surface area that is required by Dutch farming laws. It is covered by an open steel structure that is equipped with adaptable windscreens on all sides, ensuring protection from frost or harsh winds. Centrally placed 'green columns' (along which ivy is guided up along steel wiring) ensure additional cooling during hot summer days. The stall is supported by a manure cleaning robot and a milking robot that do most of the work, and it has some features that enhance the animals' welfare. The roof that covers the cow garden collects rainwater that is reused on board to flush toilets, but also to clean the barn. The repetition of the rounded profiles in the roof refers to an agricultural character and achieves a certain iconic value. Cows are able to move freely onto a quayside pasture via one of two steel bridges. These bridges act as hinges, as height differences of up to 4 metres (13 feet) can occur in the port due to the tides.

The Floating Farm Dairy is, in essence, an agricultural building based on nautical principles. This fact alone is the leitmotif for the typological organisation and corresponding appearance. Goldsmith.Company has applied the organisation of programme and machines, and the use of structural components and other materials, to enhance the buoyancy and stability. The result is a stacked organisation that places all heavy structural and technical components in the submerged part of the building. All significant and transparent functions are situated in a lightweight structure on top. The façade ranges from closed concrete to translucent polycarbonate to entirely open, giving each level a clear and distinctive character.

From the start, the client was keen to show all processes that happen on board. The building's appearance and organisation enhance this transparent character. Through all levels, visitors can circulate through the building along a route that does not interfere with the production process. The route takes them through the retail area and feeding kitchen from which they can see the entire dairy process. They can make their way up to the cow garden via the steel bridges that lead them on to the gallery. From here they can walk around and get very close to the animals without disturbing them or the milking process. The cows seem to quite like this bit of occasional extra attention. The 'feeding fences' and the transparent factory façade enhance the visitor's experience and underline the open nature of the company.

Exodus of Traditional Port Activities

Almost identical to the transition of areas for agricultural production moving outside of cities, the dynamic trading environment of the ports has left the city of Rotterdam. Scale enlargement and automation fuelled an exodus westwards towards the coast, and later on even into the sea through large land reclamation projects. For most inner-city ports the response to this industrial exodus meant an almost immediate densification through adding high-rise around the harbour basins. But the municipality of Rotterdam had alternative plans for the M4H district. This port area at the edge of the city is on the verge of transforming from a traditional port zone to a climate-proof and sustainable city district. Constructed from the 1920s as a general cargo port, it was later known for its several fruit wharfs, conditioned warehouses and a former ship wharf. Now, with the circular economy as its motor for development, it has been labelled as the 'Makers District', and the municipality aims to attract all sorts of pioneering businesses to underline this character. It is only logical that the Floating Farm Dairy is one of the projects that is situated here, and it has become one of the public pioneers of the area that gives new meaning to a previously abandoned urban space through the introduction of urban farming.

Besides trying to re-utilise many of the on-board waste flows, those from the city are upgraded from residual product to valuable ingredients for cow feed. Brewers' grains, potato scraps from local companies and grass clippings from the Feyenoord football club are all part of the menu. The rinse from the honey of a small-scale distillate company is delivered as a supplement power food for all cows that have recently given birth. Furthermore, the company tries to manage and sell most of the manure that is produced. A significant

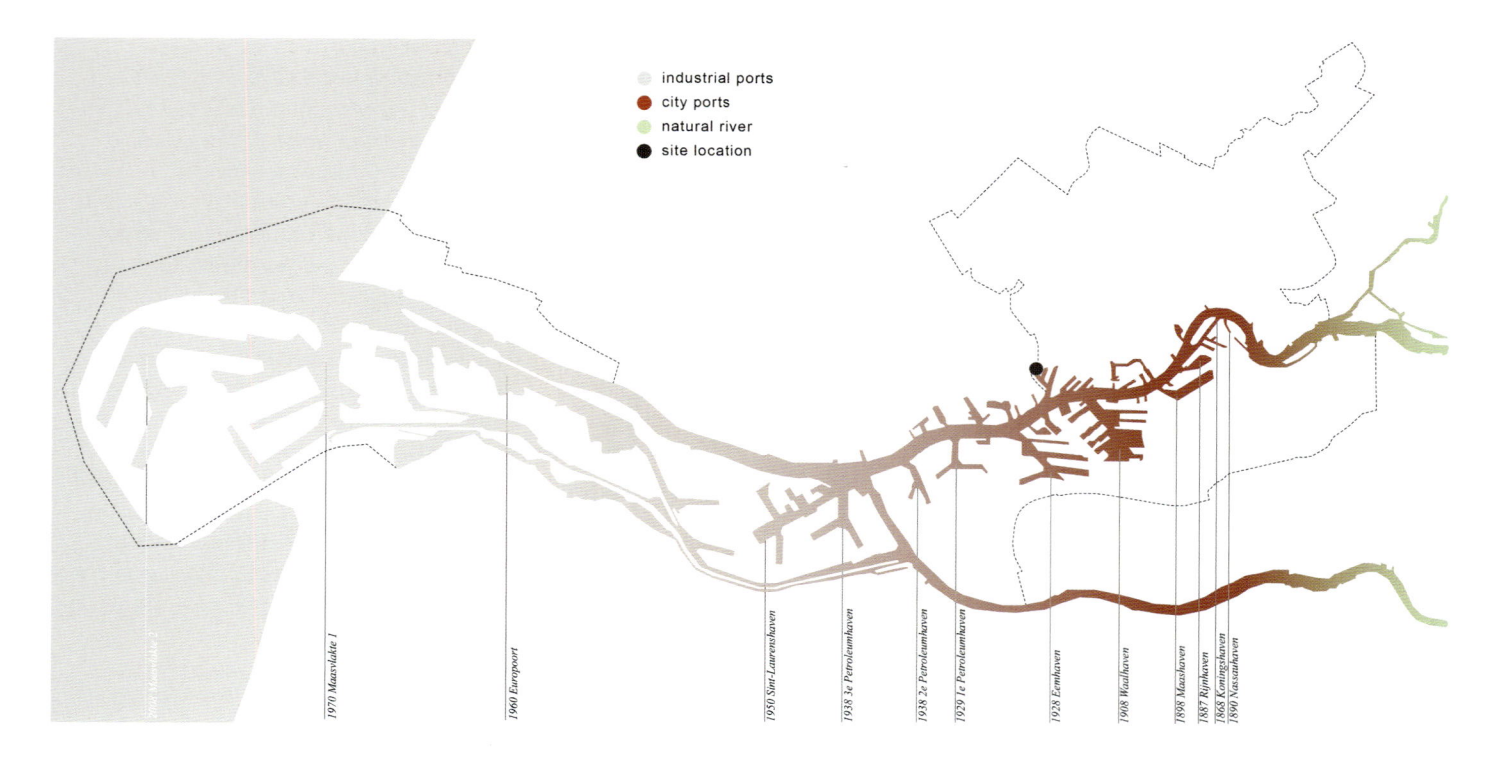

industrial ports
city ports
natural river
site location

1970 Maasvlakte 1
1960 Europoort
1950 Sint-Laurenshaven
1938 3e Petroleumhaven
1938 2e Petroleumhaven
1929 1e Petroleumhaven
1928 Eemhaven
1908 Waalhaven
1898 Maashaven
1887 Rijnhaven
1868 Koningshaven
1890 Nassauhaven

Goldsmith.Company,
Floating Farm Dairy,
M4H district,
Rotterdam,
2019

The scheme illustrates the chronological construction of the Rotterdam ports, showing an exodus westwards in combination with continuous scale enlargement.

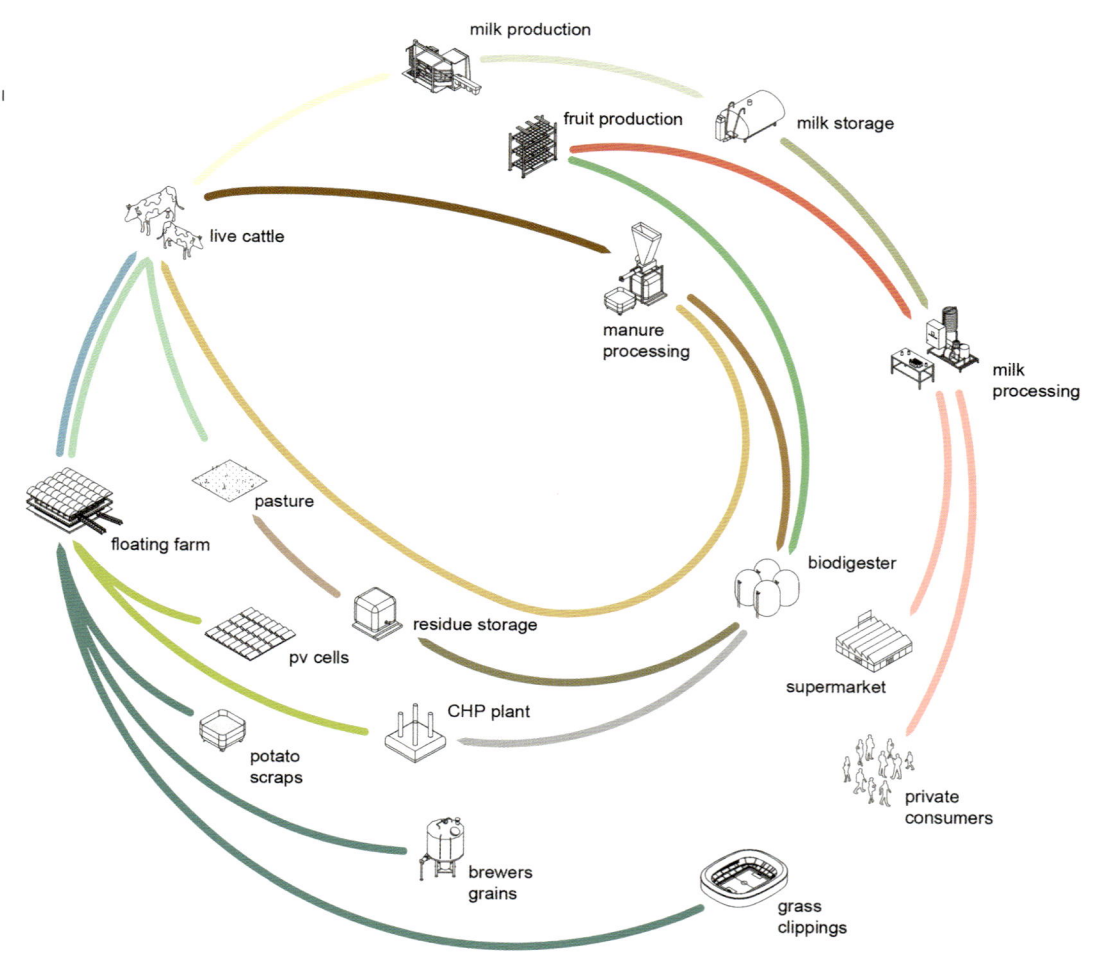

- electricity
- biogas
- cow feed
- plant clippings
- biowaste
- rainwater
- cow milk
- raw milk
- cooled raw milk
- milk products
- fresh fruits
- manure
- dehydrated manure
- cow garden bedding
- dehydrated manure
- fertilizer

milk production
fruit production
milk storage
live cattle
manure processing
milk processing
pasture
floating farm
residue storage
pv cells
biodigester
CHP plant
supermarket
potato scraps
private consumers
brewers grains
grass clippings

Sustainable cycles diagram illustrating all exchanges after the first six months of operation. These exchanges are evolving and will continue to grow over time.

percentage (once dried) is reused on board to function as cow bedding, while an even larger portion is further dried and compressed into fertiliser granules, to be sold back to the city. This adds to urban recycling and constitutes a fairly efficient form of food production, adding to the circular economy that is aimed for in the M4H district.

Since the first day of operation, the Floating Farm Dairy has been proving its worth in a dense urban environment by its economical, ecological and social contribution to the city. The operators have been creative enough to compensate for the small size of the farm and ensure economic viability. The combination of production, processing, packaging and distribution from a single farm, the transparent and educational character of the company and the intercompany relations that upgrade residual flows in the city strengthen the Floating Farm as a brand while embedding the company into the city more solidly. Because the project has a good story to tell, it makes for a relatively strong brand that appeals to consumers. For this reason they are able to add certain value to their products, thus selling them at a higher price to make up for the lack of quantity. The architectural appearance is interwoven with this brand as it underlines the dialogue between the building and its harbour context in a very literal way.

Food Strip
It will be interesting to see how this dialogue will continue to evolve in the near future. Currently, the project is a public pioneer that brings a new type of industry to a previously privatised part of the city. Its presence in this unusual context strongly contributes to social awareness, acceptance and education. Subsequent steps have already been made to design a 'Food Strip' of various food-producing floating structures next to the Floating Farm Dairy, including a poultry facility also designed by Goldsmith.Company. The aim is to represent a much wider range of food products and to strengthen and enlarge the sustainable cycles that have been begun by the introduction of the dairy farm.

Parallel to this are plans to densify and develop the quays of the M4H area around the farm with housing projects and offices. Being a Rotterdam-based office with a strong affinity for the harbour area, Goldsmith.Company thinks that an integral approach that includes food production in these future developments has high potential and relevance. A new type of city district in which living and food production co-exist should be further investigated. Meanwhile, an urban framework has already been formulated, to function as a guideline for all future developments in M4H. As long as the relationship between living, working and food production is not yet underlined in this framework, it is uncertain whether the Food Strip will obtain a permanent place of significance as part of the long-term developments to come. ⌂

Goldsmith.Company, Floating Farm Poultry, 2019

Unbuilt at the time of writing but intended for a location adjacent to the Floating Farm Dairy, this design combines a facility for 7,000 laying hens, with a LED farm for leafy greens, and a processing and packaging facility for eggs, leafy greens and combined products. This is the first development towards the subsequently planned Food Strip.

Text © 2021 John Wiley & Sons Ltd. Images: pp 84–5, 86, 87(r), 88–9 © Goldsmith.Company, photos Ruben Dario Kleimeer; pp 87(l), 90–1 © Goldsmith.Company

THE *DANWEI* SYSTEM

LIVING WITH PRODUCTION

Michele Bonino
and
Maria Paola Repellino

Respectively a professor and research fellow at the Politecnico di Torino, **Michele Bonino and Maria Paola Repellino** explore the rejuvenation, social aspirations, architectural techniques and outcomes of China's *danwei* system of industrial units. This is resulting in a revitalisation of these districts, bringing cultural, employment and amenity diversity as well as blurring older boundaries between richer areas and less privileged ones.

China Architecture Design Group (CADG)
Land-Based Rationalism Design & Research Centre,
Dahua Textile Mill renovation,
Xi'an,
2014

The large saw-tooth roof covers a new network of paths and squares, facilitating integration between the building and the urban space and inviting citizens to enter the new creative cluster.

Walking away from the Chegongzhuang subway station in Beijing towards the northwest districts of the city, just beyond the second ring road, you can find the austere silhouette of institutional buildings and a continuum of towers and anonymous residential buildings. They indicate that you are now a long way away from the dense fabric of the *hutong* of the old city. Yet a few steps further, just after the Municipal Communist Party School, everything changes again: you are approaching the area of the former Beijing Xinhua Printing Press, a state-run factory built in 1949, home to the main governmental news agency. Looking beyond the short stretches of brick walls and the leftover parts of old fences marking the perimeter, you can see low red-brick constructions, a theatre, a museum, a public park, the headquarters of several state institutions, office spaces, as well as a former factory. A sign on the tower at the entrance attests to its recent conversion into a different kind of production: the Xinhua 1949 Cultural Creative Industrial Park aims to attract investment and activities involving cultural and creative industries. Xinhua 1949 and its urban vitality testify to the legacy of former industrial *danwei* and the role they can play in contemporary Chinese cities.

Beijing Huaqing An-Design Architects,
Xinhua 1949 Cultural Creative
Industrial Park masterplan,
Beijing,
2014

A bird's-eye view of the former *danwei* of the Beijing Xinhua Printing Press shows the mixed fabric of the production area which, compared to a monolithic industrial structure, turned out to be better suited to being integrated into the city.

The *Danwei* as a 'City within a City'

The term *danwei* literally means 'unit'; it refers to the workplaces that were part of China's planned economy. The *danwei* system was at its strongest in the 1960s and 1970s.[1] In 1978, 95 per cent of urban workers in Beijing belonged to a work unit.[2] The three principal activities performed in the *danwei* either involved the military or government agencies, scholastic or research institutions and, above all, industrial activities (*qiye danwei*). The latter combined production units, as part of the national industrial chain; housing for the workers and their families; and other structures for social life and everyday needs such as canteens, schools, gymnasiums, clubs and medical assistance services, located within one or more enclosed complexes and under the watchful eye of the *danwei* management.[3] The importance of the work unit lies specifically in the reorganisation of Chinese society within a precise urban form that merged social, economic and political functions and is characterised by some recurrent elements. The layout of a *danwei* settlement tended to be designed as a micro 'city within a city': an enclosed, gated, independent block, divided into zones based on functional logic and axial symmetry, and free from vehicular traffic. Its land was often underexploited because no mechanism existed either to encourage a more intense use of the area or to establish an efficient sharing of services between neighbouring work units. Architecturally speaking, the *danwei* were frequently characterised by low-density, multi storey, Soviet-style line buildings. Despite all these recurrent points, the broad variety of sizes, spatial configurations and resources allocated by the government reveal that the adopted models differed greatly.

The location of a *danwei* was influenced by several factors, notably including specific political indications or proximity to infrastructure used to transport goods (railways or water channels). In addition, the fact the *danwei* were essentially autonomous meant they could be located at a distance from a city centre, thus promoting an urban model alternating built areas and agricultural areas; the latter were important because they fuelled the message of Chinese communism which, unlike the Soviet Union, was based on the peasant class rather than the working class. When a series of economic reforms were introduced in the 1980s, the *danwei* system became increasingly obsolete and uncompetitive; it gradually weakened until the strong link between production and housing disintegrated. Finally, when a private housing market emerged in the 1990s and a radical de-localisation of manufacturing industries was later implemented, placing the latter outside the boundaries of urban centres, the space of the *danwei* was generally no longer occupied and could therefore be exploited in another way. What remains of that system in contemporary cities? Today, former industrial *danwei* are mixed spaces, fragments more similar to the fabric of the city compared to the large complexes typically left by Western industrialisation. They are spaces ready to welcome architectural experiments and hybrid urban practices, combining conservation and renovation.

Maria Paola Repellino,
Drawing of the *danwei* of
the Beijing No 2 Textile
Factory in the late 1970s,
2021

A typical example of an industrial *danwei*. The Chaoyang Road axis divides the 1950s buildings formerly used for production (converted in 2011 to accommodate film and media enterprises – the so-called Legend Town, masterplanned by China Electronics Engineering Design Institute (CEEDI)) from the residential and service sector which has remained largely unaltered. Red lines in the factory area indicate the blocks obtained through the 2011 renovation based on Kengo Kuma & Associates' concept proposal.

Key

1. Auditorium and dining hall
2. Primary school
3. Kindergarten
4. Garden house
5. Dormitories for single staff, hospital, and halal canteen
6. Residential buildings
7. Textile training school
8. Post office
9. Playground
10. Balizhuang No 2 Middle School
11. Bathrooms
12. Garage
13. Office buildings
14. Factory workshops
15. Unused land
16. Dormitories for single mothers
17. Neighbourhood factory

Change Without Changing
The exponential growth of cultural industries has marked the shift from a production based chiefly on manufacturing (Made in China) to a production strategically focused also on innovation and the development of knowledge-based services and activities (Created in China). In the last two decades the renovation of former industrial *danwei* sites increasingly coincided with the creation and development of new creative industries – art districts, cultural areas, media bases, incubators and cultural parks. From an architectural point of view, these transformations concerned former independent blocks, therefore usually quite free from planning and protection constraints. Despite this freedom, the projects very often maintained the principal characteristics of the original layout which proved well suited to the new creative rather than material forms of production. Traces of the past were thus safeguarded by pragmatic forms of reuse, preservation or even monumentalisation.

A first recurrent approach to the *danwei* sites involves their specific nature of production and the work tools that are available on site, and can enhance certain transformations. This is the case of the precursor and world-famous 798 Art Zone, a former military factory located northeast of Beijing. In the late 1990s its large, flexible structures and the fact machinery was still available boosted the conversion of these spaces into artists' studios and workshops for the Sculpture section of the Central Academy of Fine Arts (CAFA).[4] In many other projects, old machinery – real *objets trouvés* – was instead repositioned as elements reminiscent of a glorious past; these were often important in the construction of new sophisticated narratives.

A second feature of numerous *danwei* renovation projects comes from the unique organisation and variety of functional interactions of the original site. The new creative industries nearly always reiterate the 'mixed' functional programme used previously in the *danwei*; it now combines 'lightweight' production, commercial activities, public areas and housing. These spaces propose an open but well-organised cohabitation concept, protected and permeated by a different manner of 'being in public'. In many projects, for instance, intersecting cycle paths, pedestrian walkways, ramps, platforms, stairs and footbridges connect inhomogeneous building elements. Even if not strictly a *danwei*, the OCT-Loft in Shenzhen renovated in 2012 by URBANUS is a significant example. The project redesigned the infrastructure linking the open spaces of the industrial area, and adapted the existing structures to the new functions of the art centre and to collective living. A second artificial 'ground' integrated the existing pathways thanks to a new system of public spaces, binding the various fragments of the area along its central axis; the system then extended beyond the original industrial perimeter and spreads into the adjacent environment.

URBANUS,
OCT-Loft renovation,
Shenzhen,
2012

A series of specific projects are grafted onto the existing layout creating a ductile, flexible infrastructure with new services, where the spaces can be easily adapted to new urban requirements.

A third feature frequently encountered in *danwei* renovation projects is the approach to the structure of the industrial plant. Architects are usually expected to pare down the large spaces of the factory to a more human scale so that different uses and activities can be performed, compared to the ones regarding manufacturing. The building's original volume is reduced or fragmented: its 'footprint' is recognisable although its geometry changes. The structural skeleton is often maintained to bear witness to the building's authenticity: a new infrastructure, capable of creating unusual links with the adjacent urban fabric, is just as frequently placed over it. In Beijing, for example, the new grid designed in 2011 by China Electronics Engineering Design Institute (CEEDI) for Legend Town, based on a concept proposal by Kengo Kuma, divided the big industrial plant of Beijing No 2 Textile Factory into new blocks closer in size to an urban scale. On the contrary, URBANUS's project for the Now Factory Creative Office Park completed in 2014 in Shanghai involved additions, juxtaposing new volumes that fragmented the factory's monolithic forms. The subtractions and alterations required by reuse tended to create a differentiation with what exists: they proposed new functions, but at the same time maintained traces of the building's original state.

Kengo Kuma & Associates (concept proposal) and China Electronics Engineering Design Institute (CEEDI) (design development), Legend Town masterplan, Beijing, 2011

The masterplan, based on a concept proposal by Kengo Kuma & Associates, cuts the large production floor with saw-tooth roof of the Beijing No 2 Textile Factory into independent blocks, varying in size, and separated by paths and gardens that establish a new low-density urban fabric.

URBANUS, Now Factory Creative Office Park, Shanghai, 2014

right: A new path meanders inside and outside the building, linking a network of open spaces that can be used by the public. Four new volumes nuance the monolithic appearance of the existing structures.

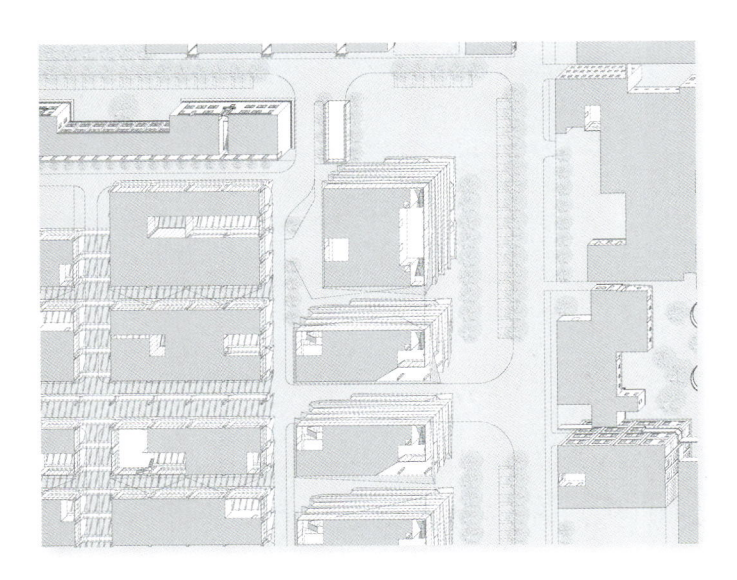

Maria Paola Repellino, Axonometric view from below of the Legend Town renovation, 2015

The renovated area still remains little accessible to the public, despite the introduction of several semi-private activities, some commercial activities and the attempt to integrate with the urban space through the creation of a public park, which was never completed.

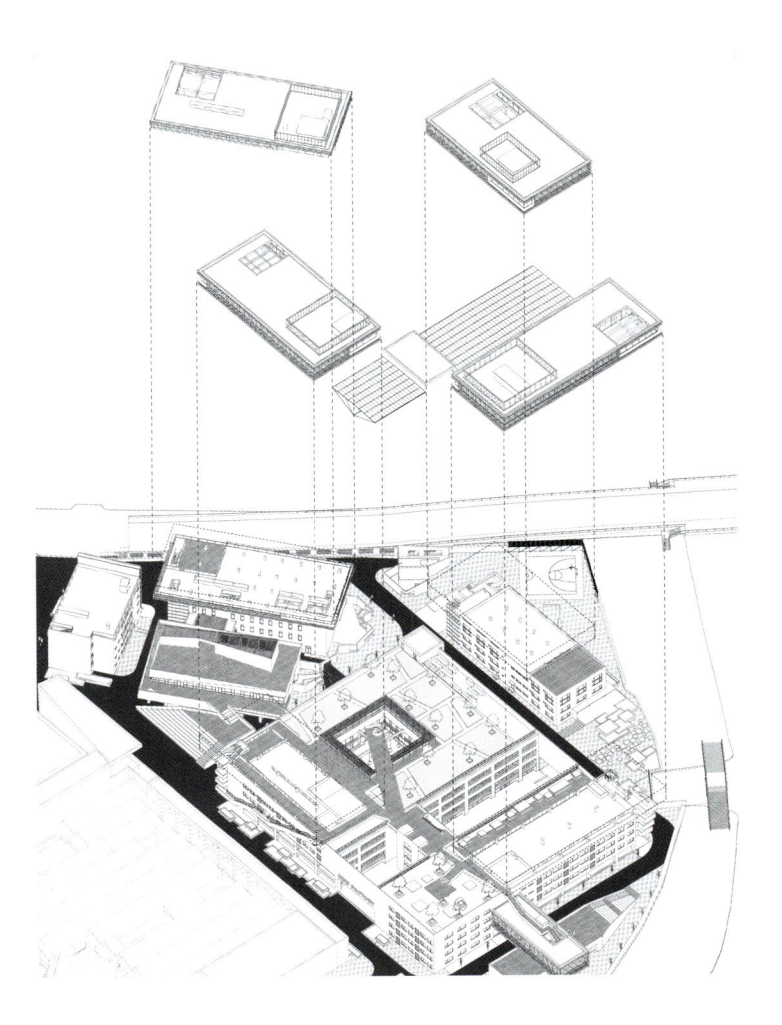

Producing Urban Centres

By renewing the legacy of collective labour, creative industries favour the aggregative form of 'clusters'. The hundreds of former factories and *danwei* settlements turned into 'creative clusters' provide Chinese cities with new spaces in which to live and work, as well as opportunities for a collaborative development between new forms of production and consumption. The quality of the cluster lies in the fact it functions like a *milieu* where several factors, enhanced by the potential of the physical space – proximity, commonalities and coexistence – generate interdependence with the city rising up around it. What sort of production can be found in these renovated sites? First and foremost culture and knowledge, features that often play a key role as the engine driving urban transformation. Starting with the prototypes of 798 Art Zone and M50 (50 Moganshan Road Art District in Shanghai), many projects exploited images linked to art and design, including museums and cultural centres. For example, the 77 Cultural and Creative Park project (2014) by Origin Architect combined the renovation of the old structures of the Offset Printing Factory in Beijing with theatrical culture in order to create a new urban centre. In fact, the theatre was the cornerstone of the project; the silhouette of the austere volume built in the heart of the complex looks like that of an ordinary industrial building. However, when the heavy front façade is lifted, it turns the courtyard in front of it into an open-air stage set, available to the city.

A second new 'production' feature is the ability of these sites to cultivate the human capital, talents and ideas needed by the city to remain competitive and produce innovation. For example, in the new tourist district of Dapeng, east of Shenzhen, in 2014, O-office Architects transformed part of the Honghua factory for the printing and dyeing of traditional silk into the iD Town International District Arts. A bankrupt factory revived as a centre for resident artists, who are invited to work and exhibit their creations in the renovated industrial space. Five years later, the success of this first transformation sparked a second project that involved converting a dozen or so structures scattered around the main nucleus in the Mingde Academy campus. The plan drawn up by O-office designed the campus and art centre as a single system of spaces for education and creativity; it revived the seamless relationship between internal spaces and open areas, once characteristic of the industrial activity.

O-office Architects,
Mingde Academy,
Shenzhen,
2019

To reach the classrooms, science centre and sports facilities that are part of the former production units of the Honghua factory layout, students and teachers leave their rooms in the residential sector and cross through a 'forest promenade' that runs past the open-air theatre behind the library.

Origin Architect,
77 Cultural and Creative Park,
Beijing,
2014

The new theatre built to replace the dilapidated old building is located in the centre of the area; it opens onto the courtyard, dilating the stage outwards to make the building more permeable to urban life.

Creative clusters prove to be efficient urban regeneration tools, seeking to fill the gaps in the urban fabric and, at the same time, producing added benefits for their surroundings. The renovation project for the Dahua Textile Mill in Xi'an is emblematic; it was completed in 2014 by the China Architecture Design Group (CADG) Land-Based Rationalism Design & Research Centre for the new Dahua 1935 creative cluster. In this case the design strategy produced public space as a catalyst of urbanity. Several different open spaces dissolved the boundaries of the enormous production plant. A new network of walkways and squares opened up under the factory's sprawling saw-tooth roof, making the former factory permeable. The transformation not only introduced a multifunctional programme for the resident community, but also promoted a more spontaneous and fluid use of the complex; it challenged the rigid spaces of production and encouraged a link between these spaces and the surrounding area.

Towards a Polycentric City

The advantage of the transformation of former industrial *danwei* into creative clusters primarily consists in a combination of the architectural renovation of the organisational characteristics of the original unit, and the insertion of new forms of production capable of extending the mechanisms once performed within the *danwei* into neighbouring areas. The localisation autonomy of the original *danwei* nowadays facilitates the creation of new urban centres even in peripheral areas; it promotes a multipolar structure in large Chinese cities and spreads elements of value, ranging from identity to real estate, to other urban areas besides privileged ones. 🐦

Notes
1. Wei Hua, 'Cong Danweizhi Xiang Shequzhi de Huigui' ('Back from the Work-Unit System to the Neighbourhood System'), *Zhanlue yu guanli* (1), 2000, pp 86–99.
2. Guojia Tongjiju Shehui Tongjisi (ed), *Zhongguo Shehui Tongji Ziliao* (*Statistical Material on Chinese Society*), Zhongguo Tongji Chubanshe (Beijing), 1994.
3. As a general reference, see the following books: Michele Bonino and Filippo De Pieri (eds), *Beijing Danwei: Industrial Heritage in the Contemporary City*, Jovis (Berlin), 2015; Duanfang Lu, *Remaking Chinese Urban Form: Modernity, Scarcity and Space, 1949–2005*, Routledge (London), 2006; David Bray, *Social Space and Governance in Urban China: The Danwei System from Origins to Reform*, Stanford University Press (Stanford, CA), 2005; Xiaobo Lü and Elizabeth J Perry, *Danwei: The Changing Chinese Workplace in Historical and Comparative Perspective*, East Gate (New York), 1997.
4. Interviews with several inhabitants living in the residential area of 798 Factory, Beijing, held on 28 November 2014 by Maria Paola Repellino with Yuan Sheng.

Text © 2021 John Wiley & Sons Ltd. Images: pp 92–3 © China Architecture Design Group (CADG) Land-Based Rationalism Design & Research Center; pp 94, 97(t) © Jia Yue; pp 95, 97(bl) © Maria Paola Repellino; p 96 © URBANUS, photo Wu Qiwei; p 97(br) © URBANUS; pp 98–9(t) © Origin Architect; pp 98–9(b) © O-office Architects

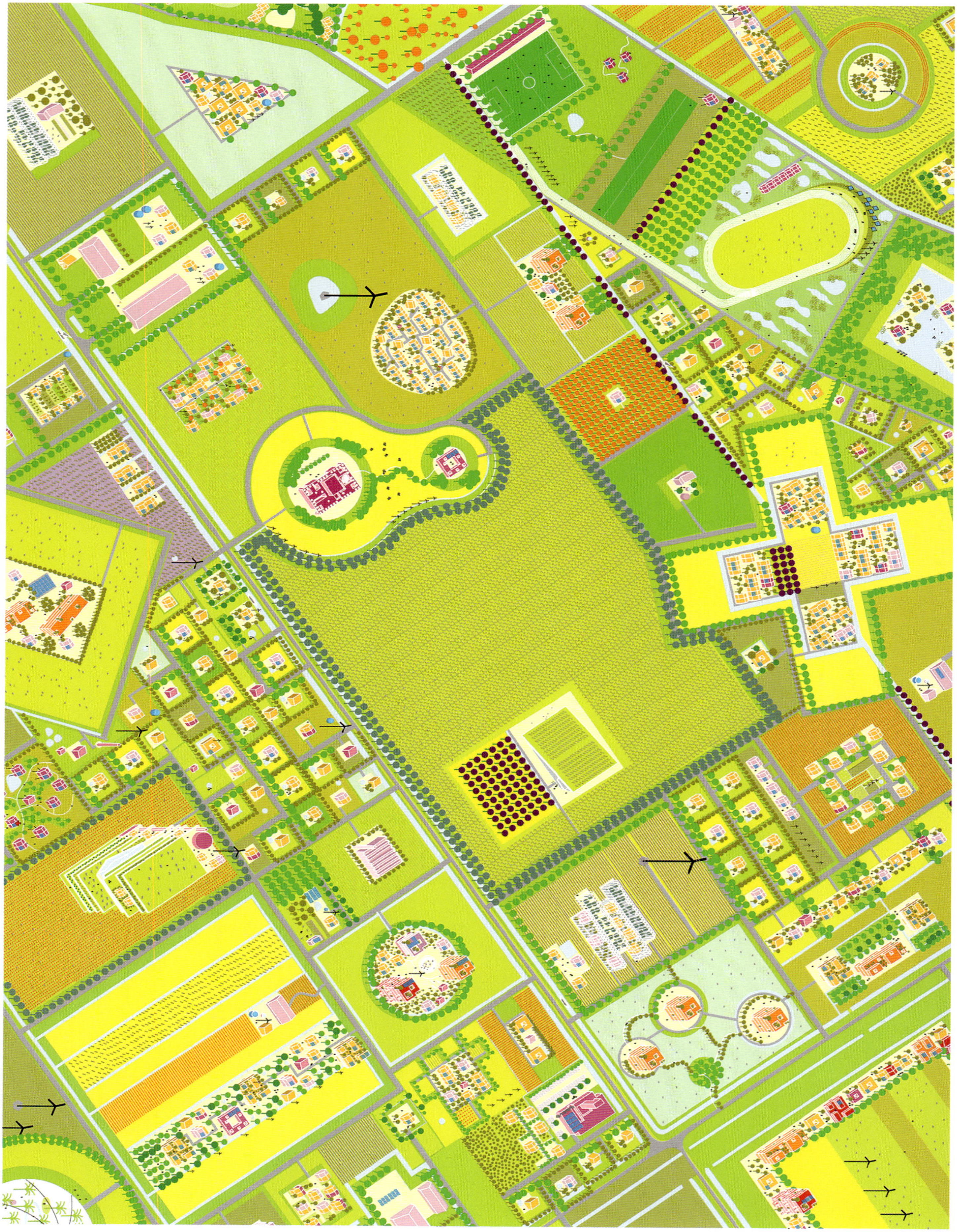

Freeland

How Residents Are Creating a Dutch City from Scratch

What would happen if residents were allowed total design control over their new town, its food production, its highways and its fuel consumption? **Winy Maas**, founding partner and Principal Architect of global practice MVRDV, introduces us to Freeland — an attempt at the total democratisation of masterplanning from the bottom up. Inhabitants can do almost anything but must also take a wider responsibility for the community.

MVRDV,
Freeland,
2011

Freeland gives residents complete freedom over their plot size and shape, leading to diverse and interesting neighbourhood layouts.

The history of the Netherlands began with the transformation of land. In the Middle Ages, farmers began to understand how to create dikes and sluices that would drain water. Using these techniques, they turned a marshy delta by the North Sea into highly productive farmland, laying the groundwork for the Netherlands to become a superpower of the early modern age. The Dutch have a unique understanding of land, in that way. Land is not immutable. Land can be whatever you want it to be.

Over time, the water works that built the Netherlands became increasingly complex. Networks of dikes grew, and windmills were added to pump water. Management of these water works shifted from individual farmers to water management boards that grew in expertise and ambition, developing increasingly large projects. Alongside, the bureaucratic, top-down management approach of these organisations – which eventually merged to become today's Rijkswaterstaat – grew too. The Dutch expertise in top-down management, which originated in their expertise in water management, created rule upon rule.

The crowning achievement of the Dutch water works is the reclamation of the entire province of Flevoland, an area of almost 1,500 square kilometres (580 square miles), from the Zuiderzee (a former inland bay of the North Sea) in the 1950s and 1960s. It was the logic of those early farmers pushed to the maximum: individual farmers once looked at marshland and saw farmland; now the country looks at the sea and sees land. However, as impressive as this achievement is, what might the position of the individual be in this system? Can we rediscover the charm of small, personal visions creating small, personal utopias?

Individual Desires, Collective Responsibilities
In this way, it is fitting that Flevoland is the setting for the first implementation of MVRDV's pioneering Freeland urban planning concept. Under the scheme, Oosterwold, to the east of the city of Almere, will soon contain around 15,000 homes designed not in a top-down fashion by a planner, but created by the residents themselves. Freeland is a place that celebrates individual desire, where you can build the home of your dreams, whatever that may be – anything from a small prefab house to a castle.

Of course, in Freeland as in the rest of the world, freedom and responsibilities are interconnected. Freedoms do not extend to the right to harm others, or to act selfishly. Residents are given the freedom to build their own home, but are expected to contribute to and be responsible for the development of the neighbourhood as a whole: its infrastructure, energy supply, waste disposal, water storage, food production and public parks. Freeland is therefore based upon a simple principle: you can do (almost) anything you want, but you have to organise everything yourself. In this way, it is an attempt to make a masterplan collectively. It will evolve bottom-up, developing into a rich assemblage where everything is possible, yet where advanced urban planning is also very basic.

```
MVRDV,
Almere Oosterwold masterplan,
Almere, Flevoland,
The Netherlands,
2012–
```

When complete, Oosterwold will contain around 15,000 houses and be home to 40,000 people.

Residents are given the freedom to build their own home, but are expected to contribute to and be responsible for the development of the neighbourhood as a whole

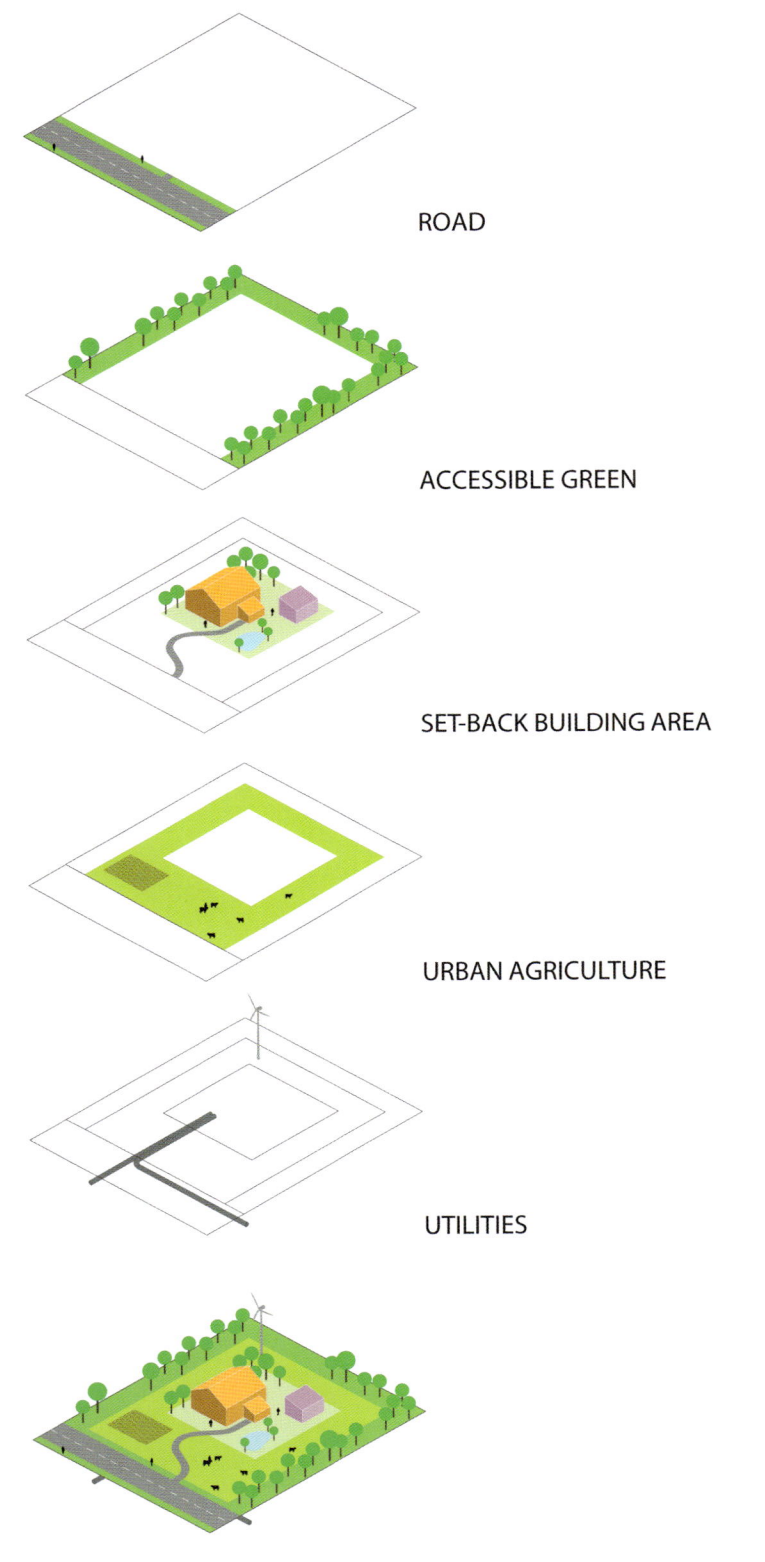

ROAD

ACCESSIBLE GREEN

SET-BACK BUILDING AREA

URBAN AGRICULTURE

UTILITIES

EXISTING PROGRAMME

NEW PROGRAMME

GENERIC PLOT

MVRDV,
Freeland,
2011

The key innovation of the masterplan is to reduce the top-down input of the designer to just a short list of rules and land-use requirements.

Designing a Masterplan from the Bottom Up

But in what sense is this an urban plan? Is it not simply anarchy? In fact, MVRDV has not entirely thrown out Dutch expertise in managing and creating rules, but simply minimised them only to what is truly necessary for a successful suburban neighbourhood: to provide self-sufficiency and encourage respect of one's neighbours. The most important of the rules are the land-use percentages: 50 per cent of each plot of land is intended for urban farming, and only 12.5 per cent can be built on. There are also requirements for public greenery, roads, water and energy production. For example, each plot must be surrounded by greenery, with public access to plots that may emerge beyond. Surrounding each development with a green ring mixes city and landscape, preventing the landscape from becoming too closed off from the rest of the city.

Decades of large-scale agriculture has created ever-more distance – both physical and psychological – between the producer and the consumer. In Freeland, the transformation of the landscape is deployed in a process of downscaling, returning in some way to the early days. The land-use rules create conditions that can in theory create a productive landscape for food, energy and water management. Whether the residents capitalise on those conditions remains to be seen. After all, they are free to make what they want of the land.

Even within the few rules, the plan allows for flexibility and creativity. If one neighbour is very interested in farming, for example, and another wants a large water feature, they can 'trade' their land-use requirements. One of the clearest examples of this negotiation in action is in the construction of streets. Neighbours along a street have to agree how they will finance it. Do they all pay an equal amount? Or do they pay for the portion of the road alongside their property? No rule stipulates this, therefore instilling community communication and cooperation in the very first stages of creating the new neighbourhood.

However, residents are not completely abandoned and left to figure all of this out by themselves. In the case of Oosterwold, they can rely on advice and support from a dedicated management team that represents five government agencies: the local water authority, Netherlands Central Government Real Estate Agency, Province of Flevoland, Municipality of Zeewolde and Municipality of Almere. This team has the challenging task of enforcing rules and settling disputes, without fundamentally undermining the residents' freedom to make their own decisions – a difficult balancing act, but one they are quickly getting used to.

Small, Personal Utopias

MVRDV has learned a lot from the Oosterwold project. However, the Freeland concept can be applied in many places elsewhere, especially in developed

Oosterwold's land-use rules were informed by a long tradition of land management in the Netherlands, ensuring adequate space for water and nature.

MVRDV,
Almere Oosterwold masterplan,
Almere, Flevoland,
The Netherlands,
2012–

above: Residents are responsible for investing in the infrastructure of their own neighbourhood – meaning they are also free to determine some of the rules that govern it.

below: Oosterwold is the first implementation of the Freeland concept, offering a development model that is unlike anything else in the Dutch housing market.

countries which, like the Netherlands, have become dominated by bureaucracy, overscaled agriculture and housing industries, and a lack of truly diverse lifestyle options for their citizens. It could even be adapted to more dense urban situations.

For some, Oosterwold allows them to realise uncomplicated dreams: a normal house that they can actually afford. Because of the cost saving on infrastructure, the municipality of Almere is able to sell land at a much lower cost, and these initial savings are passed on to new residents. Ultimately, this saving is accounted for during the construction process: construction costs are higher as residents are responsible for the development of the infrastructure, which can be paid for out of their own pockets or with their labour, but the lower upfront costs provide the flexibility crucial for those people with less money to spend. Others are drawn to the ideological pursuit of self-sufficiency, freedom and community spirit that characterises the Freeland experiment, and some to visions MVRDV could never have imagined: for example, the 'garage house', a building that incorporates a motorhome at the centre of its design. The owners spend six months each year on the road, and did not want to spend unnecessary extra money on a second kitchen and bathroom they would only use for half the year. Where else in the housing market could such a home possibly exist? ◬

Text © 2021 John Wiley & Sons Ltd. Images: pp 100, 103 © MVRDV; p 102 © Ossip van Duivenbode; pp 104–5 © Simon Lenskens

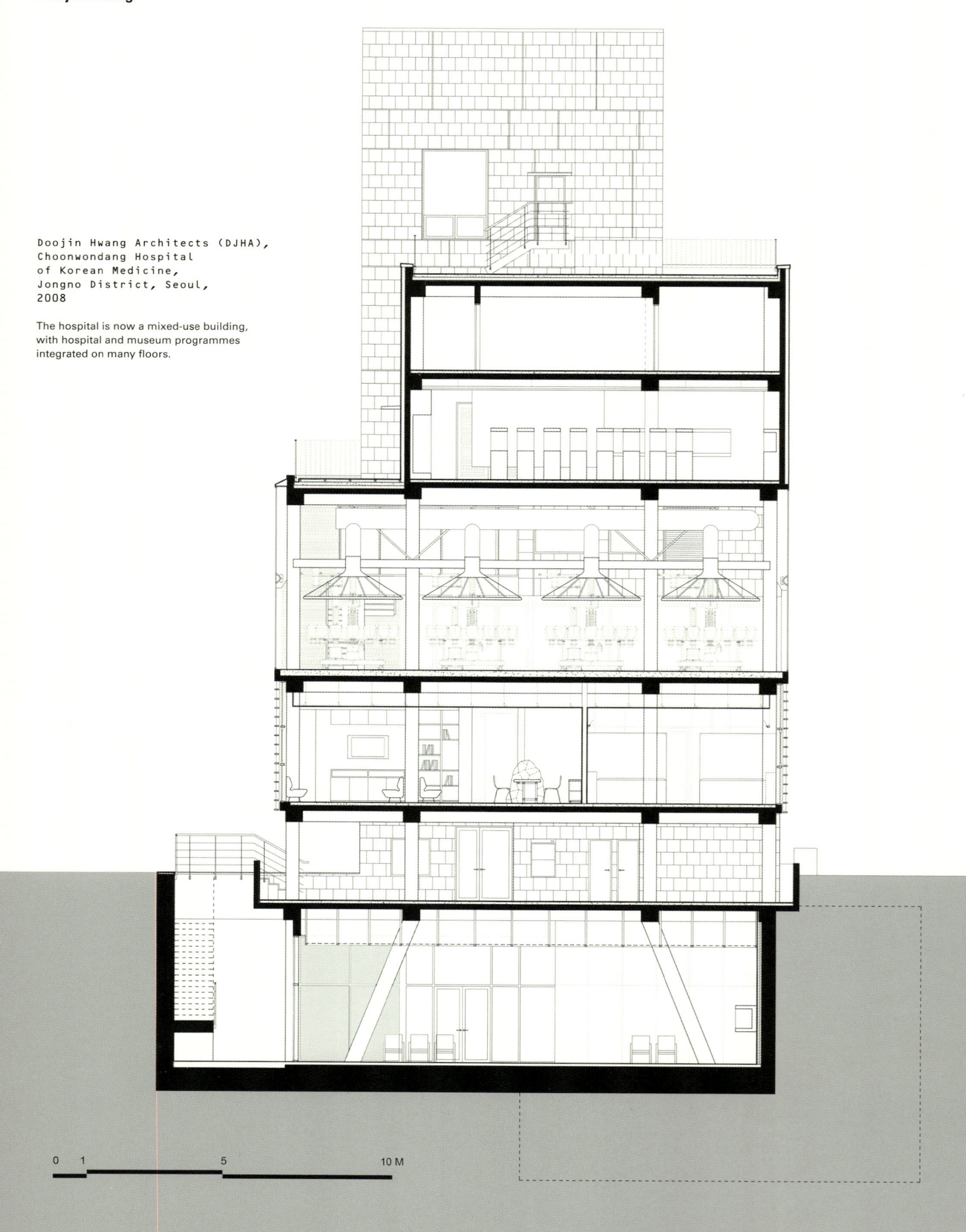

Doojin Hwang

Doojin Hwang Architects (DJHA),
Choonwondang Hospital
of Korean Medicine,
Jongno District, Seoul,
2008

The hospital is now a mixed-use building, with hospital and museum programmes integrated on many floors.

Urban Production in Seoul's Historic Centre

Choonwondang Hospital of Korean Medicine

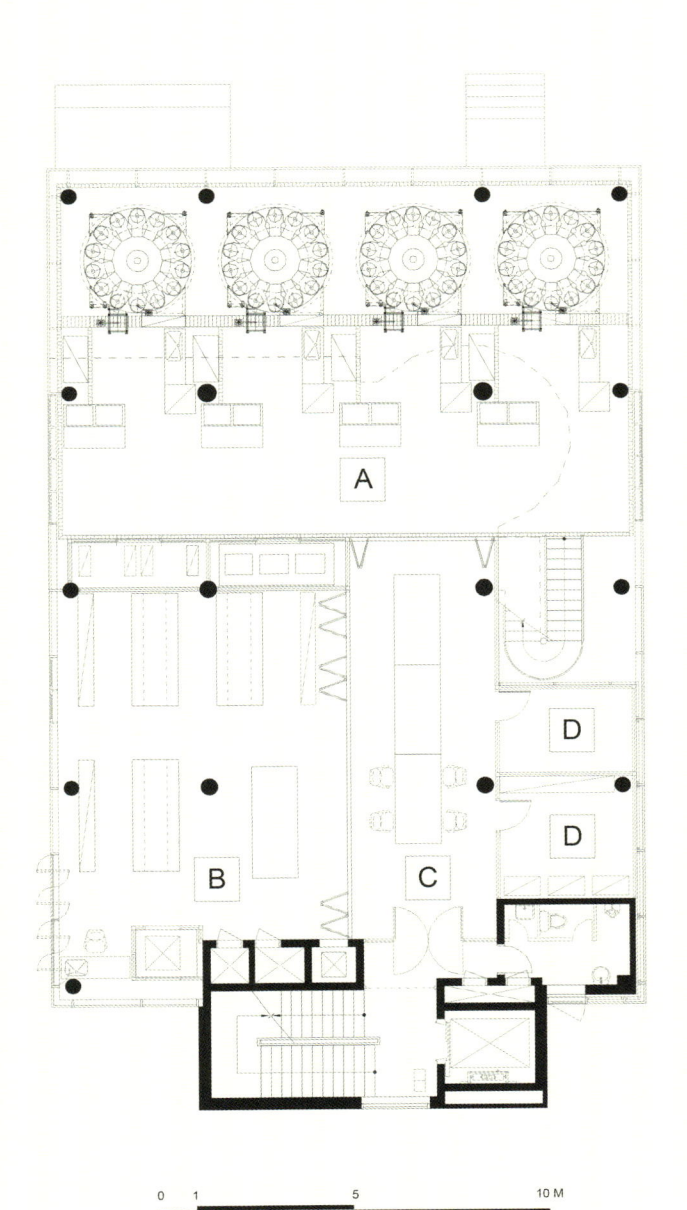

The mixing of uses in a single building or collection of buildings can function as an urban catalyst, activating regenerations to the city fabric around it. Doojin Hwang Architects' Choonwondang Hospital of Korean Medicine, Seoul, is a good example. The hospital accommodates a medical centre, museum of traditional Korean medicine and pharmaceutical herbal laboratory with back-of-house functions clearly visible to visitors. **Doojin Hwang** takes us through it.

The structural bays are determined by the four herbal medicine production machines on the third floor.

The hospital stands in the middle of an alley area a few blocks off Jongno in Seoul's historic centre.

It now includes a network of museum spaces. This particular room is where traditional medicine equipment from all over Asia is displayed.

One of the oldest and biggest thoroughfares in Seoul, Jongno runs almost due east–west through the city's historic centre. The surrounding area has long been associated with commercial and manufacturing activities, due to its proximity to the city's medieval palaces and government buildings, which demanded a constant supply of goods.

This historical industrial network started to extend out to the neighbouring areas of Cheonggyecheon and Euljiro after the 1950–53 Korean War, when the entire country began to reinvent itself as an industrial powerhouse. Unlike heavy industrial complexes planned by the government and built in the countryside, Seoul's inner-city manufacturing was mostly light industry, which sprang up in a labyrinth of urban alleys. Despite the massive urban redevelopment that has taken place since the 1960s, totally transforming the face of the city, a substantial number of small retail stores and fabrication shops still remain in business here.

Unlikely Location
The Choonwondang Hospital of Korean Medicine is located in the Donui-dong/Nakwon-dong area, a couple of blocks to the north of Jongno and only a few hundred metres from Cheonggyecheon (now an impressively renewed urban stream) and Euljiro (a recently gentrified area noted for its hip nightlife). The alley network here is twisted, complicated and narrow, like a system of veins and arteries; this is the historic centre of Seoul.

Different types of businesses have long claimed this area. 'Love motels' and gay bars are everywhere. Cheap eateries sell cold noodles for just under US$4. Some parts of the area hark back to its dark past, the once-infamous Jongsam red-light district, while more upscale stores still make and sell traditional musical instruments – another faint reminder of the nearby medieval palaces, where no one lives any more. The clock here stopped several decades ago. The ambient but frayed neighbourhood is an ideal location for a Seoul film noir, but an unlikely one for a renowned traditional medicine practice. Dr Yoon Young-seog, the director of the Choonwondang Hospital of Korean Medicine who invited Doojin Hwang Architects (DJHA) to design a new annex on the other side of the alley from the existing building, said it was his grandfather's wish to stay where they were.

He had his reasons. The hospital has been located here since 1953, when the Yoon family resettled in Seoul after the Korean War. Originally established in 1847 in a small North Korean town called Bakcheon, near Pyongyang, and handed down through seven generations, the hospital has come to regard itself as a committed guardian of its new home. Despite the overall deterioration of the area, the original building was to remain, and the new annex needed to project new visions for the future of the area and for the hospital itself.

Major Objectives
DJHA's first step was to understand the realities of a centuries-old traditional medicine practice. After a few weeks of observation, research and interviews, three main objectives were identified. The first was to double the daily production of herbal medicine, which would push the Choonwondang Hospital higher up the list of the traditional medicine practices in Korea, even ahead of university hospitals, in terms of volume prepared in-house. Among various subcategories of traditional medicine, including acupuncture and *chuna* (a cross between chiropractic and osteopathy), the hospital's

The observation deck on the fourth floor, from which patients and visitors can watch the herbal medicine being produced, is where the hospital and museum programmes overlap.

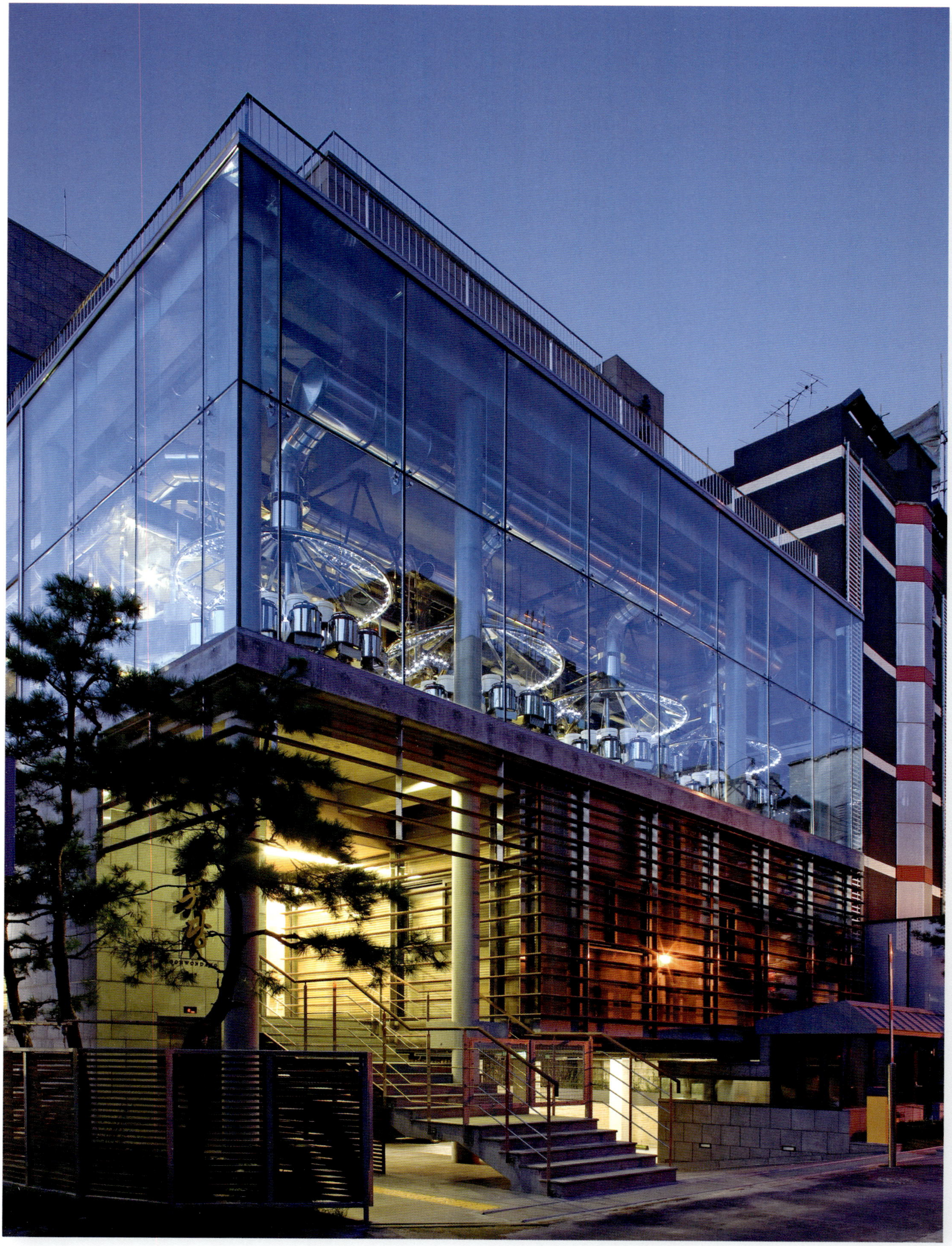

major area of expertise was herb-based preparations, and Dr Yoon wanted to further reinforce this, stressing that the entire production should take place in-house under tight supervision; not a single process was to be outsourced.

The second of the aims was to incorporate a museum of traditional medicine within the hospital to house the Yoon family's collection of traditional medical artefacts, not just from Korea, but from all over Asia. How to define a museum within a working hospital presented a particular challenge for DJHA.

The third objective was rather sensitive: traditional Asian medicine is controversial. Though many contemporary 'Western-style' doctors see it as something little better than quackery, the general public have in the main embraced it both as a time-proven medical practice and a part of traditional Korean culture. However, even they were slowly losing their trust in traditional medicine, due to a number of public scandals involving substandard quality control and the alleged use of polluted raw materials. Dr Yoon, as an heir of a prominent medical family, was seeking to bring this professional disgrace to an end – at least on his own turf.

Glass Box
DJHA's response to these challenges was to design a multipurpose building in which different programmatic elements of a hospital and a museum were integrated, often penetrating one another: a working hospital and a living museum simultaneously. For example, the proposal included a two-storey room, the Glass Box, as the main focus of the building, from which everything else unfolds. The 'box' was to contain four herbal medicine production machines: two from the existing building that were previously inside a very dark room with a low ceiling, hidden behind the scenes; and the addition of two new ones. The entire process of traditional herbal medicine production – traditionally a treasured secret – would now be exposed both externally and internally. Not only would people on the street be able to see what was going on inside the building; patients and museum visitors could also visually trace the process of preparing the herbal medicine from the observation deck above the main space. What had previously been backstage was to become the main stage.

DJHA's proposal was initially met with a shocked reaction from the client. It exceeded Dr Yoon's expectations and he needed time to dwell on it. After three days, during which DJHA wondered whether the project was now history, he approved the design concept, adding that the proposal was more than a design – it was a new business plan for him. He not only accepted the idea, but became truly committed to making it work; even going on to have staff uniforms redesigned, since now everybody was going to be 'exposed'.

The four herbal medicine production machines, visible within the Glass Box, have become part of the urban landscape.

However, a legal and administrative tug of war ensued between DJHA and the local building department. The concept of integrating a museum within a hospital was unheard of and therefore unacceptable to the authorities. One programme for each floor was their bottom line. After a great deal of negotiations, it was finally agreed that certain floors could have more than one programme.

The Glass Box was also an issue; it was deemed to be simply too big for the size of the hospital. The local building department argued that, with four machines, it was an independent production facility on its own and subject to more stringent codes. DJHA argued that the in-house production of herbal medicine had been a core element of the Choonwondang Hospital and should therefore be considered as an integral part of it, and the building department finally agreed.

The realities of urban production were more complicated than expected, resulting in other technical issues. The fumes and heat from the machines could generate environmental hazards, as well as complaints from locals. DJHA therefore came up with the idea of a 'glass canopy' for each machine that collects then passes the heat and fumes through a condenser and a filter – eventually to be vented out on the roof, where the fumes join and mingle with the area's existing urban odours.

The machines also needed to be redesigned. The hospital had invented them and held a valid patent, but had never intended to expose them. The task of making them visually presentable as well as functional was a big mechanical and aesthetical challenge. A great deal of technical coordination and visual adjustments were required to transform the mechanical contraptions into design statements. DJHA sat down with a machine fabricator from Daegu, a city well known for its long history of herbal medicine, and literally went over every major part of the machine, changing finishes, colours, details and materials.

From a planning point of view, the four machines were the major factor in the overall structural layout of the building. Each weighs more than two tonnes when fully loaded – slightly less than a Humvee. They needed space around them for operation and maintenance, which determined the structural bays. As the columns reached the basement level, however, they had to fan out to accommodate a large space for professional gatherings (as a part of the hospital) and exhibitions (as a part of the museum). The result was a cathedral-like ambience.

Dr Yoon sees his patients in his office; after an examination he writes the prescription, which is transmitted to the preparation room where rows of medicine cabinets store the raw materials. The staff then start to collect different ingredients and place them in individual non-toxic plastic containers. The herb-based raw materials are examined and tested on arrival at the hospital's lab, which is also transparent – an expression of honesty and integrity. The plastic containers are hauled to the Glass Box where the

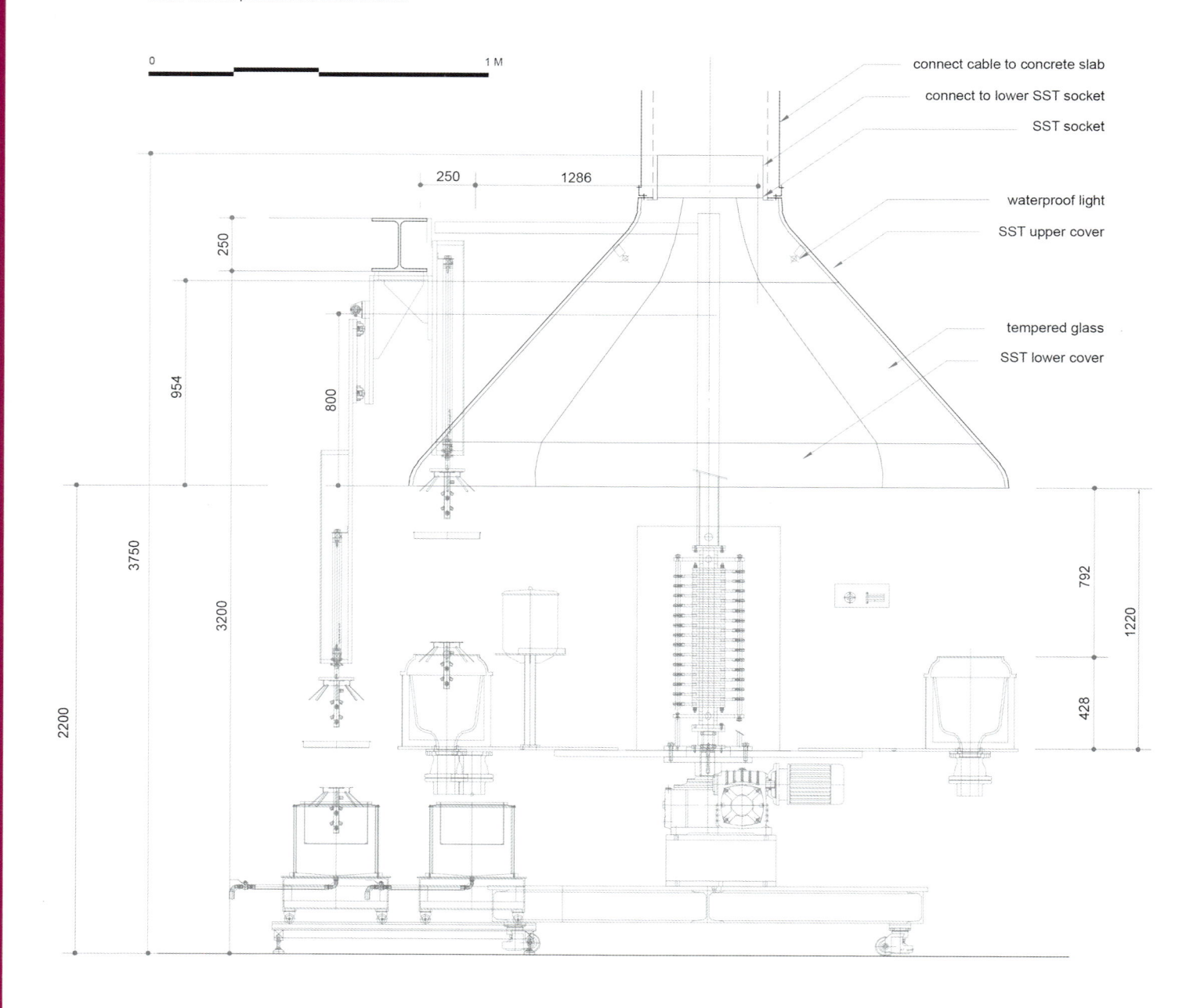

DJHA collaborated with a machine fabricator to redesign the production machines to work better with the practice's architectural ideas.

connect cable to concrete slab
connect to lower SST socket
SST socket
waterproof light
SST upper cover
tempered glass
SST lower cover

The Choonwondang Hospital of Korean Medicine, rooted in tradition but contemporary in design and spirit, marks a new stepping stone in exploring the potential of an old city centre as a testbed for new production urbanism and beyond

machines await. The raw materials are poured with water into round stainless-steel containers and then sit for two hours and 40 minutes for 'cold brewing'. They are then poured into ceramic jars, which are heated by electricity. When the medicine is ready, after another two hours and 40 minutes, the machines start rotating slowly and the contents in each ceramic jar (14 per machine) get squeezed and extracted into non-toxic PET-aluminium pouches, each containing one dose, are put in a paper box, and finally delivered to the patients' homes. What is left of the materials, called *mugeori*, is collected and transported to the hospital's medicinal herb farm on the outskirts of Seoul to be used as compost, creating a closed-circuit, self-sustaining system.

Rainbow-Cake Architecture

The concrete-and-glass architecture of the Choonwondang Hospital of Korean Medicine, standing in stark contrast to the nondescript buildings that dominate one of the oldest alley systems in Seoul, is both a testimony to urban history and a vision for the future. It is the most challenging of a series of projects in Seoul's historic core so far undertaken by DJHA. The context of the old city centre and programme of a traditional hospital has given the practice the opportunity to realise its belief in 'the old giving birth to the new'.

From the perspective of production urbanism, the Choonwondang Hospital showcases the extent of architects' role in defining a sophisticated production programme and then in designing it as an iconic element of an urban landscape. The centuries-long tradition of Korean herbal medicine practice was both a determining factor in the programming and planning, and a fertile source of inspiration in the design as well.

Seoul's historic centre is now eerily almost empty of permanent residents, a typical outcome of the doughnut effect. According to DJHA's 'rainbow-cake architecture' concept, the addition of residential programmes, if not in the same building then in the surrounding areas, could trigger much-needed urban changes: shorter average daily commutes between work and home, more free time, more diverse urban activities, reduced energy consumption and pollution levels – the key issues of urban sustainability. The city centre could be an ideal location for residential and other urban programmes to co-exist in close proximity. The Choonwondang Hospital of Korean Medicine, rooted in tradition but contemporary in design and spirit, marks a new stepping stone in exploring the potential of an old city centre as a testbed for new production urbanism and beyond. ᴅ

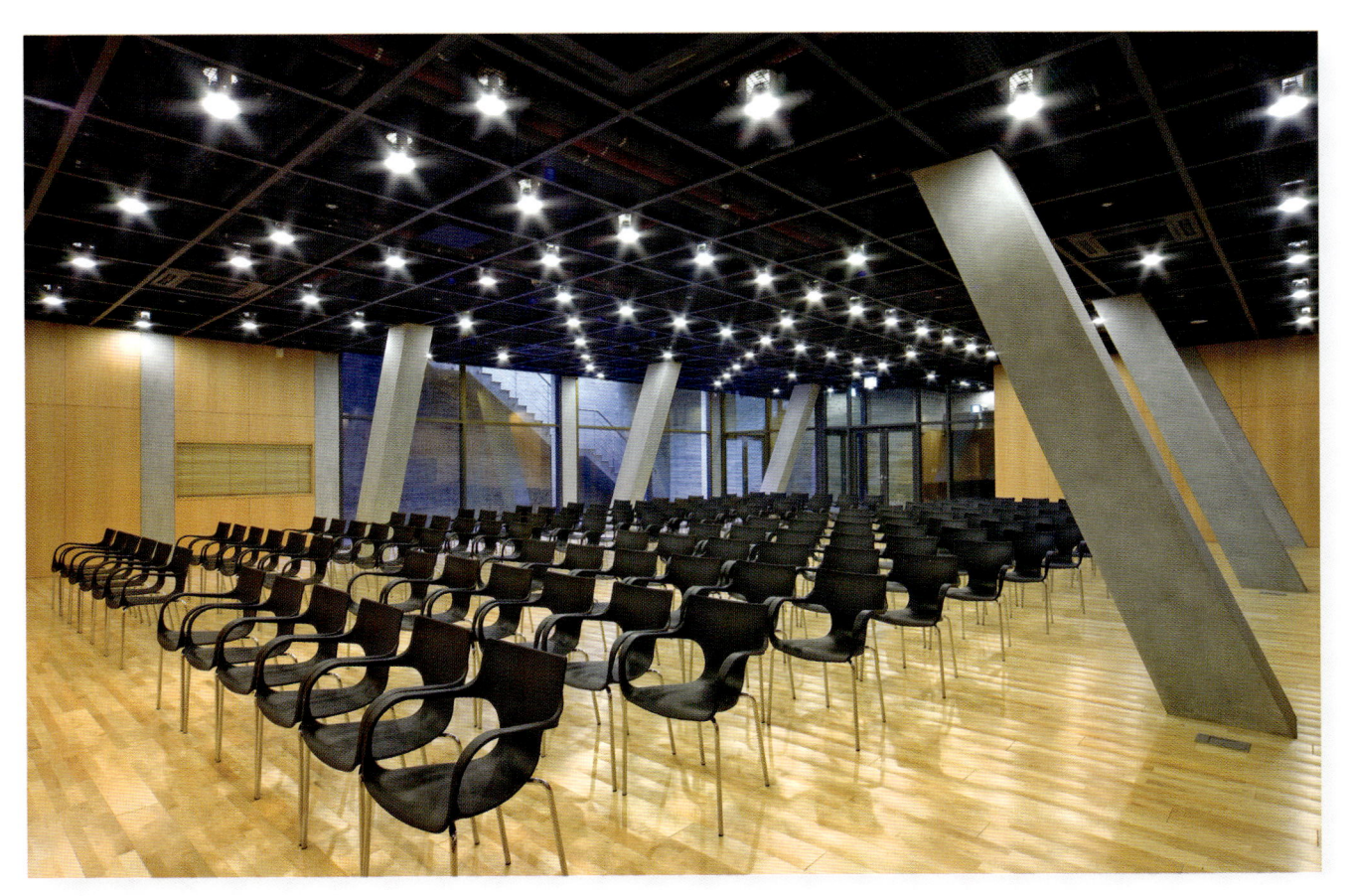

The multipurpose hall in the basement is used for social and professional gatherings and also exhibitions. The sloped columns create a cathedral-like ambience.

Text © 2021 John Wiley & Sons Ltd. Images: pp 106–7, 112 © Doojin Hwang Architects; pp 108–10, 113 © Youngchae Park

Yerin Kang and Chihoon Lee

SoA (Society of Architecture),
Seongsu-Silo,
Metropolitan Small Manufacturers'
Support Center (MSMSC),
Seoul,
2020

The urban street is integrated into the vertical movement of the building by allowing people to enter its upper levels directly from the road at the front through protruding exterior stairs and elevators.

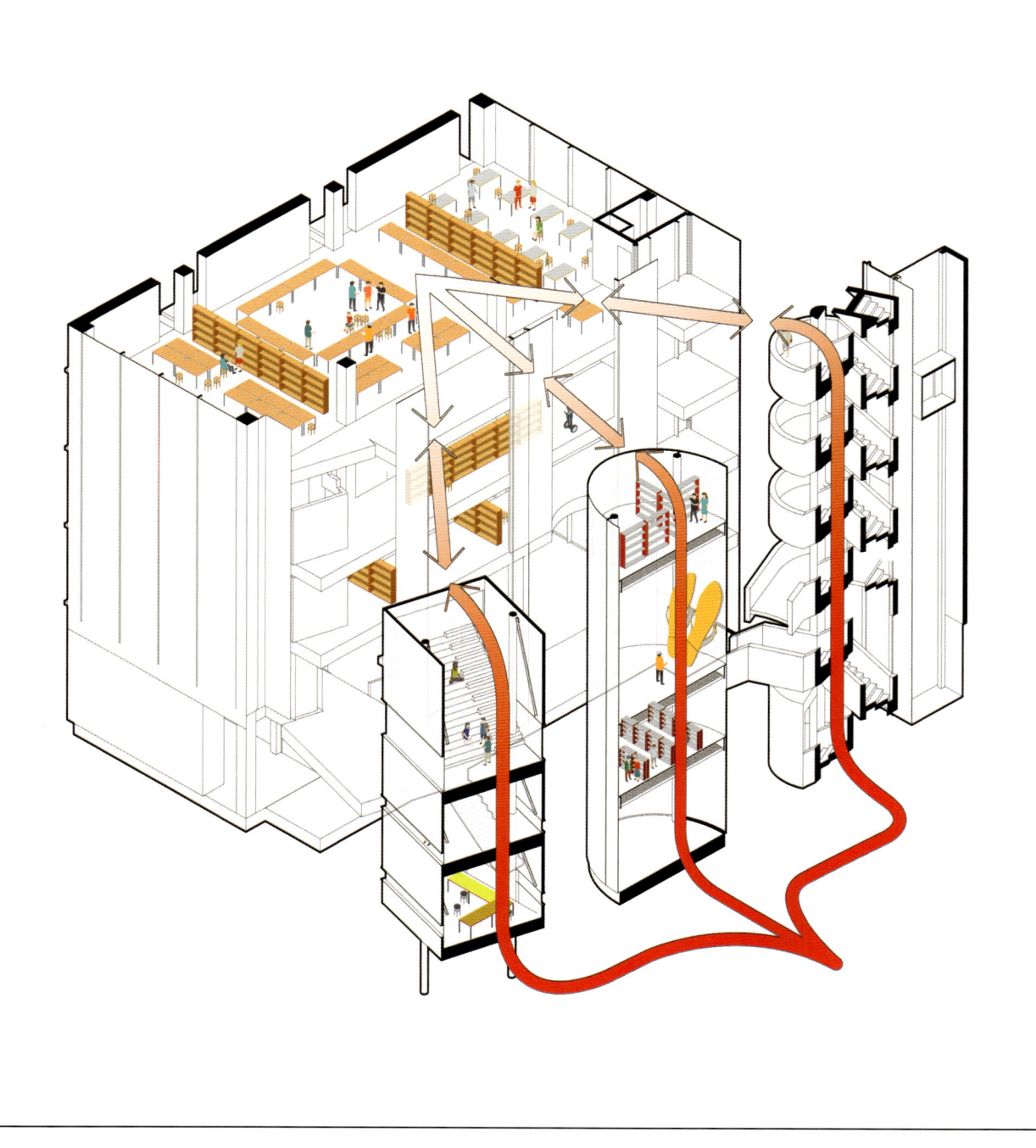

Seoul's Shoe Silo

Architects **Yerin Kang and Chihoon Lee** of Seoul practice SoA (Society of Architecture) discuss the emerging consumer and manufacturing dynamics evolving in the South Korean capital's industrial zones, particularly Seongsu-dong. The changes are partly provoked by the establishment of 'smart anchor' facilities — government-funded hubs that provide digital facilities such as 3D printing for companies to share. This also enhances cross-disciplinary collaboration and encourages small and medium-sized enterprises.

A Vertical Smart Anchor for the Small Manufacturer

Since its foundation in 1394, Seoul has transitioned from an agrarian society to a full-fledged industrialised megacity. Within this 600-year transition, it was the 20th century that saw the most drastic urban change due to a process of industrialisation. During its colonial period under Japanese imperial rule (1910–45), Yeongdeungpo, southwest of the Han River, was developed with heavy military infrastructure. This laid the groundwork for this area to transform into Seoul's largest industrial zone after liberation from Japan. Other industrial areas around Seoul followed; yet, as of 2021, only seven major semi-industrial zones in Seoul remain. They account for 3.3 per cent of the city's total area, but are essential to its industrial economy.

Seoul's industrial areas accommodate mostly light industries such as fashion, printing, fabrication of metal parts and jewellery. Although these zones are mostly made up of small businesses operating in relatively poor conditions, the Seoul Metropolitan Government is building a support system to invigorate the area with jobs production: since 2018, it has been funding ₩300 billion worth of manufacturing support to build 'smart anchor' facilities for each manufacturing industry. A 'smart anchor' is a space that allows small businesses that are burdened with purchasing high-tech facilities, like 3D printers, to have a base that they can use jointly. Smart anchors also promote collaboration between companies. Seoul City is aiming to build 20 smart anchors by 2022. Currently, five such sites have been confirmed for each autonomous district of the city, including 'Jungnang-gu Sewing', 'Jung-gu Printing', 'Guro-gu Machinery Metal' and 'Gangbuk-gu Sewing'. The Seongsu-dong neighbourhood, in the district of Seongdong-gu, is projecting to run a facility that supports small craftsmen who make handmade shoes.

The Semi-Industrial Mix
Currently, semi-industrial areas in Seoul are distributed with light industries, interacting with residential centres, financial centres and business centres in other areas of Seoul. They are filled with dynamic flows of production–consumption players. Industrial areas were originally planned to form blocks and accommodate roads that are good for factory logistics, but various consumption/leisure activities overlap in these semi-industrial areas. Relevant laws and regulations of the building code have been revised to promote diversity of land use plans, unlike the originally designed factory zones. The industrial zones are no longer solely responsible for production but also for consumption and residential functions. From the perspective of the metropolitan city of Seoul, a certain range of factory zones are perceived by people as places with very strong identities and thus considered as spaces that provide an attractive opportunity for urban experience, which is different from the uniformity of a typical residential space.

Seongsu-dong, in particular, was transformed into a place where specific images and values were recognised at a cultural level. The industrial cityscape of the factory zone is a special experience for visitors. An empty factory is gradually filled with attractive consumer products. Roads which once were occupied by raw materials, intermediate products and finished products – handmade shoes – are being filled with pedestrians visiting the neighbourhood. They are not producers in the manufacturing sector, but consumers who visit Seongsu-dong from outside. The nature of urban streets will change from a logistics system for products to a pedestrian-oriented one, which mainly focuses on consumption activities,

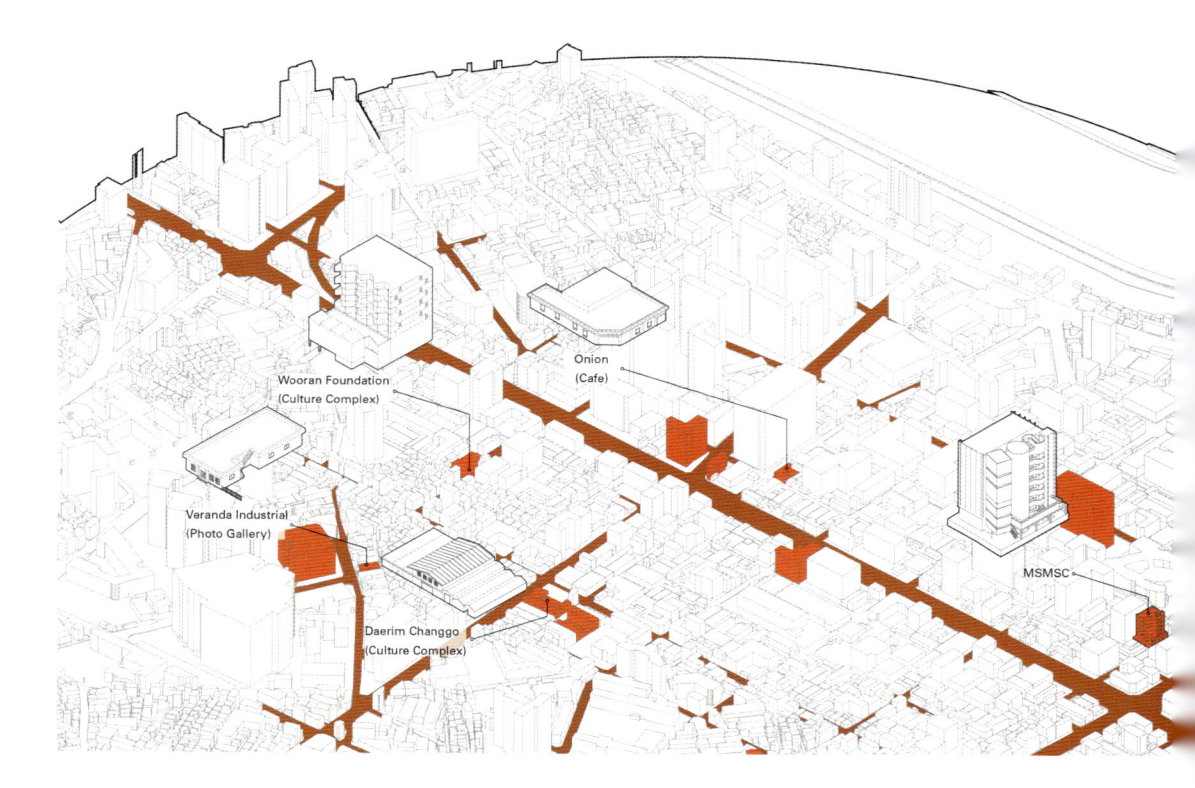

SoA (Society of Architecture), Industry and culture in Seongsu-dong, Seoul, 2020

A study of the cultural facilities and relationship of major urban streets in the semi-industrial area of Seongsu-dong reveals the density of industries mixed with new cultural venues and attractions.

and will acquire a multi-layered sense of place. Due to these changes, new building in Seongsu-dong has a different openness from the existing factory construction. A new type of architecture is needed to expand the dense walking network of urban streets beyond simple factory buildings.

In the course of the semi-industrial area's growth, the type of construction of the factory has evolved in an efficient way. Factories are vertically stacked to cope with the high density of the city centre, and are known in Korea as 'apartment-type factories'. The typical plan of this typology has a service core in the centre and open work space on the periphery of that core. The buildings are usually tailored to universal standards that increase the efficiency of integrated apartments rather than specific spaces that take into account the working characteristics of particular manufacturing industries.

On the other hand, production in small manufacturing industries is based on flexible systems, with a tacit form of information distribution that can only be obtained in the field, integrated with skilled technicians, and an organic environment for collaboration and division. Manufacturing industries concentrated in large cities also form an integrated economy, with production and consumption closely related. While typical specialised industrial areas are formed by concentration of industries or enterprises producing the same product, urban manufacturing coexists with various urban activities from production to consumption. It emphasises individuality and specificity, small production of various kinds, and specificity corresponding to individual demands of various ordering entities. 'Apartment-type factory' architecture struggles to digest the specificity of this urban manufacturing industry. As the production function of the city shifts to the knowledge industry, the backwardness of light industry and the manufacturing industry is accelerating.

Vertically Serviced Workspaces
The handmade shoe industry structure in Seongsu-dong does not allow small manufacturers to make their own brands, but instead depends on subcontractors that supply products ordered by the main office. While existing urban factories emphasise only efficient production, the Metropolitan Small Manufacturers' Support Center (MSMSC) aims to innovate production space by reflecting the recent start-up space trend in which production, planning, distribution, marketing and consumption are integrated into one space. The new tower-type factory is a three-dimensional space for consumption and production, which compresses the geography of the product distribution chain from planning, design, marketing and consumption. As part of the MSMSC, in 2019 SoA (Society of Architecture) proposed the Seongsu-Silo as an adaptive reuse project. Under development for construction at the time of writing, the Seongsu-Silo aims to foster collaboration and industrial innovation through space branding targeting small business owners.

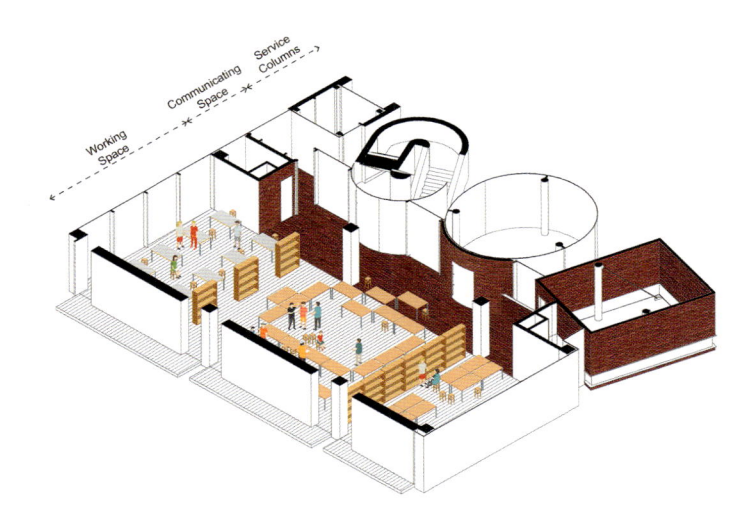

SoA (Society of Architecture),
Seongsu-Silo,
Metropolitan Small Manufacturers'
Support Center (MSMSC),
Seoul,
2020

The typical floor consists of three layers – workspace, public space and service column. A generous width is given to the corridor to define it as a space where residents can interact and exchange ideas.

SoA (Society of Architecture),
Comparison between 'apartment-type factory' and 'tower-type factory',
Seoul,
2020

A study of the plan form of an 'apartment-type factory', where service areas are centralised with workspaces placed around them, and the proposal for a new type of factory that offers flexibility, with publicly accessible service areas in separate towers in front of the workspace block.

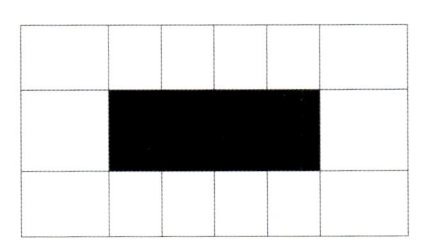

Small craftsmen's workspaces are placed on each floor within an open plan. For this to work as a vertical factory, three vertical ancillary spaces are added at the front, emphasised as independent volumes, for displays, promotional activities, storage, conferences, lectures or other customisable purposes that new factories and support centres may need, as well as an open stairway. In between, the public space allows the service areas of the front part to be opened to the outside independently.

A 'maker column' built of red brick, previously a common material for factories around Seongsu-dong, is used to extend the urban landscape of the past. A 'shoe silo' is exposed with glass to the front and brick to the rear, allowing it to be recognised as a visually open, independent space. External evacuation stairs commonly found in Seongsu-dong become a 'vertical walkway' for pedestrians to feel a vertical continuity of the urban streets.

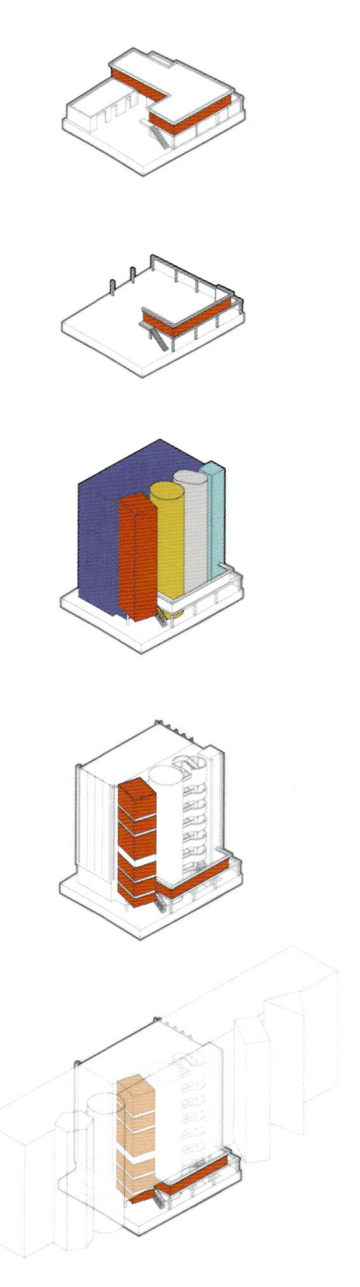

Industrial Continuity Through Renovation and Expansion

By preserving the upper face of the front – although not the interior space – of the pre-existing building, the continuity of the scenery seen on the streets of Seongsu-dong's factory zone is ensured. The construction strategy of the MSMSC is essentially one of expansion. In addition to the mitigation of the designation of building lines, the basic strategy of remodelling here was to preserve the history of Seongsu-dong by leaving the first-floor façade of the pre-existing building and its ground-floor columns, which embrace the newly created area including the service towers and make for a complex entry experience. In particular, this generates the identity of the building by establishing a relationship between the old and the new: the old building's pillars, and the multistorey 'column' elements of the new construction. It also serves as pilotis or a fence, naturally luring urban walkers into the building and lowering the psychological boundaries of the entry process.

Factory buildings constructed with the minimum requirements for use have their own industrial aesthetics. The material palettes on the streets of Seongsu-dong are filled with common architectural languages based on practicality and economy. Most of the existing factories here are modernist structures built by filling concrete frames with bricks, a typical type of construction in the area. The architecture of the MSMSC proposal uses familiar materials to preserve the landscape of the street, but it is intended to respect and develop the place by changing its use.

The core of the deployment is to place human-scale spatial elements on the road elevation at the front that can create connections between people in the manufacturing industry's branding process, such as planning, distribution and marketing. Workspaces are planned to be flexible and are located at the rear of the site.

The ground floor can be extended vertically to the first floor through the upper opening. Space is compartmentalised through a moving wall if necessary to form a flexible multi-purpose volume. Floor materials inside and out are made of the same continuous material and create a space open to the rear through the folding door. As a way to integrate the old structure, the pillars at ground level of the existing building serve as an entrance to the main office. A second entry hall is created through the new massing, which connects the public directly to the public corridor.

```
SoA (Society of Architecture),
Seongsu-Silo,
Metropolitan Small Manufacturers'
Support Center (MSMSC),
Seoul,
2020
```

Most of the old factories in Seongsu-dong are finished with red dress bricks. The Seoul Metropolitan Government defines this material as a historical asset of the city, and the guidelines for the design contest were to retain a two-storey façade of the existing building facing the front road. As a result, the project was designed in the form of façades covering the lower floors of the existing building.

The stairway located in the centre of the plan is exposed to the front road, serving as a place to pause. Visitors walking up and down the stairs will naturally find themselves looking into the exhibition space of the shoe silo.

As elements that change over time, programmes such as meetings and exhibitions, as well as vertical movement, are placed at the front. In this way, the activities inside the building are actively displayed on the urban street and the identity of the space is strengthened.

System for Flexible Work Production

As the Seongsu-Silo aims to become an industrial anchor, it requires a flexible dynamic within its context, as well as within itself. The balcony located inside the workspace and the outer curtain walls on both sides create a pleasant working environment. Reinforced-concrete walls were secured to facilitate the installation of workstations and shelves. The service columns strengthen the characteristics of the public spaces by incorporating decorative bricks used externally into indoor materials. A plane consisting of manufacturing, production space-exchange, network space-distribution, planning and marketing space enables one-stop service. Casual meetings between small business owners and consumers take place in a space at the front.

The variable planar composition reacts by organically transforming to suit the environment of various events and occupied spaces. In addition, the service space placed towards the road allows the workspace to be freely extended from side to side.

Through architectural articulation, spatial flexibility can be achieved, yet a smart anchor requires urban flexibility to be maintained. This hybrid typology encapsulates these requirements through the grafting of forms and use of materials to create a dichotomy of transparent public and opaque private areas, in order to humbly promote industry and culture. ⌀

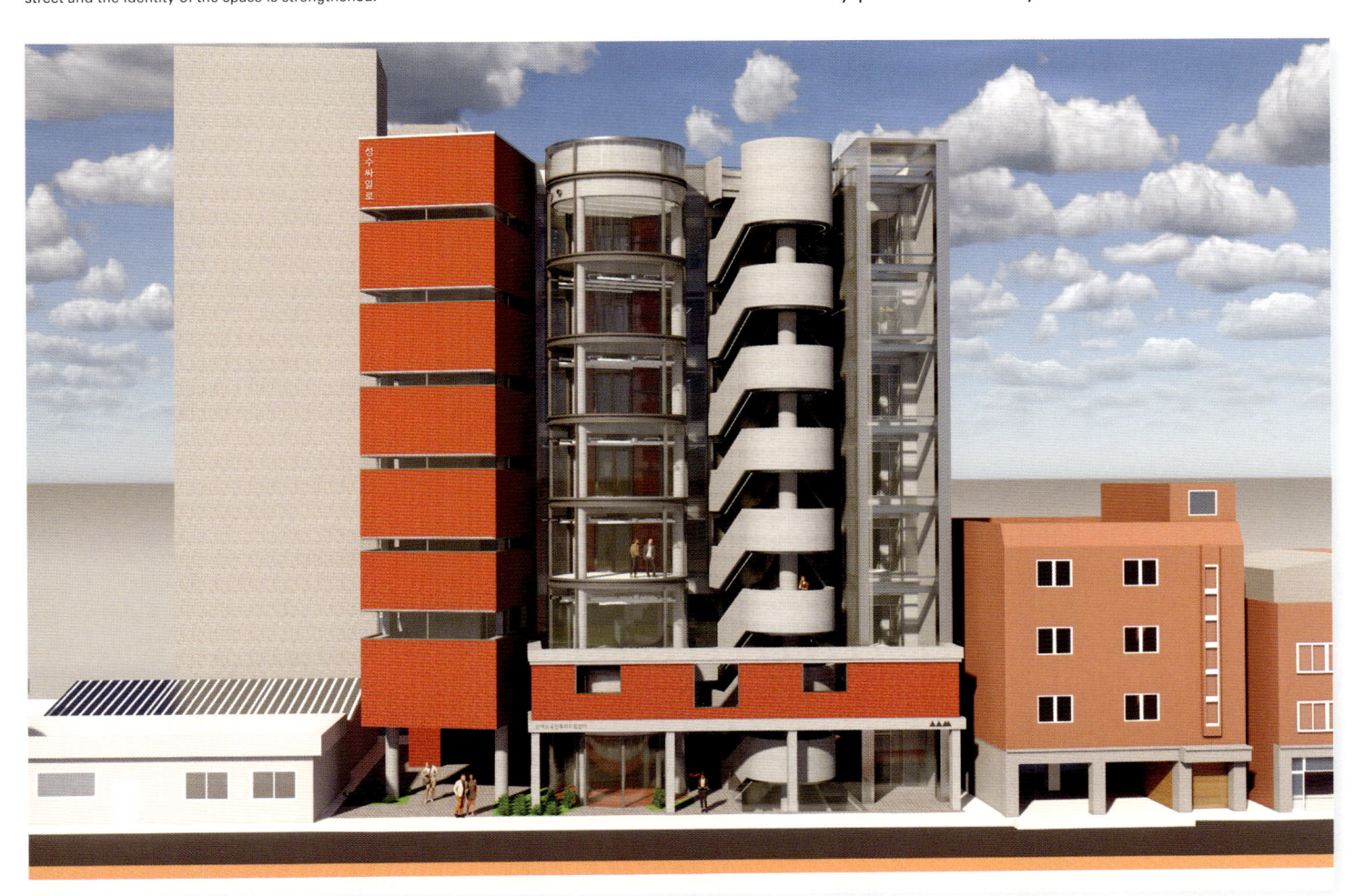

Text © 2021 John Wiley & Sons Ltd. Images © SoA (Society of Architecture)

Kristiaan Borret

OFFICE Kersten Geers David Van Severen,
Brussels Beer Project,
Brussels,
due for completion 2022

The colours of the roof are also visible in the interior – colours that recall the graphics of the labels on the beer bottles of Brussels Beer Project.

BUILDING BETTER BRUSSELS

PRODUCTION URBANISM AS A POLICY

Kristiaan Borret is *bouwmeester* (master architect) for the Brussels area. His job is to encourage and oversee the city's urban development. Here he describes the context of this development and gives various examples of creative ways to facilitate bringing production activities back into the urban zone. There is a lively public appreciation of the need to foster this integration as it is adding a new vitality of hybrid forms and functions that further animates city living.

In Brussels, awareness of the fact that productive activities also belong in the city began growing nearly 10 years ago.

Indeed, in 2012 and 2013, the universities ULB and Erasmus organised the masterclasses 'Re:Work' and 'End of Line' on the coexistence of housing and industry, logistics or infrastructure at various key sites in Brussels. The research dynamic continued later to produce many other studies, but the subject was also raised with a broader audience. In 2016–17, part of the programme in the architecture biennale IABR in Brussels's main cultural centre BOZAR was 'Atelier Brussels: A Good City Has Industry'. This diverse programme used an exhibition, debates and design-driven research to show the public why and how we can integrate a productive economy in the city.

All of these activities led to a lively discourse in Brussels on the need to integrate the productive economy in the city; a discourse that has meanwhile spread and gained support from politicians. Such support is a necessary precondition for the transition to an operational level and the realisation of projects.

Not Only Words But Also Deeds

Parallel to this growing awareness, the Belgian capital's urban planning has developed several tools that translate theoretical discourse into execution.

Brussels has experienced significant demographic growth over the past 10 years. This urgency is the reason why, in 2013, the Brussels-Capital Region decided to open up a series of mono-functional zones to housing. In these areas, however, it has become mandatory for all larger projects of 10,000 square metres (approximately 110,000 square feet) or more to include a minimum share of spaces for productive economy, which should correspond to 90 per cent of the surface area of the ground floor. This approach by means of zoning planning seeks to stimulate mixed development. Although it may seem very traditional, it helps considerably in securing space in the city for production and in protecting against otherwise fierce competition for more lucrative functions such as offices or housing.

In addition to zoning, the strategic transformation project for the canal area has proved to be a catalyst for the realisation of the Productive City in Brussels. The Charleroi–Antwerp Canal runs straight through the urban fabric of Brussels and was the city's industrial basin from early in the 19th century, but in recent decades more and more vacant buildings and urban fringe areas have emerged. It was most remarkable – certainly compared with other large European cities – that by 2010, typical waterfront development had not yet started in Brussels, for a variety of reasons. This exceptional situation allowed lessons to be learnt and the canal area to be tackled in a different way in Brussels than elsewhere.

In 2014, the Brussels authorities approved a vision for the Canal Plan which is being implemented at the time of writing. The plan puts forward as one of its strategic

Territory of the
Brussels Canal Plan,
2014–25

The Charleroi–Antwerp Canal crosses the entire city of Brussels from north to south. Historically the city's industrial basin, today the canal zone is being regenerated as a mixed urban development with integration of productive economic activities.

TETRA Architects,
Construction materials hub,
Brussels,
2018

The elegant appearance in the urban landscape of Brussels does not suggest that ordinary building materials are traded in these buildings, with a sustainable possibility of supply via the canal.

plusoffice and WRKSHP,
Tinker Tower,
'Atelier Brussels: A Good City Has Industry',
International Architecture Biennale Rotterdam (IABR),
BOZAR, Brussels,
2016-17

A provocative picture of the proposal for a Tinker Tower with vertically stacked industry on a site near to the North Station area, in order to make people realise that densification in Brussels cannot only be about offices or housing.

objectives the integration of a productive economy with new jobs for blue-collar workers, which was unusual to see approved in an official policy document at the time it was presented.

Today, the number of projects integrating productive activity in the city has increased significantly in the canal area. In this way, the old industrial basin of Brussels is being reinvented.

A Consistent Policy

While planning tools can ensure that affordable space remains available for productive economy in the city, they do not offer specific and high-quality design solutions. Even so, these are essential, since the cohabitation of working and living can cause nuisance and mutual distrust. There is work to be done because the know-how among both architects and real-estate developers is in need of reinforcement in terms of inventive solutions to reconcile homes and businesses in the same building or neighbourhood.

One of the main tasks of the Brussels chief architect is to organise design competitions. These are no longer limited to typical assignments such as public facilities or housing, but also programmes of productive economy and logistics are launched in competitions to obtain new, unexpected and high-quality proposals. At the same time, architects themselves appear to be interested in designing this type of programme. The result is that the creativity of good architects is now also applied to programmes that were previously conceived as utilitarian, thus improving their quality.

A first example of an architectural competition dates back to 2013, under the then chief architect Olivier Bastin. Because the canal runs through the centre of Brussels, it is possible to use inland navigation for the logistical supply of goods all the way into the city centre, thus keeping heavy freight traffic out of the city. This is the vision behind the design of a distributor for building materials on one of the quays along the canal. The goods can be transported there by ship, and small-scale contractors or industrious private individuals can then purchase all kinds of building materials on site without having to drive quite some distance to the sales points on the outskirts of the city. Building materials will always be needed in a city, especially in Brussels considering Belgian building habits according to which people often renovate their homes themselves, little by little.

Completed in 2018, the project site has been divided by TETRA Architects into 31 bays, each 20 metres (65 feet) long – exactly the distance between two bollards on the quay. The entire area forms a modular strip in which the buildings and open spaces are arranged. The open spaces are positioned in such a way that they offer an open vista in line with the transverse streets in the nearby urban fabric. The hustle and bustle in the warehouse also remains visible, connecting living and working, city and water. The roof structure is a variation on the typical saw-tooth roof design in which a diagonal folded seam is added. This gives a poetic

Up to 15 million beer bottles will be brewed here, within the city and in a place along the canal where a new residential area for 10,000 new inhabitants will be built.

OFFICE Kersten Geers David Van Severen,
Brussels Beer Project,
Brussels,
due for completion 2022

In addition to the production of beer itself, there is also a taproom, terrace and garden that allow people to consume beer on the spot and thus contribute to the liveliness of these new mixed places along the canal.

elegance that is not normally accorded to this kind of commercial warehouses.

Brussels Beer Project (due for completion 2022) is a local craft brewery similar to those that have emerged in many cities in recent years. While there is already a shop in a hipster neighbourhood of the city centre, the brewing process of the beer itself actually takes place somewhere else in Belgium. This is now changing, because the founders want to do the production within the city itself in the future and increase it to 35,000 hectolitres (770,000 gallons) per year. With the same pioneering flair, Brussels Beer Project chose to commission a remarkable building by the architects of OFFICE Kersten Geers David Van Severen along a southern part of the canal. The new production unit will – literally – give colour to the as yet inhospitable place and provide both employment and animation, as there will also be an accessible taproom and an open-air beer garden, further contributing to the idea behind the project, which ultimately integrates industrial production with public space.

The building itself is conceived as a compact and efficient industrial container, a rectangular box with an inclined roof which reveals its contents. The section of varying height enables a series of table-like platforms on top of which the production elements are visible through the large greenhouse façade. The roof indicates the company's graphic identity, as it is coated in stripes of characteristic colours of Brussels Beer Project beer labels.

In addition to these design competitions for individual companies, several projects are being developed in Brussels that bring together both dwelling and working on the same site. These mixed projects often tend towards compact and stacked solutions, with housing located on top of a plinth with productive activities.

The Urbanities project (due for completion 2022) is located on the opposite side of Brussels Beer Project in Biestebroeck, a large transformation area along the canal, where numerous large-scale housing projects by private developers will be established in the coming years. The architects B2Ai, MSA and plusoffice have opted for a vertical superposition of the programmes of production and housing. In total, the ground floor accommodates approximately 15,000 square metres (160,000 square feet) around a central covered courtyard where logistical flows are centralised. It forms a base from which the structural pattern and architectural form of the entire complex is developed as one single entity.

Urbanities looks like a configuration of various collective housing buildings but has in common a certain understanding of the living concept and coherence in terms of the real-estate product. The project optimises vertical superposition by including a transition and interweaving layer between the production levels and the housing units: the roof garden of the housing units opens to bring natural light into the workshops located underneath; the central skylight is positioned above the production level to become a feature of design and a communal garden area. The common spaces shared by companies and housing units will stimulate mutual interactions.

Nevertheless, it is questionable whether the repetition of this stacked typology across a whole new neighbourhood can generate sufficient activation of street life. An elevated city of residents on top of a city down under of workers risks resulting in an at times all too empty public space. That is why the competitions also investigate how horizontal mixing or juxtaposition can be used to combine living and working.

B2Ai, MSA and plusoffice,
Urbanities,
Brussels,
due for completion 2022

Housing on top of productive economy: the section shows how the two worlds are superimposed in order to create a model of urban mix.

A glimpse between different worlds: the conservatory provides daylight to the logistics downstairs and offers exchange with the inhabitants upstairs, thus creating a shared experience of space.

BOGDAN & VAN BROECK, DDS+
and Atelier EOLE Paysagistes,
NovaCity,
Brussels,
2021

Horizontal mixing by partially overlapping living and working still produces a new kind of urbanity, but less dense and less complex.

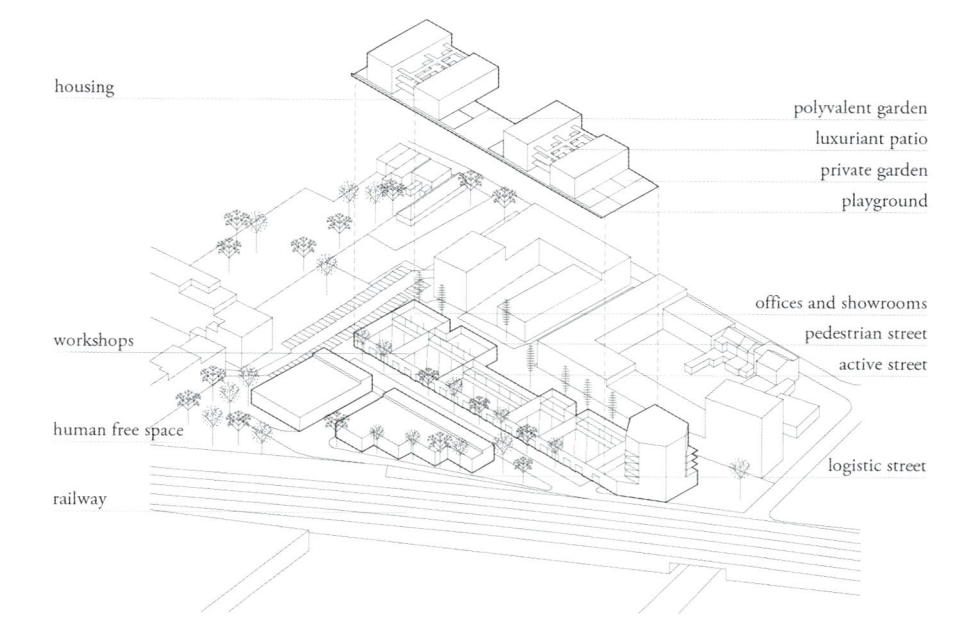

- housing
- polyvalent garden
- luxuriant patio
- private garden
- playground
- offices and showrooms
- workshops
- pedestrian street
- active street
- human free space
- logistic street
- railway

Once again, the two worlds of living and working are not separated from each other, but connected by mutual exposure. The same design language also expresses this in an architectural way.

The public real-estate operator citydev.brussels is becoming a specialist in such large mixed projects. NovaCity (2021) is a project that opts for a partially overlapping juxtaposition of the different functions. It consists of a redeveloped brownfield where on the ground floor the workshops are distributed on both sides of a street that constitutes a backbone for the different users. In direct relation with the workshops, a double height of retail and offices offer an interface with the neighbourhood, and share an address with the housing blocks. Above this plinth, a skyline of various heights of housing blocks animates the visual sequences of a new pedestrian street, and allows natural sunlight to reach the heart of the site. A small housing tower articulates the site's entrance corner, and four urban blocks are paired two by two around vertical patios where terraces constitute a convivial threshold between community and privacy. The architects BOGDAN & VAN BROECK and DDS+ have given it all a similar architectural language through a play of metal façade elements that subtly expresses how living and working are connected.

Beyond Bricks

These four projects do not form an accidental collection but illustrate a broader portfolio of initiatives under development in Brussels, thanks to a consistent policy of searching new solutions for the ideals of the Productive City by means of design competitions.

The continuation of this policy requires a next step – asking the question: For whom do we actually build? If we put all this effort into building, we need to know what kind of businesses we are aiming to attract. Which economy do we want in the city?

Of course we should not bring the steel industry back to the city. Equally, we must avoid a kind of romantic nostalgia that favours the return of pre-industrial craftsmanship.

The creative manufacturing industry is hip among millennials. Production of customised bikes, fab labs, craft breweries; these are certainly welcome in the city – but it doesn't end there. 'Ordinary' professions should also be granted a place, such as repairers, building material suppliers or the proverbial plumber. Such essential activities in the sphere of the foundational economy will always be indispensable for the daily functioning of an urban society.

In the future, it is hoped that the economy will be more equitable, ecological and local and thus have more potential to become circular. Therefore it is certainly worthwhile to create physical space for productive economy now, so that we do not have regrets later when eventually welcoming The Next Economy.

We must learn to accept the activities that take place behind the scenes of the city as an integral part of our daily urban lives, just as much as what is happening at the forefront. If we want the city to become a sustainable metabolism, then the city cannot just be the place of consumption.

Last but not least, there is also a symbolic dimension: just as we believe that city children should know where milk comes from, our children should also be able to see and understand that things are 'manufactured' somewhere by someone and that this requires jobs that we are willing to give a prominent place in our vision of an urban society. ᴅ

Text © 2021 John Wiley & Sons Ltd. Images: pp 120–1, 124 © OFFICE Kersten Geers David Van Severen; pp 122–3(t) © Plusoffice and WRKSHP; p 122(c) Image © 2021 Google, Aerodata International Surveys, CNES / Airbus, Landsat / Copernicus, Maxar Technologies, Données cartographiques; pp 122–3(b) © Filip Dujardin; p 125(t) © B2Ai-MSA-PLUSOFFICE; p 125(b) © B2Ai-MSA-PLUSOFFICE and CLAAR; pp 126–7 © BOGDAN & VAN BROECK, DDS+ and Atelier EOLE Paysagiste

FROM ANOTHER PERSPECTIVE

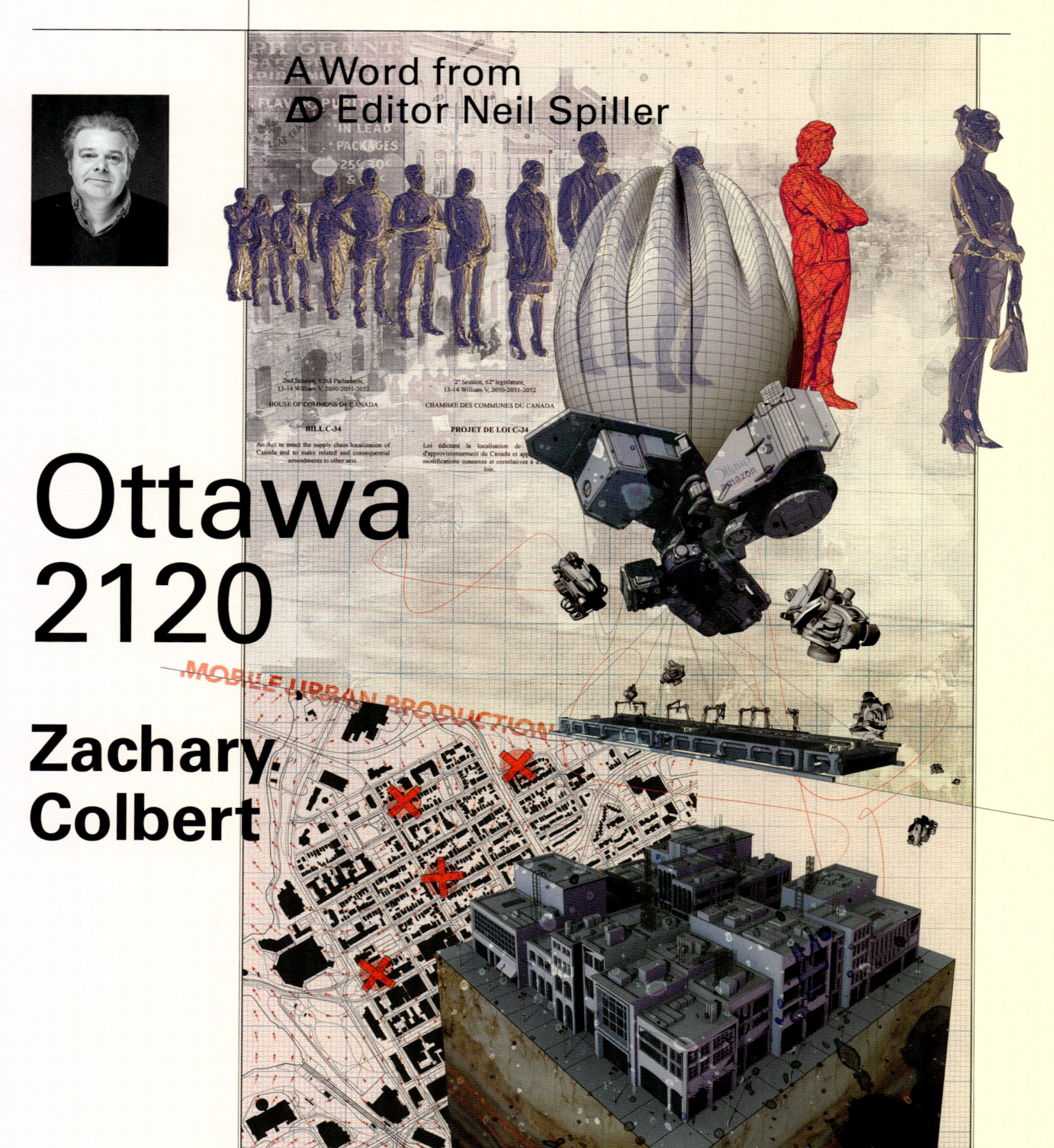

A Word from
∆ Editor Neil Spiller

Ottawa 2120

Zachary Colbert

To coincide with this issue on production urbanism and the meta-industrial city, ⌂ invited award-winning American architect Zachary Colbert to speculate on these trends and their possible impact on the city in a hundred years or so.

The nature of the cities people experience moulds them into the people they are and hence will become. Cities are highly dynamic, always in flux, forever changing, influenced by a myriad of social, political, legal, financial and human factors. Here, in a series of drawings, Colbert imagines a future city, Ottawa 2120, by exploring what the citizens of the meta-industrial city might produce and how they might interact with both local and national government.

Colbert holds a graduate degree from Columbia University Graduate School of Architecture, Planning and Preservation (GSAPP), and as an undergraduate achieved a Bachelor of Environmental Design cum laude from the University of Colorado at Boulder. Before setting up his own practice, he worked with SHoP Architects, Bernard Tschumi Architects as well as other notable US practices. He is also an accomplished architecture teacher, and currently Associate Director (Graduate Programs) and Assistant Professor at the Azrieli School of Architecture and Urbanism at Carleton University in Ottawa, Canada. On Ottawa 2120 he says: 'For each drawing, a premise is constructed through an imagined parliamentary act and corresponding piece of urban infrastructure. Six interventions in Canada's capital city, in 100 years' time, are used to explore the politics of the meta-industrial city through both the mundane moments of everyday life and the fantastic possibilities of a highly speculative urbanism.'

Changing the City
He starts by examining ideas of 'value' and how the notion of 'brand' has warped the idea of the worth of goods being about the transaction of produce in specific locales: 'Instead, value registers profoundly in notions of brand, where goods stand in for the stuff of hopes and dreams.' Into the future, he imagines this notion will become more attenuated and extreme, especially against a backdrop of climate change and highly proscriptive legal and social constraints posited by interventionist governments.

Contemporaneously, the move to reintegrate industry back into the city is a complex socioeconomic and socio-political project: 'For better or worse, architectural narratives tend to focus on the stuff of industry (logistical systems, cybernetics, economies of scale, assembly processes, etc) where pragmatic considerations like cost and function are paramount. Yet, the "factories" of production urbanism are as much factories of ideas as they are factories of products or goods. Such factories may have little impact on globalised industrial production patterns for now, but what is produced with immediate certainty is a renewed faith in the local, a resource for creating community, and a vehicle for self-actualisation – the stuff of hopes and dreams.' Such thoughts are at the core of politics, says Colbert. Ottawa 2120 is about how such imperatives might be entwined with the societal management of the meta-industrial city's citizenry (both for good and bad) and is an instructive architectural thought experiment.

The project is predicated on six fictional national legal frameworks that change the relationship between life, work, and what it means to be a socially productive participant in an imagined production urbanism economy. A suite of floating mobile automated production platforms blow around in the wind, enabled

Zachary Colbert,
Byward Market,
Ottawa, 2120

Meta-industrial citizens are continuously purchasing new fabrication instructions (within their allowable federal material budget) to be ready when they encounter the proper production platform. Upcycling previously fabricated materials replenishes a citizen's material budget. Consumption levels are mandated and any citizen who fails to meet their monthly consumption quota risks expulsion into the wilderness.

Zachary Colbert,
Rideau Canal,
Ottawa,
2120

Weekly festivals celebrate that week's harvest and restaurants operate entirely based on the reputation of their chef's ability to riff on the week's ingredients. Algorithms prompt citizens to gather at the towers to collect their weekly ration, thus creating a transient form of community.

by the Supply Chain Localisation Act; an urban agriculture system in the Rideau Canal produces all of Ottawa's food, enabled by the Federal Diet Act; an atmospheric condensation system makes use of abandoned wastewater infrastructure for water collection and treatment, enabled by the Suburban Expropriation Act; an urban reforestation plant and public indoor park are enabled by the Tree Census Act; a high-frequency democracy is enabled by the Algorithmic Voting Act; and finally, a post-truth discourse is enabled by the Narrative Control Act.

Colbert describes his drawing work as 'revealing a world of shortened supply chains and socio-political mutations, wherein daily life becomes structured by mandated consumption levels, political will is expressed through behaviour, corporate actors are embedded in urban governance, democracy is automated, and truth is obsolete'. The project is sited in six prominent areas of Ottawa: ByWard Market, the Rideau Canal, Kanata, LeBreton Flats, Centretown and Dow's Lake. Each is represented by a large composite drawing showing location, architecture and a series of vignettes in use. Colbert has even invented short biographies of some of the inhabitants. One ByWard Market inhabitant is described thus: 'Meta-industrial citizen 248812: Age: 28. Gender: female. Race: black. Consumer-citizen type: a-19. Household: 2 partners: 0214878; 214569. Favourite municipal product: dust storm gas mask. Political affiliation: ndp. Born after the merging of Amazon and the city of Ottawa – has no memory of democracy. Management note: increase pharma traffic for anxiety and depression. Self-diagnosis would optimise consumption patterns.'

Getting Down to Specifics
Imagine a world without physical retail, without cuisine, without a middle class. Imagine counting every tree in Canada, imagine voting was automated, imagine if truth was outmoded. Each location chosen by Colbert illustrates one of these conditions. ByWard Market is an example of the new 'platform' retail: 'Only the elders remember "going shopping", and most Canadians have only heard stories of the sorts of interpersonal exchanges involved with shopping. When a meta-industrial citizen needs something, they simply purchase the fabrication instructions for an item on Amazon's global online exchange and then upload this to one of many mobile production platforms that seemingly float across the city.' These platforms are wind-blown and dedicated to differing materials such as textiles, metals, plastics, wood, glass and ceramics. Some citizens wait for the appropriate platform to arrive by chance; others wander in search of the platform they need. The urban realm is transient and unpredictable.

The Rideau Canal is repurposed by Colbert as a source of continual irrigation for agri-grids: 'The canal's ancient pumphouses and locks maintain a steady flow of irrigation water to the Ottawa agriculture grid: a series of towers above the canal that grow and process food items through automated processes.' The middle class and the city's suburbs have disappeared. There is a universal basic income and urban dwellers must meet their consumption targets.

In the Kanata district of the city, for example, the suburban wastewater grids have been repurposed for water collection, treatment and storage to supply the urban core. Atmospheric condensers help to offset the arid effects of climate change in the Ottawa Valley and fill the abandoned underground water-management infrastructure with fresh water that slowly flows towards the city. The centuries-long climate restabilisation endeavour is underway, and Canada is being reforested to draw carbon out of the atmosphere. Every Canadian urban centre contains an urban reforestation plant where tree seeds are

Zachary Colbert,
LeBreton Flats,
Ottawa,
2120

LeBreton Flats is now home to an enormous indoor park where citizens plant their mandated annual tree seed allocation. They can recreate here, year-round, in a climate-controlled facility.

Zachary Colbert,
Kanata,
Ottawa,
2120

Populations within urban centres live in comfort and their lives are managed by algorithmic automation, while those in the wild subsist off the land independently.

HIGH-FRÉQUENCY DEMOCRACY

2nd Session, 87th Parliament,
15-16 William V, 2059-2060-2061

HOUSE OF COMMONS OF CANADA

BILL D-17

An Act to enact the algorithmic voting act of
Canada and to make related and consequential
amendments to other acts.

2ᵉ Session, 87ᵉ législature,
15-16 William V, 2059-2060-2061

CHAMBRE DES COMMUNES

PROJET DE LOI

Loi édictant la loi de vote algor
Canada et apportant des modification
et corrélatives à d'autres lois.

Zachary Colbert,
Centretown,
Ottawa,
2120

opposite: A bachelor apartment that happens to be next door to the data node might cost 10 times more than the penthouse in the same building. Meta-industrial citizens deeply desire to live in proximity to the data nodes in the hope that their city might better reflect them.

Zachary Colbert,
Dow's Lake,
Ottawa,
2120

Dow's Lake is utilised as a heat sink for massive narrative rigs where the federal narrative editors do their work.

cultivated and eventually planted in nature by drones. Ottawa's LeBreton Flats has become a massive urban park in this respect.

Data centres with hardline connections to the Parliament Hill servers have been built into residential towers throughout Centretown. These data centres monitor resident behaviour and cast votes, hundreds of times per microsecond, based on these demographics, to enact algorithmic legislation that governs all automated infrastructure. Living adjacent to one of these nodes means your behaviour data might reach Parliament Hill one or two microseconds sooner and is therefore more frequently used to drive policy.

Because of this, real-estate prices in the urban core are driven by proximity to these data nodes. The last professor to receive tenure passed away 25 years ago, and only a few fringe universities still cling on to relevance. Elders, who have achieved narrative-editor credentials through self-education, curate which algorithmically generated narratives are to be federally sanctioned and which are not. These narratives feed into an ever-growing ecosystem of unregulated knowledge calibrated to optimise citizen consumption levels.

Dystopic Vision
'Paper' architecture mainly attempts to speculate on utopic worlds and architecture, but perhaps there is more value sometimes in illustrating the downsides of technology, politics and social upheaval. Colbert's vision is one that contains lessons for pedagogic purpose. His work on Ottawa 2120 teaches us the potential of tyrannical power dressed up in neoliberal guises, and the fragile nature of the socially democratic political project – a situation that has become clearer in reality in recent years. His project might have been overlooked a decade or so ago, but nowadays its resonance has a much bigger impact.

Colbert describes another occupant thus: 'Meta-industrial citizen 213146: Age: 19. Gender: non-binary. Race: indigenous. Consumer-citizen type: a-8. Household: 3 partners: 0214878; 5142355; 514235. Favourite municipal product: pharma upper 3. Spent for supply chain localisation. Management notes: increase DIY fashion traffic. Additional textile interaction would optimise consumption levels. "Where are my f#@king keys … I can't believe my parents used to have to decide what to eat. What a waste of time … Lisgar Street has the best potatoes this week. I'm so tired of synth-salmon".' This resident of the Rideau Canal area sums up their existence, their boredom with the same food and their misconception that time can be wasted by choice and variety. Let us hope the future is brighter than this, and thank you Zachary Colbert for positing out this theoretical urban scenario with humorous seriousness. ᗪ

Text © 2021 John Wiley & Sons Ltd. Images © Zachary Colbert

CONTRIBUTORS

Yasmine Abbas is architecture and engineering design faculty at the Pennsylvania State University. She researches strategies for the design of living environments across contemporary conditions of expanded physical, digital and mental mobilities. She has worked in multicultural environments employing design thinking methods to generate pan-urban intelligence and drive urban innovation. She co-founded the Agbogbloshie Makerspace Platform (AMP), was the winner of the Rockefeller Foundation's Centennial Innovation Challenge 2013, and has received the 2017 SEED award for Public Interest Design, and Le Monde Urban Innovation Award – Citizen Engagement, Le Monde Cities (2020).

Frank Barkow is the founder of architectural practice Barkow Leibinger. He received his Bachelor of Architecture from Montana State University in Bozeman, and is a graduate of the Harvard University Graduate School of Design (GSD) in Cambridge, Massachusetts. He is a design and construction leader in the practice, and heads up the research group investigating both digital and analogue fabrication methods. His approach embraces design in a discursive way that allows the work to respond to advancing knowledge and technology. He has been a professor at the Princeton University School of Architecture in New Jersey since 2016, and has recently taught at Harvard GSD.

Michele Bonino is Associate Professor of Architecture and Urban Design and Vice Rector for Relations with China at the Politecnico di Torino. He was previously a visiting professor at Tsinghua University in Beijing (2013 and 2014) and a visiting scholar at the Massachusetts Institute of Technology (MIT, 2016). He was the Academic Curator (with Sun Yimin) of the 2019 Shenzhen Bi-City Biennale of Urbanism/Architecture. On behalf of the Politecnico di Torino, he is leading the design of the Shougang Visitor Centre for the XXIV Olympic Winter Games (Beijing 2022). He has co-edited a number of books including *China Goes Urban* (Skira, 2020) and *The City after Chinese New Towns* (Birkhäuser, 2019).

Kristiaan Borret is *bouwmeester – maître architecte* of the Brussels Capital Region, Belgium. The *bouwmeester* is an independent government official who stimulates and supervises the quality of urban development projects. He previously held the same position for the city of Antwerp, and in 2017 was also appointed by the city of Amsterdam for quality monitoring in two urban transformation areas in the city. He has been a Professor of Urban Design at Ghent University since 2005.

Vicente Guallart was a chief architect (2011–15) of Barcelona City Council with responsibility for the strategic vision for the city and its major projects. He also co-founded and directed the Institute for Advanced Architecture of Catalonia (2001–11). The work of his practice, Guallart Architects, has been widely published, and exhibited at the Venice Architecture Biennale and the Museum of Modern Art (MoMA) in New York. He is the author of the books *Plans and Projects for Barcelona 2011–2015* (2015) and *The Self-Sufficient City: Internet has Changed Our Lives but it Hasn't Changed Our Cities* (2010), both published by Actar, and co-author of the *Metapolis Dictionary of Advanced Architecture*. In 2010, the American Institute of Architects organised a solo exhibition of his work in Washington DC.

Tali Hatuka is an architect, urban planner and associate professor at Tel Aviv University, where she is the head and founder of the Laboratory of Contemporary Urban Planning and Design (LCUD). Her work focuses on the urban realm and society (public space, conflicts, technology) and urban development and city design (housing and industry). She graduated from the Faculty of Architecture and Town Planning at the Technion – Israel Institute of Technology in Haifa, received an MSc in Urban Design from Edinburgh College of Art/Heriot-Watt University, and a doctorate from the Technion. She was a Fulbright and a Marie Curie fellow in the Department of Urban Studies and Planning at MIT.

Doojin Hwang studied architecture at Seoul National University and at Yale University in New Haven, Connecticut. He founded Doojin Hwang Architects (DJHA) in Seoul in 2000. He has been involved in a series of projects in the city's historic centre, including a number of *hanoks* (traditional Korean houses). This inner-city experience led him to develop ideas about an urban mixed-use typology he calls 'rainbow-cake architecture', which is also the title of a book he published in 2015. He has given lectures and exhibitions extensively around the globe.

Alexis Kalagas is Urban Strategy Lead at Relative Projects, and leads an advanced architecture studies unit at Monash Art, Design and Architecture (MADA) in Melbourne. Working across research, curatorial and strategic design projects, he has explored the economic, social and technological forces reshaping our experience of urban space and the home as a Harvard GSD Richard Rogers Fellow, a Future Architecture Fellow, and a finalist in the City of Sydney's Alternative Housing Ideas Challenge. He is the co-editor of *Reactivate Athens: 101 Ideas* (Ruby Press, 2017) and exhibited at the Seoul Biennale of Architecture and Urbanism with Zurich- and Belgrade-based design research group TEN in 2019.

Yerin Kang is an architect based in Seoul, and has served as Associate Professor in Practice in the department of architecture at Seoul National University since 2019. She co-founded the design firm SoA (Society of Architecture) in 2011. Key projects include Roof Sentiment at the National Museum of Modern and Contemporary Art (MMCA, 2015); the mixed-use Paju Book City Studio M, Gyeonggi Province (2017), and the Seong-su Silo, part of the Metropolitan Small Manufacturers' Support Center (MSMSC) in Seoul (2019), which have featured in various international publications. She was the curator of the 'Production City' exhibition at the Seoul Biennale of Architecture and Urbanism in 2017.

Kengo Kuma established Kengo Kuma & Associates in 1990 in Tokyo, after his time as a visiting scholar at Columbia University in New York. He received his Master's degree in architecture from the University of Tokyo, where he is currently a University Professor and a Professor Emeritus. Since then, Kengo Kuma & Associates has designed architectural works in over 20 countries and received prestigious awards, including the Architectural Institute of Japan Award, the Spirit of Nature Wood Architecture Award (Finland), and the International Stone Architecture Award (Italy).

Chihoon Lee is an architect and a co-founder of the award-winning practice SoA (Society of Architecture) in Seoul. His work has been exhibited at international venues including the MAXXI – National Museum of 21st Century Art in Rome (2012), and published in media such as the *Architectural Review*, *Domus Korea*, *Mark* and *SPACE* magazines. With Yerin Kang he was awarded the 2015 Young Architects Program (YAP Korea) organised by the Ministry of Culture and Korea Architects Institute, MMCA, MoMA and Hyundai Card Co, Ltd. In 2016 they were finalists in the AR Emerging Architecture award.

Wesley Leeman studied at the Rotterdam Academy of Architecture, graduating in 2014. His graduation project addressed regional-scale agricultural modernisation in the Yangtze delta, China. After working at several architecture offices in the Netherlands from 2008, he joined Goldsmith.Company (founded by Klaas van der Molen) in 2017, and became a partner in 2019. The firm operates within the boundaries of architecture and urbanism, and has gained specific expertise in the fields of nautical and agricultural architecture over the last decade. He is also currently a tutor at Rotterdam.

Scott Lloyd works on architecture, publishing and curatorial projects. His design, research, teaching and writing explore the politics and aesthetics of space. He graduated from ETH Zurich, where he researched and taught urbanisation. He is currently director of the design research group TEN, which won the Swiss Art Award for Architecture in 2018 and the 2020 Foundation Award for emerging architecture practices.

Winy Maas is a founding partner and Principal Architect of MVRDV, and has received international acclaim for his broad range of urban planning and building projects across all typologies and scales. He challenges colleagues, clients, as well as students and collaborators at TU Delft's The Why Factory – an internationally engaged think tank he established in 2008 – to question the boundaries of established standards to produce solutions that reimagine how we live, work and play. He is widely published, actively engaged in the advancement of the design profession, and sits on numerous boards and juries, including the Spatial Quality Boards of Rotterdam, Eindhoven and Barcelona.

DK Osseo-Asare is principal of transatlantic architecture studio Low Design Office (LowDO), is an Architectural League of New York 2021 Emerging Voices award-winner, and assistant professor of architecture and engineering design at Pennsylvania State University where he directs the Humanitarian Materials Lab. He co-founded the pan-African open maker tech initiative Agbogbloshie Makerspace Platform (AMP) and led urban design for the Anam City and Koumbi City new town projects in Nigeria and Ghana. He is a TED Global Fellow and received his MArch from Harvard GSD. His research explores material assemblies optimised for massively scalable radical resilience.

Marina Otero Verzier is director of research at the Het Nieuwe Instituut in Rotterdam where she oversees initiatives such as Automated Landscapes, and BURN-OUT: Exhaustion on a Planetary Scale. She is also the head of the Master's programme in Social Design at the Design Academy Eindhoven. She was a member of the curatorial team of the 13th Shanghai Biennale; curator of 'Work, Body, Leisure', the Dutch Pavilion at the 2018 Venice Architecture Biennale; chief curator of the 2016 Oslo Architecture Triennale; and the director of Global Network Programming at Studio-X – Columbia University. She has co-edited a number of books, including *Work, Body, Leisure* (2018), *Architecture of Appropriation* (2019) and *More-than-Human* (2021), published by the Het Nieuwe Instituut.

Nina Rappaport is an architectural historian, curator and educator. With her consultancy, Vertical Urban Factory, she focuses on industrial urbanism, encouraging urban production spaces, and the role of the factory worker. She is the author of *Vertical Urban Factory* (Actar, 2015) and co-editor of *Design of Urban Manufacturing* (Routledge, 2020). Her exhibition 'Vertical Urban Factory' has travelled to 12 cities since 2011. Her ongoing film project, *A Worker's Lunch Box*, features interviews with factory workers. She is Publications Director at the Yale School of Architecture, has been a visiting professor at the Politecnio di Torino, and teaches at the College of Public Architecture at Kean University in Union, New Jersey.

Maria Paola Repellino has a PhD in architecture and building design, is a research fellow at the Politecnico di Torino where she is Executive Director of the China Room research group and a member of the Future Urban Legacy Lab. She was previously a visiting scholar at the School of Architecture at Tsinghua University. Her research work focuses on the role of industrial legacy in redefining the relationships between architecture, city and production in contemporary China. Recent books include *Fun Mill: The Architecture of Creative Industry in Contemporary China* (ORO Editions, 2021) and *The City after Chinese New Towns* (Birkhäuser, 2019).

Neil Spiller is Editor of *⌂*, and was previously Hawksmoor Chair of Architecture and Landscape and Deputy Pro Vice Chancellor at the University of Greenwich. Prior to this he was Vice Dean at the Bartlett School of Architecture, University College London (UCL). He has made an international reputation as an architect, designer, artist, teacher, writer and polemicist. He is the founding director of the Advanced Virtual and Technological Architecture Research (AVATAR) group, which continues to push the boundaries of architectural design and discourse in the face of the impact of 21st-century technologies. Its current preoccupations include augmented and mixed realities and other metamorphic technologies.

Shohei Shigematsu is a partner at OMA, based in the practice's New York office. He leads the firm's diverse portfolio in the Americas and Japan. His cultural projects across North America include the New Museum and Albright-Knox Art Gallery extensions in New York, Sotheby's Headquarters, the Quebec National Museum of Beaux-Arts and the Faena Art Center in Miami. He has also designed exhibitions for Prada, the Venice Architecture Biennale, Metropolitan Museum of Art, Park Avenue Armory, and Dior's first US retrospective at the Denver Art Museum and Dallas Museum of Art. He is currently overseeing the construction of OMA's projects in Japan, including the Tenjin Business Center in Fukuoka and a mixed-use tower in Tokyo.

What is *Architectural Design*?

Founded in 1930, *Architectural Design* (⌂) is an influential and prestigious publication. It combines the currency and topicality of a newsstand journal with the rigour and production qualities of a book. With an almost unrivalled reputation worldwide, it is consistently at the forefront of cultural thought and design.

Issues of ⌂ are edited either by the journal Editor, Neil Spiller, or by an invited Guest-Editor. Renowned for being at the leading edge of design and new technologies, ⌂ also covers themes as diverse as architectural history, the environment, interior design, landscape architecture and urban design.

Provocative and pioneering, ⌂ inspires theoretical, creative and technological advances. It questions the outcome of technical innovations as well as the far-reaching social, cultural and environmental challenges that present themselves today.

For further information on ⌂, subscriptions and purchasing single issues see:

https://onlinelibrary.wiley.com/journal/15542769

Volume 90 No 5
ISBN 978 1119 651581

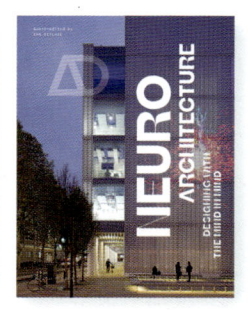

Volume 90 No 6
ISBN 978 1119 685371

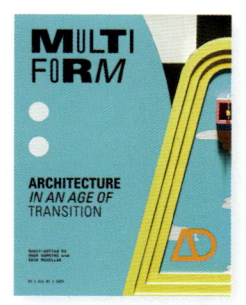

Volume 91 No 1
ISBN 978 1119 717669

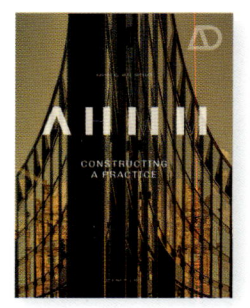

Volume 91 No 2
ISBN 978 1119 717485

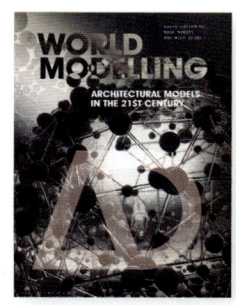

Volume 91 No 3
ISBN 978 1119 747222

Volume 91 No 4
ISBN 978 1119 717522

Individual backlist issues of ⌂ are available as books for purchase starting at £29.99 / US$45.00

www.wiley.com

How to Subscribe
With 6 issues a year, you can subscribe to ⌂ (either print, online or through the ⌂ App for iPad)

Institutional subscription
£346 / $646
print or online

Institutional subscription
£433 / $808
combined print and online

Personal-rate subscription
£146 / $229
print and iPad access

Student-rate subscription
£93 / $147
print only

⌂ App for iPad
6-issue subscription:
£44.99 / US$64.99
Individual issue:
£9.99 / US$13.99

To subscribe to print or online
E: cs-journals@wiley.com
W: https://onlinelibrary.wiley.com/journal/15542769

Americas
E: cs-journals@wiley.com
T: +1 877 762 2974

Europe, Middle East and Africa
E: cs-journals@wiley.com
T: +44 (0) 1865 778315

Asia Pacific
E: cs-journals@wiley.com
T: +65 6511 8000

Japan (for Japanese-speaking support)
E: cs-japan@wiley.com
T: +65 6511 8010

Visit our Online Customer Help
available in 7 languages at www.wileycustomerhelp.com/ask

NOW available on the iPad!

- Buy single issues or subscribe
- Store all downloaded issues to your personal library
- Easily navigable format brings new life to ⌂ articles
- Free to personal print subscribers

Available on the App Store